the PSYCHOLOGY of
from divided self to integrated self

Dr Danesh is Rector of Landegg Academy, an international private university in Switzerland. He is a writer and an international consultant with over thirty years of experience in the fields of psychiatry and family medicine, community development, ethics, and world order studies. His areas of research and expertise include the psychology of spirituality, anger and violence, marriage and family, cross-cultural issues, death and dying, and consultation and conflict resolution.

In 1985, after being elected to the post of Secretary-General of the Bahá'í Community of Canada, Dr Danesh left his academic position as an Associate Professor of Psychiatry at the University of Ottawa in order to dedicate himself to work in the areas of peace, human rights, the plight of refugees, conflict resolution, and community development. In 1994 Dr Danesh resumed his academic career at Landegg Academy.

The Psychology of Spirituality, now being reprinted both in English and Chinese, is one of four books by Dr Danesh. His other books are: *The Violence-Free Society: A Gift for Our Children; The Violence-Free Family: Building Block of a Peaceful Civilization;* and *Unity: The Creative Foundation of Peace.* He presently has five other books in preparation on the themes of violence, marriage and family, consultation and conflict resolution, as well as a book for children on death and dying entitled *The Mysterious Case of the I.W.'s.*

As an international speaker and consultant, Dr Danesh has addressed many audiences at numerous universities and public forums throughout North, Central, and South America, Europe, Russia, India, Malaysia, the Middle East, Australia, New Zealand, Japan, and China. In addition, he has produced several television programs along the themes of marriage, family, and violence.

Of allied interest

1. **Mysteries: Ancient and Modern**
   Sai Grafio
2. **Spiritual Lessons from Life**
   Rakesh K. Mittal
3. **Spiritual Sayings of Sri Ram**
   Sri Ram
4. **Destiny, Science & Spiritual Awakening**
   Ravindra Kumar
5. **Meditation, Oneness & Physics: A Journey through the Laboratories of Physics and Meditation**
   Glen Kezwer
6. **Yoga, Meditation and the Guru**
   Purusotamma Bilimoria
7. **Enlightened Views**
   Alan Bryson
8. **Kundalini Yoga: In Search of the Miraculous**
   Osho (2 vol. set)
9. **The Art of Sadhana: In the stories of Sri Ramakrishna**
   M. Sivaramkrishna & Sumita Roy
10. **New Series of 108 Names of Gods**
    Ganesha • Vishnu • Shiva • Krishna • Rama • Hanuman • Lakshmi • Durga • Shirdi Sai Baba
    Vijaya Kumar

Published by
Sterling Publishers Private Limited

the PSYCHOLOGY of SPIRITUALITY

from divided self to integrated self

H. B. Danesh, M.D.

A Sterling Paperback

STERLING PAPERBACKS
An imprint of
Sterling Publishers (P) Ltd.
A-59, Okhla Industrial Area, Phase-II,
New Delhi-110020.
Tel: 26387070, 26386209; Fax: 91-11-26383788
E-mail: sterlingpublishers@touchtelindia.net
ghai@nde.vsnl.net.in
www.sterlingpublishers.com

The Psychology of Spirituality
© 1997, H.B. Danesh, M.D.
ISBN 81 207 2132 2

Originally Published by
Paradigm Publishing (Canada)
Nine Pines Publishing (Canada) and
Landegg Academy Press
Switzerland
First Indian Edition 1998
Reprint 2006

All rights are reserved. No part of this publication may be reproduced, stored in a retrieval system or transmitted, in any form or by any means, mechanical, photocopying, recording or otherwise, without prior written permission of the original publisher.

Published by Sterling Publishers Pvt. Ltd., New Delhi-110 020.
Printed at Sterling Publishers Pvt. Ltd., New Delhi-110020.

To
my parents for their gift of life and love
and
my wife Michele for her gift of love and life

Acknowledgement

This book was researched and written over several years in the midst of many other activities. A number of individuals assisted and encouraged me throughout this long period. I am deeply indebted to my wife Michele and our sons Arman and Roshan for their penetrating insights, understanding, patience, and help. The editorial work and many suggestions of Christine Zerbinis, Bruce Filson, and Linda O'Neil have been invaluable, and I am filled with gratitude. Suggestions offered by Dr. Peter Morgan and Susan Lyons greatly helped in the reorganization and presentation of this book, and I wish to thank them for their thoughtful recommendations. Susan Lyons also helped in the preparation of the manuscript. My abiding thanks to all of them.

Table of Contents

●

PREFACE xi

PART ONE: BEGINNINGS

    Basic Questions 3
    In Search of Meaning: The Case of Carol 7
    Towards a Psychology of Spirituality 13

PART TWO: SELF AND SOUL

    On Human Nature 23
    Our Experience of Self 33
    The Nature of Soul and Consciousness 41

PART THREE: THE FUNDAMENTALS

    Being and Becoming: The Case of Dawn 53
    Fundamental Human Characteristics 63
    Primary Human Concerns 75
    Integration of Knowledge, Love and Will, and Concerns about Self 83
    Integration of Knowledge, Love and Will, and Concerns about Relationships 91
    Integration of Knowledge, Love and Will, and Concerns about Time 99

PART FOUR: WHEN THINGS GO WRONG

    On the Purpose of Life and the Process of Healing 111
    Disorders of Knowledge 115
    Disorders of Love 123
    Disorders of Will 133

Freedom and Human Will 139

PART FIVE: FROM ADOLESCENCE TO MATURITY

From Adolescence to Adulthood 147
Towards a Universal Code of Ethics 161
The Brain, Consciousness and Spirituality 167
Human Brain and Human Soul: Dynamics of Spiritual Evolution 181

PART SIX: ON BECOMING AN INTEGRATED PERSON

The Challenge of Unity 197
Life Modification and Limits of the "Therapeutic" 211
Spiritual Transformation: Concepts and Practice 227
On Becoming an Integrated Person: a Postscript 237

Notes 249

Bibliography 257

Index 261

Preface

This book is written for those who ask difficult questions: What is the nature of human reality? What is the purpose of human life? What is love? What is reality? Do we have a free will? What is the secret of happiness? Is transcendence real? Could it be that our quest for goodness is merely an attempt on our part to conceal our evil nature? And could it be that our attraction to Godhood is simply rooted in our childlike fears and our need for an authority figure? These and many other equally important questions have always been asked, and answers to them still are sought by inquiring minds and searching hearts everywhere.

The principles of spiritual psychology, as presented in this book, provide us with an integrated and comprehensive framework for understanding ourselves and our behaviour, both individually and collectively. Towards this end, the biological, psychosocial, and spiritual dimensions of human reality are all taken into consideration, and their essential relationships, emanating from the single and indivisible human reality, are identified.

Through case histories, in-depth analyses, and practical examples, *The Psychology of Spirituality* unfolds new ways of looking at ourselves, our relationships, our problems, and our world. It shows that life can truly be good, happy, and fruitful, and that we human beings are indeed noble beings, if only we knew.

H.B.D.
Victoria, October, 1993

PART ONE

Beginnings

In the beginning was the Word,...
Gospel of John 1:1

Basic Questions

Forty years ago on the first day of my training to become a physician, I was assigned to the emergency room. Our medical school had a six year program that combined pre-medical and medical training. The students had just finished high school, and many of us were quite young. I was sixteen.

Moments after I arrived in the emergency room, an ambulance brought in five members of one family, ranging in age from fourteen to eighty-one, all suffering from carbon monoxide poisoning. In the urgent atmosphere of the emergency room, everyone was given a responsibility, and mine was to administer oxygen, give mouth-to-mouth resuscitation, and do whatever else might be necessary by following the example of the physician next to me who was working on another victim. Three hours later, after an intense experience that seemed to last a lifetime, we stopped. All five patients were dead. I was totally numb, unable and unwilling to think about this, my first medical experience. However, my inactivity was not destined to last for long. Several more patients were brought in, and I was given the task of cleaning, under a nurse's supervision, the severely lacerated, bloodstained face of a young bicycle accident victim to prepare him for examination by the doctor. As I gently and cautiously worked the blood and debris away from the young man's face, I realized with horror that he was one of my best friends. Fear and pain engulfed me, but I had to continue to fulfill my responsibility. I was deeply relieved when he uttered his first words and it became clear he would recover.

Later that afternoon a number of us gathered to share our first day's experience as medical students. Many of our experiences were dramatic, or at least so they seemed. One of my classmates had had a particularly unusual experience. He had been given the task of taking the vital signs (pulse, respiration, temperature) of a number of patients. One of his patients was from a nomadic tribe and had never been in a hospital. My friend had placed a thermometer in the patient's mouth and left him briefly to speak with the patient in the next bed. When he returned, the thermometer was gone. The tribesman had simply eaten it. The nurses and doctors immediately began to treat him for mercury poisoning and gave the bewildered student the task of separating the whites of many eggs to be fed to the patient as part of the treatment.

When I reflected on these events, I realized they were more than purely medical happenings. Those who had died of carbon monoxide poisoning were also victims of poverty and ignorance. Their deaths brought the realities of life and death very close to me. I realized how easy it was to die and how preventable their deaths might have been. The injustice of it all and the knowledge that these deaths need not have happened made me angry. The bicycle accident victim aroused in me yet another feeling, the fear of losing loved ones. I began to think of all those whom I loved and who could easily get injured, fall ill, or die. Finally, the case of the tribesman caused feelings of embarrassment. The incident clearly showed the immense gulf that can exist between people. This gap, resulting primarily from differences in education and life experience, made my novice friend so unaware of the need to communicate with another human being that he simply assumed everyone knew what was obvious to him. I would probably have done the same thing under similar circumstances. Though I had always believed that in reality we are all one, I saw that in practice we can still be quite far apart.

In the years since, many such events have occurred in my practice as a physician and as a psychiatrist, dealing with some of the crucial issues of concern to us all. Cardinal among these are the issues of life and death; followed closely by the quest for happiness, love, and acceptance; the fear of pain, illness, loss, and rejection; and such concerns as the purpose of life, the nature of relationships and the mystery of suffering. The list goes on, and I have come to the conclusion that human concerns are exceedingly diverse and virtually limitless.

All these concerns, however, can be classified into two groups: those that involve physical survival, and those concerned with the purpose of existence. The former group motivates us to feed, protect, and shelter ourselves. The latter group challenges us to find purpose and meaning in all that we do. One connects us to the animal world and reminds us of our biological heritage; the other points to our spiritual nature and its significant role in our lives. In fact, without meaning and purpose, life becomes extremely painful, an unwanted and at times intolerable burden. Healing professionals have long known that many suicides and even homicides take place in the context of meaningless, aimless lives.

✧ ✧ ✧

One morning several years ago, I was called to the neurosurgery ward for a psychiatric consultation. There I encountered a middle-aged man sitting in bed, bewildered yet somehow bemused. He told me that all his life he had lived as a loner. He had never married because he could not find anyone willing to marry him. He had not done well in school, and had not continued his studies after high school. He secured a simple job and lived (as he described it) an uneventful, boring, purposeless life. In the fifty-fifth year of his life, he decided that there was no reason for him to continue living. As far as he was concerned, his life had been a miserable, meaningless burden, and he decided to kill himself.

This decision had created a certain degree of excitement and sense of anticipation in him. He had always viewed himself as a complete failure, but this time he planned to be successful. He devised his suicide in a way that appeared foolproof. After doing some thinking and research he decided that the surest method would be to put a gun in his mouth and pull the trigger. He bought a gun and did just that. To his utter amazement, however, not only did he not die, but he did not even severely damage his brain. The bullet had lodged between the two hemispheres of his brain without causing any apparent lasting or significant damage. As he recalled this bizarre tale, he smiled and said, "Once a loser, always a loser."

In my subsequent work with this man it became evident that he was very kind. In fact, he considered kindness to be his greatest quality, and having faced death he lost his shyness in admitting that he was in fact a considerate, kind, and loving person. However, he had always considered these qualities to be of secondary value to those of aggressiveness, drive, forcefulness, and success, which he felt he did not possess. He was, in many ways, reflecting the value system of our society and what that society considers to be important signs of worth, prestige, and success. After fifty-five years of mere survival and an unsuccessful suicide attempt, he decided to do volunteer work at the hospital and thereby gave a purpose to his life. He discovered his own spiritual dimension.

We all possess a spiritual dimension. Human nature is distinct from that of the animal by virtue of its special spiritual qualities. Although humans are physically similar to animals, we become truly human when our biological and instinctual capacities become the *means* through which we live lives of knowledge, love, reflection, search, and purpose, and we discover our humanity when we begin to search for answers to many challenging questions: Why are we here? How did we get here? Where are we going from here? What is the nature of our minds, feelings, and thoughts? What is the nature of human love and how is it related to our relationships? Is there a Creator, life after death, a purpose in all that happens in our lives?

One of my patients, Carol, single-handedly focused my attention on all such questions.

In Search of Meaning: The Case of Carol

●

Carol, a thirty-five-year-old married mother of a four-year-old son, asked for help in dealing with her deep distress over her serious illness. Some four years earlier, while she was still breastfeeding her son, her physician telephoned to inform her that she had been diagnosed with breast cancer. The shock of the diagnosis and the manner in which her doctor informed her made Carol very angry, fearful, and depressed. She was angry not only because of her illness but also because she believed her physician had conveyed the diagnosis in an inhumane manner. She felt betrayed not only by God but also by her fellow human beings. In many ways she felt helpless and alone. She believed her very existence was in jeopardy and that there was little she could do about her situation. Her fear subsided somewhat when she was assured by her physicians and surgeons that with a mastectomy and a course of anticancer drugs she would be cured. She would be able to continue her life in an "almost normal" manner. Being a highly educated person and placing a lot of importance on the "scientific," Carol felt reassured about her future and underwent a mastectomy followed by chemotherapy. In the process she lost her hair and was acutely sick and exhausted, all of which made her miserable. But she considered this worthwhile because she believed the outcome would mean freedom from cancer.

CASE STUDY

CASE STUDY

During this period, Carol had several transitory thoughts about God, death, and life after death, but she did not spend much time pondering such issues. As far as she was concerned, death meant the end of her existence, nothing less and nothing more; and if God existed, it did not matter much as far as her life and death were concerned. So Carol continued to focus on her cure and avoided thinking about death and other related issues.

After two years of treatment, her cancer reappeared. The promised cure had not taken place. Instead, her cancer had spread. This turn of events put Carol in an unenviable position. She felt totally betrayed. Science had failed her. In her opinion, the medical profession had lied to her, and she was totally alone. Nonetheless, she returned to her physician for possible new forms of assistance. He told her the treatment would be more of the same, only with stronger, more debilitating drugs. The doctor also said that when she began to have pain, he would make sure that she would receive painkillers, tranquilizers and, if necessary, some psychological counselling.

In response to this news, Carol began exhaustive research into all aspects of cancer, its causes and cures. She read and became educated about most of the issues related to cancer, studied the relationship between cancer and emotions, diet and vitamins, and in particular Vitamin C. She studied alternative modes of treatment unavailable through medical institutions, and she sought advice of various other physicians and agencies with regard to her condition. She began to take megadoses of Vitamin C and other vitamin supplements. She changed her diet, stopped chemotherapy and radiotherapy, and decided to consult a psychiatrist about the emotional aspects of her illness.

It was at this time that Carol made an appointment to see me professionally. I found her to be extremely unhappy, distraught, disappointed, and angry. First, we had to deal with her anger towards the medical profession. I pointed out that physicians are, like herself, basically impotent in the face of death. Doctors also try to avoid death, and that is why most of them focus exclusively on curing the disease. When they fail, they focus on the physical comfort of their patients. Unfortunately, doctors often avoid dealing with related issues that accompany a serious illness, issues such as the purpose of life, the reason for suffering, or the nature of death. Many members of the medical profession feel physicians need not address the psychosocial or spiritual dimensions of illness.

CASE STUDY

Modern medicine has become, for the most part, a mechanistic and inhumane practice, focusing almost exclusively on the body and its diseases. It pays little attention to the psychological consequences of illness and still less to its spiritual dimensions. Patients who ask for assistance in either of these two areas are referred to psychiatrists and psychologists for psychological and emotional support, and to the clergy for spiritual support. This schism in patient care is highly unsatisfactory, especially for those facing their own death or the death of a loved one.

Carol and her family were in extreme crisis when our sessions began. She wanted to know what medical science could do for her, what she herself could do to control her disease, how she could prepare herself for the future, if there was anything in her past that had made her susceptible to cancer, and whether there were different forms of treatment not yet scientifically proven but reportedly effective. If, despite all her physician's efforts, as well as her own, she did not recover, she wanted to know how she should prepare herself for death. Moreover, she needed to know how she should prepare her young son, husband, and parents for her death.

One could object that most of these questions do not belong in the realm of "legitimate" medicine and psychiatry, that no member of the medical profession could possibly be competent to answer such questions, which extend beyond the domain of medicine to psychology, sociology, and religion. This objection is legitimate at one level, but before we completely dismiss the questions of this patient and those like her as inappropriate or irrelevant, it would be valuable to review her situation in a more integrated manner.

Carol's case was approached along these lines. We began by looking at all these issues simultaneously. In the course of subsequent sessions, it emerged that Carol was reared in a middle-class, conservative family. Her father was basically reserved and emotionally aloof, while her mother was overprotective and excessively critical. In spite of this emotional environment, her early years were uneventful. She was physically healthy and attractive, socially outgoing and likable, and intellectually superior and successful. She had done well at anything she tried. She attended church but derived little satisfaction from religion and was unable to integrate

The Psychology of Spirituality

CASE STUDY

religious doctrines with her logical reasoning and thinking. Consequently, she gradually lost interest in religious concepts but retained an interest and affinity for religious music, architecture, and rituals. Her adolescence was relatively uncomplicated. During those years, she was gradually able to choose her own direction and to become more independent of her parents, especially in lifestyle. She became a socially conscious person, showing considerable concern for social and individual injustices. She held several jobs in the field of social services at hospitals and in the government.

In their marriage, Carol and her husband were able to deal successfully with the challenges of life until the diagnosis of cancer. The appearance of cancer (especially its metastasis two years later) caused serious disruption to their lives. Their views about themselves and the world were no longer sufficient to explain and deal with this crisis.

For Carol herself, the dilemma was even more devastating. She suddenly realized that not only was her life in jeopardy, she was also in danger of losing everyone—her husband, son, parents, relatives, and friends. To her horror she found that she was not able to make any sense of these events. Faced with death, all that she had learned about life's challenges and threats and coping methods were inadequate. She began to read more books on cancer and its treatment, and also books on death, dying, and bereavement. She had many questions and actively tried to formulate a new framework within which her life, her disease, and her death would all be meaningful and understandable. Her attempts to do so met with considerable obstacles. Basically, the answers were neither forthcoming nor adequate. She fully understood the physical and medical aspects of her illness and began to search for physicians who would provide her with a type of treatment she felt was more appropriate. She did not hesitate to ask for consultations, explanations, and new treatments from her physicians.

However, in the emotional sphere she did better. She was able to understand and deal with her feelings of anger, fear, and sadness. She fully understood the psychological explanations of these emotional states, and she was able to identify the dynamics at work in her own case. Nonetheless, in spite of these insights, she remained dissatisfied. Detailed, complex, and seemingly plausible medical and psychological explanations did not satisfactorily explain the mystery of life and death to her nor did they answer her questions about the purpose of life, the meaning and purpose of human suffering, the wisdom of an untimely death, and similar issues.

> CASE STUDY

These were, of course, spiritual questions that she ultimately had to answer for herself. Such tasks are enormously difficult and the individual in crisis requires help and encouragement to deal with them In the context of regular and frequent interviews, help and encouragement can be provided, given the willingness of the physician or the therapist to discuss such matters, acknowledge their legitimacy, recognize their importance, and share with the patient information and experience that would clarify these issues.

Carol became wholeheartedly and enthusiastically involved in the process. She began to relax and embarked upon the all-important task of facing the ultimate—her own death. Gradually she was able to understand and express her feelings about her own death. She did not back away from pondering her reality and the condition of that reality after death.

Naturally, she had hoped for a longer life. At first she bargained for more years, then months, and finally weeks. A noticeable change then occurred. She began to talk about her own death as not a very frightening event. She came to feel that her life had a purpose and would continue to be purposeful. She became more at ease with the whole situation, except that she still wanted to know more, especially about the condition of the human reality after death. Once again she followed her own approach to this matter and began to read many books on this topic. One day, when she had difficulty breathing and was exhausted, she said that it felt as though her body was a burden to her, and she thought that her reality was independent from her exhausted, diseased, and uncomfortable body. She was surprised at these feelings. She had never thought that she would come to believe that life had a spiritual as well as a physical dimension.

As her cancer spread and her physical health deteriorated, her understanding of her own life increased. One day she told me that as far as she was concerned she had a soul that was different and separate from her body. She was nevertheless very afraid to mention this to anybody. Her greatest fear was that her relatives and close friends would discount her understanding of her own spiritual reality. She feared they would analyze everything along psychological lines and

The Psychology of Spirituality

CASE STUDY discard her insights as wishful thinking in response to her illness and imminent death. In spite of this overwhelming possibility, she decided to share her views and thoughts with her relatives and friends and even went so far as to make those views and thoughts a part of plans for her funeral. To her relief, responses were extremely positive, and she was showered with encouraging affirmations.

Carol's case provides us with many challenges to our common understanding of human nature and our attitudes regarding the purpose of life. It poses questions regarding self-love, interpersonal relationships, human feelings of fear and anger, and finally those of life and death. It challenges our concepts of anxiety and depression and does not allow us to explain away the rich phenomena of our lives through biological and psychological explanations alone. It calls for answers to eternal questions about knowledge, love, freedom, justice, happiness, existence, and nonexistence.

These issues all belong to the spiritual domain which is addressed in the following section.

Towards a Psychology of Spirituality

●

In the case history just reviewed, several fundamental questions were raised, among them: What is true human nature? How do body and mind interact? Is there a soul, and, if so, what are its properties and characteristics? Is there an existence after death and if so, what kind of existence? And, finally, does spirituality have a reality and if so, what is it?

These questions have been with us for as long as we can trace back into human history. As early as a hundred thousand years ago, our ancestors had burial rituals, made amulets, and were concerned about death, evil spirits and forces beyond human comprehension. This was sixty thousand years before language was invented. In ancient times no distinctions were made between physical, psychological and spiritual experiences. Physical, psychological, and spiritual problems were identified as the work of the devil or acts of the gods, attributed to magic, exorcism, shamanism, punishment, and sacrifice.

At the dawn of civilization, in various ancient cultures, the belief in spirits and their influence on the hearts and minds of people was widespread. In the Bible we come across references to madness being caused as a punishment for disobeying God's commandments. For example, Saul has unusual childhood experiences,* later becomes distraught, and finally commits suicide. In the Greek, Roman, Persian, Egyptian and Chinese cultures, popular belief in supernatural causes of mental disorders was widespread.

The concept of soul divorced from the qualities of the body was expressed in philosophical terms for the first time by Heraclitus, who lived between 540 and 475 B.C.. Soon thereafter, Hippocrates (460-355 B.C.) asserted that human sorrow and grief, vision and knowledge, and various senses all came from the brain. He furthermore stated that when the brain is not healthy we experience "sorrows, griefs, despondency, lamentations" and other abnormal conditions.[1] Later, Plato stated that the soul has three parts—appetite, reason, and temper—which closely resemble Freud's Id, Ego, and Superego.

The belief in the relationship between emotional or mental conditions and spiritual concepts has continued throughout history and has affected the lives of individuals and societies of all cultures. Remarkably enlightened, although limited, views on the nature of human psychology arose from the earliest times. However, frighteningly destructive views and practices were held by the general population as well as by ecclesiastical and political authorities. In the fifteenth century, witchcraft mania swept over Europe and caused the death of more than two hundred thousand innocent women and children (and some men) in Germany and France alone. Smaller numbers of victims were put to death in England, Spain, and elsewhere in Europe.[2]

The central preoccupation of the ecclesiastical authorities dealing with witchcraft was supposed sexual activities between women and the devil. In 1484, Pope Innocent VIII issued a decree that removed any reluctance to persecute those accused of witchcraft. The infamous *Witches' Hammer (Malleus Maleficarum)* was published in the latter part of the fifteenth century. This book is replete with sexual detail as well as religious superstition about mental illness, and the fear and hatred of women.

In the first half of the sixteenth century, several noted individuals began to refute the claims of the exponents of witchcraft and rose to defend the rights of women. Among them was Juan Luis Vives (1492-1540), who in 1524 wrote a treatise on the education of women. Vives has the distinction of being called the father of modern empirical psychology.[3] Cornelius Agrippa (1486-1535) also defended the rights of women. His book *On the Nobility and Preeminence of the Feminine Sex* is of considerable interest with respect to the struggle against misogyny. Another prominent figure of this era was Johann Weyer (1515-1588), a physician with extraordinary psychiatric insights. Through his clinical work he demonstrated the fallacy of the witchcraft doctrine and outlined, for the first time, some of the fundamentals of the relationship between patient and doctor in psychotherapy. He is considered by some to be the first psychiatrist.[4]

These contributions gradually separated the unhealthy mix of religious doctrine and clinical findings. Slowly, a scientific approach to understanding the human emotional state began to develop. Human behaviour increasingly became the domain of clinical practitioners and behavioural scientists. Treatment methods became more humane. The German philosopher Göckel (1547-1628) coined the word "psychology" and emphasized the importance of the dynamics of the body-mind relationship.

In 1793, Philippe Pinel (1745-1826), the father of modern psychology, became the Superintendent of Bicêtre and later Salpêtrière, two institutes for the care of insane men and women respectively. It was Pinel who freed the mentally ill from their chains.

However, the most significant advance in modern psychology occurred at the beginning of this century when Freud published *The Interpretation of Dreams* in 1900, and, later, many other of his books. Freud spoke of his struggles to achieve greater self-awareness. According to Bruno Bettelheim, Professor Emeritus of both Psychology and Psychiatry at the University of Chicago, "The English rendition of Freud's writings distorts much of the essential humanism that permeates the originals." These distortions are especially significant with respect to the manner in which the original concepts of psychoanalysis, which are "deeply personal appeals to our common humanity", are presented in depersonalized and dehumanized "scientific" language. Bettelheim points out that in the original German language the emphasis is on the first part of the word "psychoanalysis." "'Psyche' is the soul—a term full of the richest meaning." In English translation, the emphasis is on "analysis" and the enormous significance of the fact that we are dealing with the human soul is generally ignored. Bettelheim points out that "Freud often spoke of the soul—of its nature and structure, its development, its attributes, how it reveals itself in all we do and dream."[5]

The original objective of psychoanalysis was to encourage people to reflect introspectively on their inner lives and the life of their souls. However, as Western society, and particularly North American society, became more materialistic in its orientation, it changed the character and initial aims of psychoanalysis and created new schools of psychiatry, which are "behaviorally, cognitively or physiologically oriented and concentrate almost exclusively on what can be measured or observed from the outside...."[6]

During this century, psychology has emerged as a legitimate and significant area of study. Psychotherapeutic approaches have multiplied. Educational, industrial, institutional, individual and group psychologies have infiltrated all segments of our lives. Psychological terminology has permeated common speech and the folk wisdom of Western societies. Much of human behaviour, particularly the sexual and aggressive aspects of behaviour, is now discussed in psychological terms and dealt with accordingly. Parallel to the ascendancy of psychological concepts in these societies has been a marked decline in the influence and relevance of the teachings of mainstream religions. With the rise of psychology and the fall of religion, spiritual aspects of life have received little or no attention.

Together with psychoanalytic schools, the behavioural, cognitive, existential, developmental, humanistic, and other major schools of psychology have all made great contributions to our understanding of the instinctual, biological, and psychosocial forces that affect the formation of our personalities and life styles. We are now more fully aware of the importance of our childhood experiences in forming our personalities. We know the genetic roots of some major psychiatric disorders. We are beginning to understand the biochemical configuration of affective disorders, schizophrenia and some other major psychiatric illnesses. We have developed novel and effective methods of psychotherapy, marriage and family therapy, and group therapy. We have also begun, with some success, to apply our psychological insights into socio-economic and political aspects of human life.

However, along with these major achievements, modern psychology has become increasingly mechanistic and lifeless in its orientation and approaches. An ever greater and all-inclusive emphasis is placed on the development of chemical agents that will calm our anxieties, counter our depression, and decrease our confusion. We are increasingly offered new techniques and steps to overcome our addictions to drugs, to food, to work, to our relationships, to God—to everything. We are told unhesitatingly that we are victims and have to take revenge and discharge our anger at those who have wronged us, be they our parents, family members, friends, or strangers. In their attempts to analyze and explain away the root causes of such disturbing behaviour as violence, cruelty, inequality, prejudice, greed, selfishness, war, and so on, psychologists and psychiatrists have resorted to instinctual, hereditary, biophysiological, and ethological (the scientific study of animal behaviour) explanations.

Many people, disappointed and mistrustful of mainstream schools of psychology, are turning to fringe movements with fantastic claims and fanatical approaches. In many instances, the rational is giving way to the irrational, and loving therapeutic encounter is being replaced by indulgent and self-gratifying counsels.

These conditions exist because the fundamental dimension of human nature—the spiritual dimension—is either missing or misunderstood. The absence of the spiritual dimension in current therapeutic approaches has also caused moral and ethical bankruptcy. Consequently, the therapeutic sanctum has become a battlefield. In therapy, love and trust—unconditional, pure, and unadulterated—are essential prerequisites. Without them, anger and mistrust will dominate. Both the therapist and the client will be wary, the former for fear of being accused, the latter for fear of being abused. Each enters the relationship with discomfort and suspicion, and little, if any, healing takes place.

Having freed itself from the chains and locked gates of the asylums, having replaced witchcraft with analytic insight, and having refined the crude alchemy of the past to a substantive understanding of the chemistry of the brain, modern psychology is now ready to focus on the spiritual dimension of human reality.

The central objective of the psychology of spirituality is to integrate the biological, psychosocial, and spiritual aspects of our reality into a fuller and more balanced understanding of human nature and human needs. We have, by now, laid a solid foundation for understanding the human person in health and in illness. We now know that the separation between the biological and psychological, the body and mind, is arbitrary. Every human condition is both biological and psychological. The body affects the psyche and the psyche influences the body. While the body takes prominence in some conditions and the psyche in others, all human conditions are a combination of both. This does not mean, however, that the same approach can be applied to all conditions.

At the present time, one of three general approaches is advocated. On the one extreme are those who contend that all human conditions, whether in health or illness, are physical in nature and should therefore be treated physically, through chemicals, surgical interventions, diet, exercise, and other means and modalities that alter the functions and conditions of the body. On the other extreme are those who argue that all human conditions, whether in health or illness, are psychical in nature and should therefore be dealt with through psychical means such as psychological interventions, mind-affecting substances, mental exercises, religious rituals, and magic. The exponents of both orientations are adamant in their views. They seem, at times, prepared to go to the bitter end, even if it means further injury to the person or persons involved. Somewhere between these extremes is the largest group—those practitioners and people who are willing to use the knowledge and insight of both groups.

An interesting and highly consequential aspect of all three approaches is the way they deal with the dilemma of dualism. The doctrine of dualism considers human reality to consist of two opposing and irreducible elements: matter and mind, body and soul, or the material and the spiritual. This doctrine is problematic because it divides reality. In its essence, reality is one. In order to overcome this thorny issue, most scientists of our time have chosen simply to reduce the mind to a configuration of extremely complex chemical and electrical activities in the brain, hence material in its essence. Likewise, they have resolved the body–soul, material–spiritual dichotomies by denying the reality of soul and the validity of the spiritual. Similarly, those who consider all reality to be psychical have made the same error as the material scientists, by attempting to explain all objective reality in psychological terms, have made the same error as the physical scientists. The third group has basically abandoned any hope of resolving this difficult issue.

As we will see with the psychology of spirituality, there is no dualism at the level of the living human being. The living person is one, as there is total unity and integration between the two distinctive expressions of reality, i.e., the material and the spiritual. The psychology of spirituality, therefore, perceives human nature as an integrated and unified human reality with three fundamental powers: to know, to love, and to will.

All human conditions, both in health and illness, and with respect to life and death, are experienced and understood by us through our capacities to know, love, and will. The way we live, experience our existence, and understand and deal with opportunities and challenges all depend on these three capacities. The psychology of spirituality explains human reality and life experiences within this framework. As such, our discussion will focus on knowledge, love and will, which are the properties of our psyche. We will first begin with a review of human nature and concepts of self and soul.

PART TWO

Self

and

Soul

*There is no history but that of soul,
no place but that of soul.*
St. John Perse

On Human Nature

●

In the contemporary world many view human nature as essentially material and entirely the product of the biological and evolutionary processes of life. Our first objective in this book, then, is to define human spiritual nature in order to show that at the core of the major problems of our individual and collective lives lies the denial and neglect of this basic aspect of reality. The second objective, equally important, is to present the principles of the psychology of spirituality.

The intense study of the field of psychology that I have pursued from that eventful first day in the emergency room has resulted in what I feel is a valid new approach—the fourth approach, if you like—to distinguish it from the three previously mentioned prescientific, analytic, and biological approaches. I call this new formulation the psychology of spirituality, an approach that unifies the biological, psychosocial, and spiritual dimensions of human nature and offers an integrated and comprehensive understanding of human behaviour and psychological problems.

We begin with a review of the materialistic and spiritual views of human nature and the consequences of materialism and a spiritual way of life. This will be followed by observations about life experiences and what we can learn from these observations with respect to human nature.

I will then focus on the issue of duality in the light of our understanding of human consciousness. Consciousness is at the core of all spiritual realities, in the same way that energy is the basis of all physical realities. Consciousness, therefore, plays a central role in our understanding of human nature.

This discussion of consciousness is followed by a section on the concept of self and the role of feelings and emotions in our lives. It is at the level of feelings that the body and mind function in a truly integrated and complete manner. This is probably one important reason why coming in touch with our feelings and understanding them is so important and plays such a crucial role in creating a wholesome and happy life. The remaining part of the book outlines the principles of the psychology of spirituality and their application to our life challenges and opportunities.

THE MATERIALISTIC VIEW OF HUMAN NATURE

The basic concepts of the materialistic view of human nature are that existence and life are both accidents; that humans are the chance product of the process of evolution; that matter is the basic constituent of the universe; and that therefore human thoughts and feelings are the by-products of human biological activities. This materialistic philosophy has existed since pre-Socratic times. Referring to this philosophy, Erich Fromm says:

> This materialism claimed that "the" substratum of all mental and spiritual phenomena was to be found in matter and material processes. In its most vulgar and superficial form, this kind of materialism taught that feelings and ideas are sufficiently explained as results of chemical bodily processes, and "thought is to the brain what urine is to the kidneys."[1]

Furthermore, this view of human nature holds that we are basically animals at the mercy of our instincts and that we are driven in our lives to obtain pleasure and avoid pain at all costs. Put differently, human actions are motivated by greed and selfishness, empowered by aggressive and sexual drives. Alternatively, materialism views human beings as machines. Paul Davies and John Gribbin, in their book *The Matter Myth*, point out that Richard

Dawkins, an ardent promoter of the biological machines theory, describes all living entities, including human beings as the "gene machines."[2] They then reject such a materialistic and deterministic view of the world and observe that

> a machine can have no "free will"; its future is rigidly determined from the beginning of time. Indeed, time ceases to have much physical significance in this picture, for the future is already contained in the present (and so, for that matter, is the past). As Ilya Prigogine has eloquently expressed it, God is reduced to a mere archivist, turning the pages of a cosmic history book that is already written.[3]

The materialistic view denies the existence of soul or spirit; the soul does not exist because we cannot prove its existence as we can prove the existence of the planets, for example. We can neither see, hear, taste, smell, nor touch the spirit or soul; nor do we have instruments that can demonstrate its existence or measure its powers. However, we do have our five senses, and through these we experience the world. We each have a mind through which we understand the world. This mind is the product of the brain, and once the brain is dead, the mind no longer exists. The materialistic school further holds that human existence is limited to this life. There is no scientific evidence of life after death, and therefore when we die we no longer exist. The purpose of life is to stay alive, be happy, seek pleasure, accomplish what we can, and be successful. As such, life is basically a power struggle and an arena for the survival of the fittest.

The Marxist, psychoanalytic, existential, behavioural, ethnological, and Darwinian schools of thought all define human nature within the materialistic framework described above. These philosophies have greatly influenced our thinking in the twentieth century and have shaped our views about ourselves, our world, and our lives.

In 1859 Marx wrote: "It is not the consciousness of men that determines their social being, but, on the contrary, their social being that determines their consciousness."[4] On another occasion, Marx elaborated on this theme and concluded that human beings are what they produce:

> As individuals express their life, so they are. What they are, therefore, coincides with their production, both with what they produce and with how they produce. The nature of the individuals thus depends on the material conditions determining their production.[5]

With the advantage of historical hindsight, we are now gradually apprehending the enormous cost to humanity as followers of Marxist ideology tried to put these concepts into practice.

Freud is another individual whose ideas have had far reaching influence in our way of thinking about ourselves. Freud believed that our thoughts, feelings, and actions are determined by two powerful instincts: Eros, the life instinct and Thanatos, the death instinct. According to this perspective there is no such thing as free will, and all our actions can be explained (and justified) through analysis of the conscious and primarily unconscious dynamics of our psyche.

Such an approach to personal responsibility is now quite common. Many therapists help their clients absolve themselves of guilt and shame about their actions, and many destructive and violent forms of behaviour are justified and sanctioned on the basis of these perspectives on human nature.[6]

A different, but similarly widespread, notion about human nature and the reasons for our troubled lives came from the existentialist school of thought. Jean-Paul Sartre, one of the leading existential thinkers, like Marx and Freud, did not believe in the existence of God or human spiritual nature. In his work, Sartre concluded that because God does not exist, everything is permitted. Indeed, without God or spirituality, the logical conclusion is that there are no transcendent or objective values. According to Sartre, there is no such thing as human nature. We do not exist because of God, or evolution, or any other reason. We just simply exist. We are here for no reason, and we have the freedom to decide the nature of our lives. Sartre believed that much of human misery is due to the fact that we are free, that our freedom is painful, and that we try to avoid this pain. In a word, he pointed out that we cannot avoid the pain of freedom because we are free.[7]

Almost diametrically opposed to the views of Sartre, but still within the confines of materialism, are the ideas put forward by B.F. Skinner, one of the main exponents of the school of behaviourism. Behaviourism presumes to apply, in a very strict and narrow way, the scientific method (which has proven so useful in the study of the physical world) to the study of human nature. Skinner categorically stated that there is no scientific basis for belief in God, nor, for that matter, is there any reality to human desires, intentions, and decisions. The only real thing is our behaviour, because only behaviour can be empirically studied and manipulated. He believed that all human behaviour is basically in response to the environment and an attempt to avoid pain or have pleasure. While Sartre saw our freedom as the main characteristic of humanness and at the same time the basic cause of existential pain, Skinner posited that we are determined by nature and the main cause of our problems is that we like to think we are free. According to Skinner, the answer to all our problems is to abandon the illusion of our freedom, change our environment, and modify our behaviour.[8]

Konrad Lorenz is another modern thinker who views human nature essentially in materialistic terms. An ethnologist, Lorenz studied animal behaviour while incorporating many of Darwin's ideas in a formulation of human nature. Lorenz's main conclusions are that humans are innately aggressive, free will and virtue are illusions, human behaviour is the same as animal behaviour, and humans differ from animals only in degree and with respect to functions. Lorenz went so far as to believe that all great dangers threatening the human race with extinction are direct consequences of our capacity to think conceptually and to communicate through speech. He held little hope for improving the human condition because of the innate aggression easily aroused by many factors in our environment.[9]

Although these five materialistic views conflict in many respects, they do have one important idea in common. In their view, humans, both as individuals and societies, have very limited potential or scope for personal development. Humans are subject to enormous biological, evolutionary, historical, and social forces over which they have little control. These viewpoints have profoundly affected the way modern people think of themselves and deal with their problems.

Humans as Spiritual Beings

It is not easy to discuss human spiritual nature. To begin with, the very concept of spirituality is suspect. We live at a time when many scientists deny or question the validity of such concepts as soul, spirit, or spirituality. Furthermore, many religions have lost their respectability because of their reliance on blind faith and because many of their practices are (or seem to be) superstitious or prejudiced. In addition, religious definitions of spirituality do not always agree and are usually vague and unclear. Moreover, people of our time have lost their confidence, buried their hope, and can no longer bring themselves to believe firmly in the existence of a benevolent and just God, or in a loving and spiritual human race. We live in a century that has seen two World Wars and several major regional wars in which millions of people have been killed, starved to death, or allowed to die totally preventable deaths. This is a century in which science has given us destructive weapons that are used in turn by upholders of ideologies of the left and right, and of secular and religious persuasions. This is a century in which a concerted effort has been made (and continues to be made) to prove that human beings are animals, that animals are aggressive, and that humans are therefore aggressive by nature. These are the times in which people have lowered their standards of morality and ethics to such a degree that almost any behaviour is sanctioned as long as, on the surface, it does not "harm" other human beings or, if it does, that at least it is not noticed. These are times in which, in the name of security and democracy, order and freedom, and state rights and human rights, practically all forms of deviant and unjust behaviour are sanctioned and condoned.

These developments have so separated us from our spiritual nature that the study of spirituality is very difficult, viewed as it is with a cynical and hostile air. Generally speaking, the view of humans as spiritual beings is based on the notion that there is a Creator—single, unknowable, all-knowing, and all-loving—who has created us, with capacities for knowledge, love, and will. The purpose of our lives is to use these capacities to acquire knowledge and wisdom, to become loving and just, and to use our will in the service of good rather than evil.

My main objective in this book is to put forward a framework within which we can study the spiritual aspects of human reality in a coherent and logical manner, appropriately employing the scientific method.

As self-aware human beings, we study ourselves, and in so doing we are, of necessity, both subjective and objective. In my work as a psychiatrist, I have been privileged to witness the most profound experiences, thoughts, and feelings of many people from several different cultures under various circumstances. A study of these lives provides us with invaluable data about the characteristics, qualities, and workings of human nature. A combination of knowledge derived from these clinical studies and the cross-cultural work in which I have been engaged for the past three decades, as well as insights drawn from years of study and practice of both science and religion, form the core of the concepts about human nature presented here.

Let us now return to our discussion of the two main perspectives on human nature—the materialistic and the spiritual—and consider the actual impact of these two views on our daily lives.

MATERIALISM AS A WAY OF LIFE

The materialistic philosophy, which holds that humans are advanced animals with little potential for deliberate self development and change, has immediate consequences for the way people lead their lives. It disclaims any purpose in life and encourages people to live according to their desires, feelings, and instincts. This approach uses all human capacities in the service of self-gratification and self-aggrandizement. As a result, greed, injustice, extremes of wealth and poverty, aggression, and war are seen as inevitable and perhaps even necessary.

Materialistic philosophy encourages people to compete for and consume the world's limited resources without thought to generations yet to come. In this materialistic context, interpersonal relationships are greatly troubled. The natural human tendencies toward love, care, and kindness are often misunderstood or abused. Love relationships are usually disturbed because people are self-centred and unwilling to give or to care.

In individual life, a dramatic inner conflict develops. By nature human beings are drawn to ever higher and more refined degrees of knowledge, love, compassion, justice, and beauty. However, a materialistic view of life and human nature incites us to use our knowledge to acquire wealth and power, to love ourselves foremost and to excess, and to consider justice and beauty secondary to issues of self-interest and gratification. These views cause a profound degree of inner conflict. Many accept the ways of materialism and live their lives in an unending quest for happiness, peace of mind, love, and calmness, none of which they ever attain. Others try to have both a materialistic way of life and spiritual fulfillment. These are people who want to have their cake and eat it too. They live their lives in pursuit of gratification, wealth, and power on the one hand, and try to offset this lifestyle by performing certain acts of charity and service on the other hand. But at the core of their being they experience a schism and dividedness. There is no fulfillment in this type of life either.

A less obvious, but equally negative, consequence of materialistic philosophy is that the creative, artistic, and intuitive aspects of life are given far less importance than the scientific, logical, and technological aspects, partly because the latter gives us much greater opportunity to accumulate wealth and power. The consequent inner disaffection and impoverishment of the soul may be temporarily forgotten through use of alcohol, other mind-altering drugs, mind-numbing music, and a variety of excessive life experiences. However, in the long run these conditions take their toll. Because life is considered to be limited in duration, with nothingness looming at the end, the materialistic lifestyle causes us a profound degree of fear and anxiety. Our greatest fear under these circumstances is, of course, fear of death. Consequently, a materialistic society becomes preoccupied with death. Its sciences, politics, industry, art, literature, music, and entertainment all become death oriented. Bombs are made, war industries are created, and artistic, literary and entertainment activities are all centred on death—its inevitability on the one hand and its unreality on the other, as though death were a black hole of nothingness into which we are all sinking. As a result an attitude of cynicism and pointlessness becomes pervasive.

It is this inability to accept the reality of death that breeds aggression and violence and that sanctions the organized killing of millions in the name of security, freedom, justice, democracy, or law and order. Ultimately, materialism takes joy, hope, and creativity out of life. It makes life a struggle, love a burden, knowledge a commodity, beauty a luxury, and peace an unattainable fantasy.

SPIRITUALITY AS A WAY OF LIFE

It is difficult to give a single definition of the spiritual way of life because there is such a wide range of views on the issue. It should be pointed out that being religious and living a spiritual way of life are not necessarily synonymous. There are many religious people who, despite belief in such things as the existence of God, the human soul, and life after death, nevertheless live a life that is basically materialistic. For them, God is both a provider and withholder of gifts, a Being who gives through divine love and punishes through divine anger. These people relate to God as they do to any other authority, trying to appease God, to receive favours, and to avoid disclosure of their inner thoughts and intentions. Their purpose in life is to obtain personal salvation and to be admitted into a heaven they have created in their imaginations. Their main objective is to get something—in this case God's favour, admittance into an everlasting paradise, and preference over the ungodly. In form, if not also in substance, this attitude parallels the materialistic approach to life, in that it likewise concentrates on the accumulation of wealth, attainment of ongoing pleasure, and power over others.

Another segment of the population approaches spirituality as a justification for personal shortcomings and failure, as well as their own unwillingness to face the challenges of social life. Under the guise of detachment from worldly things, these individuals may isolate themselves from the mainstream of society, assume little or no responsibility for dealing with the challenges of human existence, and live basically self-centred, parasitic lives. Some in this group are lazy or self-indulgent, but many have simply misunderstood a spiritual lifestyle to mean avoidance of the day-to-day affairs of human society, as though all human affairs were by definition materialistic.

Spirituality, however, is not simply the opposite or the negation of materialism. Far from it. Spirituality is an active process that is inherently purposeful. Its objectives are growth, development, and transcendence. Through our spirituality we seek to achieve the highest and noblest in ourselves and to create a united and ever-advancing civilization.

We human beings are at the crossroads of material and spiritual realities—the junction at which the material and spiritual meet. We have one foot in the animal world and the other in the spiritual. We can live totally materialistic, animalistic lives, or we can choose to transcend our animal nature and enter the realms of spirituality. This choice is the essence of our freedom. As humans we are endowed with the capacities to know, to love, and to will. We have to decide what to learn and how to use our knowledge. We can use our knowledge to wage war or peace. If we choose peace and dedicate ourselves to its cause, we have chosen a spiritual lifestyle. The same holds true for other choices such as truthfulness, trust, justice, compassion, cooperation, beauty, humility, service, and all other spiritual qualities. If we make the objective of life to use our minds to learn about these spiritual qualities, to focus the power of our love and attraction on them, and to employ our will to commit acts according to them, we will have embarked on a spiritual lifestyle.

But this is not all. A spiritual life is a life of growth and detachment, purpose and reflection, discipline and creativity, immediacy and farsightedness, prayer and social action, determination and resignation—seemingly irreconcilable opposites. Ultimately, a spiritual life transcends the limits of time, place, and person. It follows that a spiritual lifestyle calls for a major review of our thinking about our life experiences and perspectives. It examines not only our inner personal processes but also our interpersonal relationships and our relationship with God—a process that inevitably helps us to search for and establish a transcendent meaning for our existence.

Our Experience of Self

●

Theories of human nature must be applicable to everyday life. How do we perceive our nature? What do our life experiences tell us about our body and mind? What are our major struggles in actualizing our potential? Why do we have feelings? These are some of the questions that need to be addressed.

HUMAN EXPERIENCE AND HUMAN NATURE

One way of understanding our true nature is to reflect on our daily life experiences and to think about the choices that are open to us. Take, for example, the experience of writing. As I write these words, I have several simultaneous experiences. I am using my hand, eyes, and brain to write. As such, writing is a physical experience. I am also thinking about what I write and using my mind. Writing, therefore, is an intellectual experience. As I write, I am fully aware of my attempts to relate to those who will be reading these words, and this brings me simultaneous feelings of joy because of the readers' attention, fear that the reader will not approve, and hope that what I write will be meaningful to those who read it. As such, writing is an emotional experience. Finally, I have a choice about what I write. I can focus my soul and my readers' souls on subjects that will bring us together and allow us to understand ourselves better, or I can exploit the readers' baser instincts and focus them on their primal fears, suspicions, and instincts. Furthermore, as I write these lines and the reader reads them, we are both transcending the limits of time, person, and place, and we are communicating soul to soul. These are spiritual dimensions of the simple act of writing these lines. In doing so, I have clearly used my powers of mind and consciousness, which are far more than my instincts. It is this spiritual dimension that we need to understand better, because it gives meaning and purpose to our lives, and shapes our understanding of ourselves and relationships to each other, the universe, and ultimately, God.

Let us look at another human experience, for example, pain caused by a broken arm. Such pain is usually intense enough to force us to seek immediate treatment. Our first (and appropriate) concern is to decrease the pain and to avoid any activity that would cause a greater degree of discomfort or injury. However, if we were to sustain the fracture in an earthquake in which others were buried alive under the rubble or were suffering from more severe injuries, we would have several distinct choices. We could abandon all others and become preoccupied with our own well-being. Or we could take advantage of the situation and abuse the rights and properties of others. Or we could put aside our self-concern and become actively involved in saving other lives, perhaps even to the detriment of our own well-being. Obviously, all of these different forms of behaviour are not the result of the human instincts of self-preservation and pain avoidance that we share with animals. These responses are uniquely human.

The pain we experience as a result of a broken arm is usually accompanied by a variety of emotions. If the accident occurred on a ski slope we may have feelings of sadness because of the injury and our inability to continue skiing, anger because of our own or someone else's negligence, fear that such an accident could occur again, happiness that a more serious injury did not happen, relief that in time of need there are always those to take care of us, or a combination of these and other feelings.

Likewise, if we were injured in an earthquake, we could have experienced a variety of feelings such as self-pity, fear, anger, and withdrawal, as well as empathy, closeness, joy, love, and ecstasy if we were able to be loving and helpful to others. This range of responses and feelings clearly indicates that human behaviour cannot be fully understood in the light of biological and psychological explanations alone. Rather, any human experience assumes its complete and comprehensive significance when in addition to the biological and psychological dimensions, spiritual factors are also taken into consideration.

The spiritual dimension gives meaning to all our experiences and integrates them into a cohesive form that includes the present, past, and future. This unique human capacity allows us to transcend our instincts and to respond to life experiences with knowledge, choice, and creativity.

FROM DUALITY TO INTEGRATION

One of the most challenging aspects of human nature is the mystery of the relationship between the body and the mind. We experience ourselves and others both as a duality and as a whole, and we view our world both in dichotomies and in an integrated manner. For example, we are aware of having a body and a mind. We are able to move, see, hear, and smell while our body is asleep. We have the ability to discover distant planets through mathematical calculations without actually seeing or touching these planets. These are a few examples of our constant experiences with duality. These experiences are further strengthened by our observation of dying people.

Those who have been with dying people are well aware of the remarkable change that occurs at the time of death. At one moment we are communicating with a human being; at the next moment we are in the presence of a dead body knowing that the person is no longer there. We experience a sense that the person has departed and that now the body is simply like an empty house with no inhabitant or an empty cage without a bird. What happens at the moment of death that results in such a change? Is this experience an indication that body and soul are independent of each other? Is this proof of the validity of theories of duality? A partial answer to this question lies in the way in which we look at our world.

The Psychology of Spirituality

We tend to see the world in dichotomies or dualities. We speak of light and darkness, good and evil, love and hate, as though there are indeed two realities, that of light and that of darkness, that of good and that of evil, that of love and that of hate, and so on. However, in the case of light and darkness, science clearly demonstrates that only light has a reality, and what we experience as darkness is simply the absence of light. The same is true of good and evil. In reality, what we experience as evil is the nonexistence of good. When there is no truthfulness, there is falsehood; when there is no mercy, there is cruelty.

In the context of values, there is no neutral condition in which neither good nor evil exists. From this perspective there is only one reality in the realm of human values and that is good. When good is partially or totally absent, evil with varying degrees of destructiveness is experienced. The same is true of love and hate. Love has a reality and existence of its own. It brings life and creativity, while the absence of love results in destruction and hate. These examples show that our experiences and observations of duality are not sufficient proof that duality exists. In fact, there is always one reality, the absence of which is experienced as the negative image of that same reality.

With this in mind, let us now turn to the puzzling issue of the body/soul duality. New insights into the function of the brain, the nature of consciousness, and the nature of physical reality, combined with new perspectives on the nature of soul and the definition of spirituality, now allow us to understand human nature from a perspective of unity. In the light of these new understandings, the dilemma of body/soul duality is resolved.

We must remember that reality is one, although expressed in many forms. This is both a scientific and a spiritual truth. For example, energy is a material reality that can be expressed in several forms: force, light, solidity, heat, etc. In like manner, consciousness is a spiritual reality which is expressed in several forms: thoughts, feelings, hopes, and desires.

There is now considerable evidence in scientific, philosophical, and religious thought that human reality is the human soul, which enables us to have consciousness. Theoretical physicist John Wheeler is of the view that "the world cannot be a giant machine, ruled by any pre-established continuum physical law." Rather, he sees information as the basis of everything and has coined a slogan "It from bit" to express the view that matter comes from information, which we may for all intents and purposes define as consciousness.[10]

Paul Davies and John Gribbin refer to the above statement and observe that from the perspective of the "participatory universe" philosophy of Wheeler, "observers are central to the nature of physical reality, and matter is ultimately relegated to mind."[11]

The same authors, in the concluding paragraph of their book, *The Matter Myth* state:

> Descartes founded the image of the human mind as a sort of nebulous substance that exists independently of the body. Much later, in the 1930's, Gilbert Ryle derided this dualism in a pithy reference to the mind as "the ghost in the machine." Ryle articulated his criticism during the triumphal phase of materialism and mechanism. The "machine" he referred to was the human body and the human brain, themselves just parts of the larger cosmic machine. But already, when he coined that pithy expression, the new physics was at work, undermining the world view on which Ryle's philosophy was based. Today, on the brink of the twenty-first century, we can see that Ryle was right to dismiss the notion of the ghost in the machine—not because there is no ghost, but because there is no machine.[12]

In the same spirit, Gregory Bateson says that "mind is the essence of being alive."[13] This is particularly true about the human mind, which is the power of the human soul. The human soul is the human capacity to understand and to know. Knowledge here is used in the broadest sense of the word and refers to consciousness, self-awareness, feelings, desires, as well as to our ability to think, use symbols, create language, and imagine. These are just some of the soul's qualities. There are other names given to the soul, such as psyche, human spirit, and the rational soul. But they all refer to the same thing: our ability to know, be conscious, experience, and understand.

Human beings are human beings because they know, and know that they know, and know that they want to know more. This human yearning and love for knowledge is not bound by the limitations of time and space. The human soul is on an ongoing journey of discovery and creativity and in the process uses all the available resources at its disposal to achieve its objective to acquire more knowledge, awareness, and insight.

In its journey through this life, the human soul is aided by the marvelous and magnificent tool of the human body. Various organs and parts of the body become instruments through which a person achieves great heights of knowledge, love, and creativity. For example, human eyes are used by the soul to behold the beauty of the beloved, to perceive the qualities of the world of nature, and to create new forms of art and technology. Likewise, the human ear is the tool of the soul in helping to compose music, hear the melodies of love, and receive communications conveyed to it by the words of others. These are only two examples of how the human body is used by the human soul to achieve its objectives and acquire greater heights of knowledge, understanding, awareness, and love.

The human soul not only uses the body and its various organs in their natural state but also creates new tools that greatly enhance the capacities of the body. These tools are then used for the purpose of acquiring additional knowledge and understanding by the soul. For example, we create the microscope and telescope to function as adjuncts to our eyes, allowing our mind to penetrate deeper and further and helping us understand the mysteries of nature to a much fuller extent. Likewise, the airplane is an extension of our feet that allows us to travel long distances and to increase our knowledge of different lands, peoples, and cultures. There are, in fact, a large number of tools produced by the creative forces of the human soul. Of all the tools our soul has created so far, the computer, which is the extension of the human brain, has the most far-reaching consequences. The human brain is the site of the human mind and the organ through which the human soul operates. There is no doubt that proper use of computers facilitates and accelerates the rate of human learning and provides us with higher capacities in various aspects of our intellectual functioning. From these examples it should be clear that the interaction of the human soul and body is ongoing and ever present, comprising all that a person knows, feels, and does.

Before we continue our discussion of duality and the nature of the human soul and consciousness, one more note of explanation is in order. Throughout this book I will use terms soul, spirit, and mind interchangeably. These words all refer to the same reality—the human reality—but each with specific emphasis. The following statement by 'Abdu'l-Bahá (1844-1921), one of the most outstanding spiritual leaders of all time, explains the delicate nature of these terms. Referring to the human reality 'Abdu'l-Bahá stated that:

> it [the Human Reality] is the same reality which is given different names, according to the different conditions wherein it becomes manifest. Because of its attachment to matter and the phenomenal world, when it governs the physical functions of the body, it is called the human soul. When it manifests itself as the thinker, the comprehender, it is called the mind. And when it soars into the atmosphere of God, and travels in the spiritual world, it becomes designated as spirit.[14]

In addition to the terms soul, mind, and spirit, at least three other terms—psyche, heart, and consciousness—need to be mentioned here. These three terms also refer to the human reality, each with its own specific emphasis. Psyche is a Greek mythological maiden, personifying the soul. She is loved by Eros, the Greek mythological god of love. In its contemporary usage, *psyche* means the soul. In psychology, it means the mind, both conscious and unconscious.

Heart is a word rich in meaning, including: the seat of life, the vital part or principle, life; the seat of feeling, understanding and thought; the mind in its widest sense; the seat of one's inmost being; the soul, the spirit, intent, will, purpose, inclination, desire; the seat of love or affection; the seat of courage; the seat of intellectual faculties, understanding, intellect, mind; the moral sense, conscience (*Oxford Dictionary*).

This review of the meanings of the word *heart* helps us to see the absurdity of the dichotomy that many people create between their thoughts, feelings, and desires. All these diverse human experiences and qualities are expressions of the human reality, which is one in its essence.

Finally, consciousness refers to a state of being in which the mind is functioning in its clear, rational, and inquisitive state. As such, consciousness is the expression of the human soul in its most immediate, accessible condition and therefore, merits close attention.

The Nature of Soul and Consciousness

•

The best way to understand the soul is to identify its characteristics and properties, because understanding the nature of the soul itself is beyond our capacity. Historically, there have been two views as to the nature of the soul or consciousness. The materialistic view considers matter as primary and consciousness as a property of complex material patterns that emerge at a certain stage of biological evolution. The spiritual view considers consciousness to be the primary reality, the essence of life in general and of humanness in particular. It is this consciousness (soul) that animates matter at the level of the human body and makes human life possible. A number of scientific developments and conceptual formulations in recent years offer us a better understanding of this interface of matter and consciousness.

Paul Davies, writing about mind and soul in his book *God and the New Physics*, states, "The fact that a concept is abstract rather than substantial does not render it somehow unreal or illusory."[15] Later he goes on to the specific question of body and soul, observing that "the fundamental error of dualism is to treat body and soul as rather like two sides of a coin, whereas they belong to totally different categories.... Mind and body are not two components of a duality, but two entirely different concepts drawn from different levels in a hierarchy of description."[16] In other words, the human body belongs to one level of reality, the human soul to another, and they interact at the site of the human brain. The nature of this interaction is not yet known and may never be completely understood. However, new discoveries in the field of quantum physics clearly indicate that there exists a very real and demonstrable relationship between consciousness and matter. This is most interestingly observed at the level of subatomic particles. "Quantum theory has shown that subatomic particles are not isolated grains of matter but are probability patterns, interconnections in an inseparable cosmic web that includes the human observer and her consciousness."[17] These and other similar observations are gradually shifting attention from the concepts of duality to the dynamics of integration of the body and the soul.

The result of this integration is the emergence of "self." The human "self" is simultaneously a body and a soul. There is no duality. Our sense of duality is due to the fact that our body and soul evolve differently. The evolution of the human body has been studied quite extensively and consequently, is better understood:

> According to generally accepted anthropological findings, the anatomical evolution of human nature was virtually completed some fifty thousand years ago. Since then the human body and brain have remained essentially the same in structure and size. On the other hand, the conditions of life have changed profoundly during this period and continue to change at a rapid pace. To adapt to these changes the human species used its faculties of consciousness, conceptual thought, and symbolic language to shift from genetic evolution to social evolution, which takes place much faster and provides far more variety.[18]

These two stages in human evolution—biological and psychological evolution—are now being followed by the third stage in human evolution: spiritual evolution. These evolutionary stages are represented in the structure of the brain. The brain stem, which is the innermost part of the brain and the oldest in the evolutionary process, is concerned with instincts, biological drives, and various kinds of compulsive behaviour. The limbic system, well developed in all mammals, surrounds the brain stem and is responsible for emotional experiences and expressions. The third part of the brain, the neocortex, is the most developed and distinctive in the human species and is connected with higher order abstract functions such as thought and language. The development of the neocortex was stabilized some fifty thousand years ago.

We are now evolving towards a new level of our collective evolution, in which our instincts, emotions, and thoughts are to be integrated into a whole, unified process. This is possible as we learn to expand the human mind and connect it with the Universal Mind. This is a spiritual process. It makes use of our freedom of choice and challenges us to change our values and attitudes. Many people believe that values are constant and do not change. However, this is not the case. Everything in the universe, including our values, changes and evolves. Evolution is the very stuff of creation. For example, science tells us that the evolution of our material universe probably began with an enormous explosion releasing an awesome amount of energy. From then on our physical world has been on its journey of development. The epitome of this material evolution is the human body and, in particular, the human brain. The same principle applies to the evolution of metaphysical and spiritual realities such as consciousness, love, and creativity. It will be helpful to review briefly the emerging views and theories on the evolution of consciousness and spirituality.

Ken Wilber identified four levels of consciousness: ego, biosocial, existential, and transpersonal.[19] The transpersonal level is similar to the above mentioned concept of spirituality.

Grof identifies three major domains of consciousness: psychodynamic experiences (past and present), prenatal experiences (process of birth), and transpersonal experiences (beyond individual boundaries).[20] These views are similar in essence to views put forward by Jung, Maslow, and others. These thinkers all attempt to introduce spiritual concepts into our formulations about the nature of human reality and to find conditions under which we human beings can function at a higher level of maturity, insight, integration, creativity, and wholeness. Similar views are found in various religious writings. The following is a concise and comprehensive statement by 'Abdu'l-Bahá on the relationship of body and soul and the process of spiritualization:

> There are in the world of humanity three degrees; those of the body, the soul, and spirit. The body is the physical or animal degree of man.

From the bodily point of view man is a sharer of the animal kingdom. The bodies alike of men and animals are composed of elements held together by the law of attraction.

Like the animal, man possesses the faculties of the senses, is subject to heat, cold, hunger, thirst, etc.; unlike the animal, man has a rational soul, the human intelligence....

When man allows the spirit,* through his soul, to enlighten his understanding, then does he contain all Creation; because man, being the culmination of all that went before and thus superior to all previous evolutions, contains all the lower world within himself. Illumined by the spirit through the instrumentality of the soul, man's radiant intelligence makes him the crowning-point of Creation.

But on the other hand, when man does not open his mind and heart to the blessing of the spirit, but turns his soul towards the material side, towards the bodily part of his nature, then is he fallen from his high place and he becomes inferior to the inhabitants of the lower animal kingdom. In this case the man is in a sorry plight! For if the spiritual qualities of the soul, open to the breath of the Divine Spirit, are never used, they become atrophied, enfeebled, and at last incapable; whilst the soul's material qualities alone being exercised, they become terribly powerful—and the unhappy, misguided man, becomes more savage, more unjust, more vile, more cruel, more malevolent than the lower animals themselves. All his aspirations and desires being strengthened by the lower side of the soul's nature, he becomes more and more brutal, until his whole being is in no way superior to that of the beasts that perish. Men such as this, plan to work evil, to hurt and to destroy; they are entirely without the spirit of Divine compassion, for the celestial quality of the soul has been dominated by that of the material. If, on the contrary, the spiritual nature of the soul has been so strengthened that it holds the material side in subjection, then does the man approach the Divine; his humanity becomes so glorified that the virtues of the Celestial Assembly are manifested in him; he radiates the Mercy of God; he stimulates the spiritual progress of mankind, for he becomes a lamp to show light on their path.[21]

From this discussion of the relationship between human consciousness and the human body, one thing is clear. We have at least two distinctive experiences of our being—the physical and the

---

*Spirit here means the Divine Spirit, which affects the human soul through the teachings of the founders of major religions such as Buddha, Moses, Christ, Muhammad, and Bahá'u'lláh.

spiritual. Our physical experiences come from the body's five senses of touch, taste, smell, hearing, and smell. Our spiritual experiences are properties of the mind. These experiences include imagination, thought, comprehension, and memory. Furthermore, we have the capacity to integrate the powers of mind and body—we have the ability to bring the five senses and the qualities of the mind together in such a manner that our experience of ourselves is that of wholeness.[22]

So, on the one hand, we think of ourselves in terms of body and mind, as two entities, and, on the other hand, we experience ourselves as a *self*, undivided, whole, and complete. It is towards this integrated and whole self that we are attracted. We all want to achieve such wholeness.

THE CONCEPT OF SELF

Experience of selfhood is uniquely human. When we speak of *self*, we are talking about our awareness that we exist now, have existed in the past, and will continue to exist in the future and that this experience has been, is, and will remain constant and whole. This definition includes components of our self such as the conscious and unconscious parts of our psyche; the physical, mental, and emotional dimensions of our personality; and both the egoistical and the universal aspects of our behaviour.

When we use the term *self*, we are talking about our being as we experience it and as it is perceived by others. This concept of *self* resolves the dilemma of the body/soul duality and allows us to study the human self in its fully integrated totality. Ego is the conscious experience and expression of *self* and its evolution is determined by genetic and biological factors on the one hand, and psychological and spiritual factors on the other.

Let us look at *self* in a more specific way. As human beings, we all have certain instincts that we share with animals. These instincts are essential for the survival and continuation of the species. We get hungry and search for food; we experience pain, realize something is wrong, and seek remedy for the pain. We have the capacity to sense danger, so we either face the danger and fight it, or escape the danger and seek a secure situation. We also have sexual drives, which under normal circumstances attract us to a member of the opposite sex, frequently resulting in pregnancy and the continuation of our species. Furthermore, we have bonding instincts that connect us very firmly to our newly born and motivate us to care, protect, and nurture our young.

At the instinctual level most advanced animals do the same. There is, however, a very fundamental difference between humans and animals. Animals do not deviate from instinctual laws. Humans, clearly, have a choice. Our response to basic instincts of hunger, pain, fight or flight, and sex are quite different from animals. We may decide to fast or diet rather than eat. Some may decide to fast until death in order to make a point, often to seek justice. Some people eat even when they are not hungry. Others do not eat even though hunger and food is accessible (as in anorexia nervosa). Still others do not share food with the starving masses even when they themselves have more food than they need. These are all unique to human behaviour.

The same is true of pain. It should be added here that not all pain is a sign of illness. For example, growth is painful. The same is true for the pain we experience following strenuous physical activity. Masochistic human beings intentionally inflict pain upon themselves. Sadistic people inflict pain upon other people. From these few examples it is very clear that the human approach to pain is very complex and does not follow the simple laws of instincts.

The fight or flight reaction is also different in humans. There are many occasions in which we choose to face a dangerous situation even though we know that we would not be able to protect ourselves. This is the way the followers of Ghandi faced the threat of the British forces. In South Africa today, unarmed or poorly armed black children, youth, and adults face the powerful, heavily armed police, knowing full well that they are in physical danger.

Conversely, there are phobics who fear harmless things or situations. Some are afraid of heights, dogs, bees, or flies. Some are afraid of crowds; others fear being left alone. There is a wide range of phobias and a large number of phobic individuals in this world.

With regard to sex, humans also do not exclusively follow the laws of instincts. There are people who choose to be celibate. There are those who choose to have sex but not to procreate, those who go the route of homosexuality, and still others who combine sex with violence and death. Human sexual behaviour is very complex. There is a huge industry dedicated to sexual matters, and beyond making my point I shall not add further to it.

We may ask why human beings respond so differently to these basic instincts. The answer, of course, lies in the fact that humans have consciousness and will. We have the capacity to choose, and our choices are influenced not only by our instincts but also by our consciousness, feelings, and knowledge. During our childhood and adolescence we have a range of experiences that help us develop a worldview and to have specific feelings about ourselves, our world, and our relationship to the world. People's worldviews vary considerably. Some see the world as a dangerous place, others as a safe one. Some avoid involvement with the world; others become fully involved with it. Some feel helpless in the face of the world; others relate to the world as a challenge and an opportunity.

These and other worldviews greatly affect how we live, and how we understand and relate to the *self*. We also acquire certain feelings towards *self* and the world. As we grow, we greatly expand our abilities and transcend the limitations of the instinctual level of our existence. We become less animal and more human. The mind begins to have greater power and initiative, and there develops a mind/body struggle that is at the core of many human endeavours and the cause of much distress. This struggle has resulted in the development of materialistic and parapsychological schools of thought and the conflicted lifestyles of the contemporary world.

In order to understand the root causes of these conditions and in our attempt to find an integrated and wholesome approach to self-understanding, we need to understand the nature and function of our feelings. This is required because emotions play such an important role in all our activities.

THE PURPOSE OF FEELINGS

We are all familiar with feelings and emotions[23] because we all experience them. When we speak of feelings, we usually think of bad and good feelings. We consider sadness, anger, fear, and anxiety to be bad; while happiness, kindness, and calmness are good feelings. But this description does not really help us to understand the nature of feelings and their role in our lives. A definition of feelings will help. To do so, let us review some of the characteristics and functions of feelings.

First, feelings are conscious human experiences. We cannot feel without awareness. Whenever we feel something, it is because we are aware of that feeling. When we are in a coma or under anaesthetic, we do not feel anything because we are not conscious. To feel, we need consciousness.

Second, feelings are experienced in our bodies as well as our minds. We not only know that we are feeling in a certain way but also experience that feeling physically. For example, when afraid, we know that we are afraid, and at the same time experience certain changes in our body. Our heart rate increases; we may become pale and sometimes tremble. We have an urge to escape and experience a number of physical and physiological changes. Finally, feelings have a purpose and fulfill a function. There are some feelings that tell us about our state of health, such as pain or weakness. Other feelings warn us of impending danger, like feelings of anger, fear, or anxiety. Still other feelings tell us things are well. To this category belong feelings of wellness, happiness, and calmness.

As we study feelings, it becomes even clearer that they are, in fact, complex human experiences. Human emotions (feelings) are complex because they are the bridge between our instinctual and intellectual powers. Feelings result from the interface of body and mind and are an indispensable part of the *self*. They have both physical and metaphysical characteristics, and affect both body and mind.

Some feelings are primarily physical, others primarily psychological, and a third group is a mixture of both physical and psychological. It should be noted, however, that in human life the physical can become psychological, and the psychological can be experienced as merely physical. While this classification is not rigid, it can nonetheless be helpful in understanding a very important aspect of our being.

The primary physical feelings are related to our instincts for self-preservation, pain avoidance, and gratification. We experience these feelings as hunger, fear, pain, and pleasure. We become motivated to find food, avoid a fight or danger, seek remedy for pain, and achieve gratification, usually of a sexual nature. If life becomes limited to this level of functioning, then we live a basically animal existence. It does not matter how comfortable or easy such a life becomes, it does not fulfill our fundamental human needs. We remain dissatisfied. Under healthy conditions we will eventually seek a greater degree of fulfillment. However, to change the animal-like pattern of life we need to grow, and growth is painful. We have to accept responsibility, postpone gratification, face life challenges with courage, discipline our appetites, and channel our desires into new directions.

These are difficult tasks, and in the process we will experience certain uniquely human emotions. If we face obstacles in our quest to grow, we will feel anxiety, fear, and anger. We may become frustrated and sad. We may feel unhappy with ourselves and/or with others. We may even become paranoid and suspect that people are against us. Once we begin to grow and evolve, however, negative feelings are eventually replaced by feelings of calm and certitude, and we become creative, encouraged, and happy.

To achieve this transformation, we must eliminate the root cause of our discontent. In recent years it has become very popular to learn techniques to remove our undesirable feelings. For example, many people try to learn how to manage stress. Stress, like all other feelings, has a physical component, and stress management has focused on such practices as recreational physical activity, biofeedback, and relaxation techniques. These techniques do help to rid the body of stress, but the effects of such techniques are temporary unless the underlying psychological and spiritual causes are also treated. It is important to find out what caused the stress in the first place. Stress could be due to an interpersonal conflict, a life-threatening situation such as an illness, or a spiritual crisis such as the recognition that one is living a meaningless life. Therefore, it is clear that to focus on relaxation alone will not be sufficient. In the same way, tranquilizers will not eradicate the root causes of anxiety, nor will an antidepressant alone bring us everlasting happiness. These conditions all have physical, psychological, as well as spiritual causes. In dealing with our emotions, we have to ensure that all these important causes are considered. Through this process we acquire a greater degree of self-knowledge that includes the physical, psychological, and spiritual aspects of our life.

To summarize, the unique aspect of human nature is its spiritual component. As humans, we have the capacities of knowledge, love, and will, the properties of our souls that distinguish us from animals. Despite similarities to the more advanced animals, the human brain alone has the capacity to respond to the specific demands of the human soul. It is this interface between the human body and soul that is the foundation of *selfhood* and of being a unique individual. At the level of self the powers of the mind, such as imagination, thought, comprehension, and memory are integrated with our bodily senses of sight, hearing, smell, taste, and touch. At this level feelings play their crucial role by integrating our instincts and thoughts.

We have seen that the human self is the unique result of the soul/body interface and interplay. In spite of this axiomatic principle, this integration is not a closed and deterministic formula. It simply allows the individual to be a person. The type of person we become is our choice, and this choice is usually made the hard way. Dawn, whose case is discussed in the next chapter, is a good example of this process of *becoming*.

PART THREE

The

Fundamentals

Noble have I created thee.
Bahá'u'lláh

Being and Becoming: The Case of Dawn

•

CASE STUDY

Dawn was thirty-three, a journalist, highly intelligent, a free spirit. She was married to a cautious and dependent man. She had two children, five and eight years of age. She was quite successful, well liked by her friends and colleagues. Psychologically she was well and had no past history of psychological disorder requiring therapy.

When she asked for an appointment with me, it was in connection with her leukemia, which was not responding to treatment and had caused her concern about several issues. First and foremost, she wanted to know how to prepare her children for her imminent death. Second, she wondered what she could do to help other cancer patients who suffer in helplessness and horror. She had organized her friends into a circle of helpers who were looking after many of her concerns, but not everyone had such a large number of helpers. She consequently felt something had to be done to develop a program of help. She was also concerned about her mother. She felt that the loss of a child is the most painful loss, and because she was an only child she expected her mother to be unable to cope with such a devastating loss.

In addition, of course, she was preoccupied with her own death. Even though she had been very courageous in dealing with her

CASE STUDY illness she was nevertheless filled with deep feelings of apprehension and worry. She was also angry because she considered her death to be fundamentally unjust. "If there is a God," she would say, "then that God is unjust and unkind. And if there is no God then this whole thing is a sham." She had heard of my interest in helping those facing death and decided to come for one or two sessions, "to look at these issues and do something about them." I saw her for nine months until she died, and I continued to be in touch with her family for a few years after her death.

Instead of giving a chronological account of the developments of this case, let me point out the most significant issues that eme ged during my work with Dawn. Each of these issues has an integrity of its own, and I have observed that these issues arise continually in many other situations. Of particular importance here is that Dawn did not have a psychiatric illness nor did most of my other patients facing death. They were normal, happy, loving, successful, optimistic people, but they were facing the ultimate challenge—death.

If we wish to understand human nature, we must study humans, not rats or mice or geese. Study of animals helps us to understand human physiology but not the human psyche. To understand the human psyche, it is preferable to study psychologically healthy people so that our conclusions are not unduly influenced by the peculiarities of various emotional and mental disorders. Also, the study of human nature is greatly facilitated in circumstances when we are tested. Death provides such circumstances.

Under ordinary circumstances, we have both a private life and a public one. Our private lives are filled with hopes, aspirations, thoughts, and feelings we do not usually divulge. These are too private, too personal, and too precious to be shared. However, when we suffer pain and face death, we are more willing to share at a deeper and more meaningful level. This is especially true if we are in contact with someone who is willing to try to understand us and who is unafraid to face his or her own mortality. Under these circumstances we can share some of our special private thoughts, feelings, and hopes and become more connected with and insightful about our inner selves.

Disease forces us to come in touch with both body and soul. Our powers of knowledge, love, and will are tested. Our views about life

The Fundamentals

CASE STUDY

and death are scrutinized. The purpose and meaning of our existence is questioned. The strength of our souls in the face of the weakness of our bodies is measured. Our ability to handle our many different feelings is taxed in the extreme. We have to face love in its most profound and painful reality. We have to acknowledge our utter ignorance so that we may gain some glimpses of insight into the mysteries of life. We gradually have to let go of our will and begin to develop a new will that transcends our mortality and connects us to the Immortal. The drama of human life is the account of human nature, and it is most intensely played out when we have to face death.

For these reasons, I believe the study of cases such as Dawn's are most helpful in our attempt to understand human nature. Here I will focus on Dawn's need to acquire more knowledge, particularly self-knowledge, to strengthen the bonds of her love, employ her powers of will, and find a purpose and meaning for her life.

TO KNOW IS HUMAN

Three days before her death, Dawn was involved in making a videotape about her disease, suffering, and death. She wanted to convey to others what she had learned about these aspects of life. At that time she was very weak and had begun to bleed into her joints. We were talking about anger, fear, and anxiety. She wanted to know whether there was a relationship among these three feelings. I told her that these feelings always occur together. They are our emotional responses to the experience of threat, whether to our life, identity, or values and ideas. Whenever we are threatened, we automatically respond with these three feelings, usually with one assuming a predominant position. In the face of a threat, depending on the nature of the threat, our personality, and life circumstances, we respond with either anger, fear, or anxiety being predominant. However, always behind the more predominant of the three feelings are the other two lurking in the background of our awareness. Dawn became very interested in this description of human response to threats and said, "Wait. Let me write this down. I need to review this later." Then she stopped and said, "Isn't this silly. I know I'm dying in a few days. What's the use of making notes?"

The Psychology of Spirituality

CASE STUDY

But she made a note of it anyway.

We then began to talk about the need to know. As human beings, we are always in search of knowledge. However, because knowledge can be unsettling and painful, especially self-knowledge, we busy our minds with lesser issues and preoccupy ourselves with trivia. I will discuss these matters more fully in the section on knowledge. Here I will briefly outline Dawn's attempts at understanding herself.

One of the earliest things Dawn wanted to know was whether or not she could be cured. Accepting that she could not was not difficult. Prior to my first encounter with her, she had already struggled with this matter. She admitted she had already gone through the denial stage. By this she meant that the knowledge that her disease was not curable was so painful and unacceptable that her first response was disbelief. This denial is a not fully conscious psychological process. We human beings have a great capacity for denial of the painful, the unacceptable, and the dangerous. Of course, because the human soul in its very essence is driven to know and to become more aware, all efforts at denial ultimately fail.

After a period of denial, Dawn began to face the reality of her situation and became quite angry, anxious, and fearful. She was afraid and anxious not only about her own situation but also about her children and her mother. Dawn wanted to know what she could do to lessen the traumatic effects of her death on her children. She would say, "I know there is no life after this one, but how can I tell my children such a thing? How can I help them to understand that we should live a good and moral life if I also tell them that in the end they will become nothing?" She struggled with these questions, spoke with members of the clergy in the hospital, disclosed her thoughts to a number of friends, but could not find a satisfactory explanation for her death. This quandary helped her to plunge into ever deeper questions like the meaning of life and what our real nature is. She used to say she did not feel she was dying, but that her "wretched body behaved differently."

During the same episode of videotaping, a nurse brought in Dawn's tray of food. She ate a little, then picked up a package of cheese that she struggled unsuccessfully to open. She would not accept help and said that surely she should be able to open a package of cheese. Finally she turned to me in desperation and said that this was what she had meant earlier—that she was willing to open the package, but her body was not. She had come to make a distinction between herself and her body. The soul was willing, but the body was weak. Her soul continued to gain knowledge, become excited about new discoveries, and plan the future, but her body could not carry out these activities.

I pointed out that the way we conceive of our nature has a crucial impact on how we live. If we think of ourselves as only our bodies and our minds as part of our bodies, then of course with death we become nothing, or, to put it more accurately, we decompose into the elements that compose our body. However, if we realize that the soul is the real self and that our bodies are the vehicles for the expression of the soul in this life, then with the death of the body our consciousness (soul) remains as a reality, although it is no longer observable through our body.

I gave Dawn the following two examples to elucidate the relationship between the body and soul. The relationship of the soul to the body is like the relationship of electricity to the light bulb. The only way we can have light (life) is to have electricity (soul) pass into the light bulb (body). Without this connection, the electricity and the bulb have their own separate existence, but light does not exist. Another example is that of a computer. For the computer to function it needs both software (soul) and hardware (body). When the software and the hardware function together, the computer is able to perform its remarkable feats. Likewise, when body and soul come together, the miracle of life takes place.

After a while, she admitted I might be right but asked what happened to consciousness, or the "soul" after death. I said no one knows what happens to the soul or consciousness after death, but the fact that we do not know something does not mean it does not exist.

Although Dawn had quite a struggle to understand who she was and what her true nature was, she persevered nevertheless. She wanted to know. If we were to summarize Dawn's quest for self-knowledge and establish a hierarchy of significance, the following order would emerge: (1) Learning about the facts of the disease and its causes, (2) understanding pain and its remedies, (3) looking into her feelings and how to deal with them, (4) reviewing her relationships and how to face separation and loss, and, finally, (5) reflecting on the issues of life, death, mortality, and immortality in order to

CASE STUDY

have a better understanding of them. The first two (i.e., disease and pain) deal with the human body, the next two (feelings and relationships) are in the domain of the psychological and psychosocial, and the final theme (life, death, mortality, and immortality) is spiritual in nature. During the course of her illness, Dawn faced all of these issues thoroughly.

Two days before her death, Dawn said she was ready to go but didn't know where. She then began a lengthy and very loving discussion with one of her favourite caregiver friends. A few hours before her death Dawn announced that she had resolved her quandary but would not say more. She just gave a teasing smile.

TO LOVE IS HUMAN

Dawn had several different love relationships. Her love for her children was unconditional, all-encompassing, and without reservation. She loved her mother deeply, and this love had grown stronger, mainly because through exceptional effort, Dawn had managed to free herself of the conflicts of her childhood years. Her parents had a poor relationship, and Dawn was caught between loyalties and demands. When she became ill, Dawn immediately began to work on her relationship with her mother and in essence put the past behind her. Her father was out of the picture. Dawn had a certain degree of affinity with her husband but not "love". She could not relate to his dependent, aloof ways. They related as friends and parents of their children but little else. For years, Dawn had had a lover with whom she was very close. This relationship was satisfactory to her in many respects, and they supported each other to the end. In addition, Dawn had many friends whom she loved and who loved her. These friends remained loyal and helpful throughout her illness.

Dawn handled her illness differently in regard to each of these love relationships. She did not know how to inform her mother about her illness and imminent death. I pointed out to her that because love is the most powerful source of human relationships, it is probably also the most painful. Love demands truthfulness, honesty, and openness of us. We all know that facing the truth and being totally honest and open is not only difficult but also very painful. Furthermore, the more we love someone the more painful losing them is. This particular pain is not mixed with feelings of guilt, shame, and resentment. However, if our relationship is poor, we will also experience such difficult feelings as anger and guilt in addition to the pain of the loss. Many people have a notion that love means ease, happiness, and an absence of concerns. It is true that love does make life easy and happy, freeing us from cares and woes. But love is, at the same time, painful and demanding. This is so because love is basic to life, and life requires growth and development. We do not grow without the pain of self-knowledge and the powerful impact of truth.

As we discussed these and other related matters, Dawn developed a strategy to communicate with her mother. She and her mother began to share their thoughts and feelings about her illness. Gradually, their relationship not only became stronger but also much more open and at ease. Dawn applied the same principle to everyone else, including her children.

To Will is Human

Dawn had a very strong will. She had made it a goal of her life to battle injustice, resist unreasonable demands, do what she wanted to do, and assert her freedom. She perceived her cancer to be an ultimate case of personal injustice and strongly protested against it. For the first several months of her illness, she single-mindedly concentrated on this injustice. As her disease became more painful and her strength began to decrease, her willpower became a source of conflict for her. She could not accept the situation as it was, nor was she able to cure herself and remedy the situation.

It was at this time that I began to talk with her about human will and the issue of free choice. I pointed out to her that while she was not free to choose between illness and health (because she was already ill), she was free to choose the nature of her approach to her illness. This choice meant that she had to use her will differently. Instead of trying to get what she wanted, she had to try to accomplish what she could within the context of her situation. More specifically, she could use her will to seek the best treatment for her illness, increase her knowledge about herself, and

The Psychology of Spirituality

CASE STUDY

strengthen the bonds of her love. This process requires willingness to change, letting go of pride, and the acceptance of a new perspective. In a way, we have to relinquish our will in order to strengthen it. This is exactly what occurred with Dawn. She could not have accomplished what she did, if she had continued to be stubbornly willful. Rather, she shifted the focus of her will from being to becoming. In other words, she began to develop and grow in the face of her illness and in response to it. The seeming disaster of her illness became the main opportunity for her life, and her will played a central role in this transformation.

TO SEARCH FOR MEANING IS HUMAN

Dawn's attempt to find meaning for her life was too extensive and complex to be described here. All I can do is to make rather broad allusions to it. This search was closely interwoven with her desire to help her children be prepared for her death. More than anything else, it was this issue that compelled her to look into "spiritual" matters.

One day, several months prior to her death, Dawn asked me to help her children understand the idea of death. I suggested an analogy that might be helpful. She wanted to think about it and discuss the matter with her husband, mother, and some friends before making a final decision. Eventually, she agreed that telling the children about death by using the analogy I had suggested would be a good idea. In fact, she was enthusiastic about it and stated that it had also been of help with respect to her own struggle with death. One evening in the presence of both parents I shared the following with John, five, and Robert, eight:

> *As you know, life begins in the mother's womb when the ovum from the mother and the sperm from the father come together to become a fertilized egg. This little egg then begins to grow and divide until it gradually takes the shape of a child with a head, two eyes, two ears, a nose, a mouth, hands, legs, and all the other parts of the body.*
>
> *Now imagine if there were little beings living in the womb. We'll call them the "I.W.s," (the Inhabitants of the Womb). These I.W.s have a good life in the womb. They swim around, hide in the corners of the womb, and come together to play and talk.*

The Fundamentals

CASE STUDY

One day an older I.W. was very sad, and a younger one asked why. The older I.W. said that he was sad because of this little baby in the womb. The other I.W.s were surprised. "Why?" they asked. "She is in good shape. We counted her fingers, and they are the right number. We looked at her eyes, and they are in the right place. So are her ears, nose, and mouth. Everything about her is just right. Why are you sad about her?"

The older I.W. said, "Yes, I know everything is right with the baby. I'm so sad because she is going to die." The other I.W.s said "What do you mean, she's going to die?" And the older I.W. responded, "We have seen this happen before. These babies grow up here and when they are perfect then they die—they go away, and we never see them again. That is why I'm so sad."

Another I.W. said, "But I have heard that there is another world after the womb, and these babies die from here to go to a bigger world. They say that in that world there is a sun and a moon and many stars, and trees, lakes, and seas, and cities, and flowers, and people, and animals. They say it is beautiful." And another I.W. said, "Do you have proof that another world exists after the womb? Have you seen the sun, the moon, and all those things you described? They are not real; they are figments of your imagination." And yet another I.W. said, "But this doesn't make sense. If this baby came here and grew up for a while and is now going to die, what was the purpose? And why did this baby grow eyes and legs and hands and ears and the many other parts of her body? She didn't need them to live here. Could it be that she grew them for life in the world after the womb?"

The I.W.s got into a heated discussion about whether or not a world existed after the womb. While they were arguing, the little baby died. Or did she? She definitely died from the world of the womb. She would not be able to go back, and the I.W.s would not hear from her again. So as far as they were concerned, that was the end of her.

But the little baby is now in this world and is growing up and living here. And she will continue her life here until a time comes that it will no longer be possible for her to live in this world. Then she will die from this world and will be born into another world. You see, death is a birth at the same time. So in this world we are also I.W.s, the "Inhabitants of the World," asking ourselves, "Is there life after this world?" the same way that the I.W.s were asking whether there was a world after the womb.

The children then discussed the issue of their mother's death within the framework of this analogy. The younger child stated, "When mommy dies, she will be like a little baby in the next world, and somebody has to take care of her." His older brother thought that death was "neat." "Wow! I'm ready to die." To which I said,

CASE STUDY

"First you have to grow, enjoy this life, and accomplish all you can, as well as grow those things you will need for the next life. In the womb we grow eyes, ears, hands, legs, etc., because we need them for this life. Without them we would be incomplete. The same is true of this life. While living in this life and enjoying all it can offer us, we should also develop what we need for this life as well as the next—things such as love, knowledge, kindness, happiness, service, patience, justice, honesty, and so on."

The children wanted the story repeated to them several times. Two years after their mother's death, they were still talking about it with clarity and understanding.

For her part, Dawn began to ponder the mysteries of life and death. After contemplating what we know about life in this world, she answered, "We know as much about death as we knew about this world when we were in the womb—nothing." It seems that our knowledge of life is all about the past and present, and it is through this knowledge and our observation of the laws of life that we reach conclusions about the future.

Fundamental Human Characteristics

●

When we speak of our *self*, we are talking about the very essence of our being—that reality which makes us who and what we are. Our knowledge of this reality is very limited at the beginning of our lives, and unless we intentionally and systematically try to understand and develop the *self* we usually remain ignorant of its most precious and important qualities. Given that the *self* is the inevitable result of the interface of body and soul, as soon as life begins, the *self* comes into being. It stands to reason, then, that *life* and *self* are totally interdependent. There can be no self where there is no life, and there can be no life where there is no self.

THREE MAIN HUMAN CAPACITIES

The human self has three main capacities: to know, to love, and to will. These capacities are spiritual in nature and are properties of the soul.[1] However, they develop and express themselves in the context of the self. To understand selfhood better, it will be useful to consider these capacities separately. Later I will discuss how they are interrelated and how they become integrated.

1 Knowledge

One essential quality of being human is our capacity to know in its broadest and most comprehensive sense. Knowledge here refers to all kinds of knowing, such as conscious, subconscious and unconscious forms of knowing, intuition, and the knowledge we gain through the less well understood phenomena of inspiration and insight.

We acquire knowledge through life experience, cognitive and intellectual pursuits, self-reflection, prayer, and meditation. Our reservoir of knowledge is made up of rational and logical, intuitive and creative, and spiritual and divine forms of knowing. The rational and logical belong to the realm of science and are particularly important in our understanding of the laws governing the physical world as well as, for example, the purely medical, legal, and economic aspects of our personal and social lives. Intuitive and creative knowledge is specially suited to the development of the arts and the refinement of human relationships. Spiritual and divine forms of knowing give purpose and meaning to our lives and provide us with insight into good and evil.

Although these various forms of knowing have been accessible to humankind from the dawn of consciousness, our understanding of them has been vague, disjointed and uneven. However, we are now arriving at a new phase in our capacity for knowledge in general and self-knowledge in particular. Even though the remarkable growth of science during the last one hundred and fifty years has, for all practical purposes, dominated all other forms of human knowledge relegating them to either secondary status or irrelevancy, nevertheless there are now strong indications that this imbalance is beginning to be corrected. For example, today there is little argument about the importance and validity of human sciences such as psychology, sociology, and anthropology. Although these sciences are still in their infancy, significant contributions have nevertheless been made to our self-understanding by these disciplines. The very fact that the scientific method, even in its very mechanistic and restricted form, is employed toward better understanding human nature, itself, is a major step forward.

In the moral, ethical, and spiritual domains, human knowledge is sadly and dangerously lagging behind. In our times, humanity has lost much of its sense of trust and hope with regard to spiritual matters. When modern philosophers pronounced God dead, it was the Divine-in-human that died, not God. God indeed continues a loving relationship with humanity. Unfortunately many people no longer allow themselves to receive this love, because they do not feel that they deserve it. In psychotherapy, quite often we encounter people who feel unloved. When we look into the reasons, it emerges that these people do not feel worthy of love and therefore do not allow themselves to receive love.

The same is true about humanity's relationship with God. With the rise of science and the decline of religion, which began gradually and reached its peak during the last hundred years, humanity changed its relationship with God. Previously, this relationship was of a parent-child nature. The parent was all-powerful, all-knowing, and frequently punitive, and the child weak, ignorant, and submissive. This was the era of the collective infancy and childhood of humanity. Our ancestors responded to the challenges of life and to what they perceived to be the powers of gods even as children do, namely, with awe, hope, fear, anxiety, and bewilderment. The age of science freed humanity from many of its fears and superstitions and inaugurated the last phase of humanity's collective adolescence.[2]

Adolescent Humanity

The greatly empowered adolescent humanity, in keeping with the unique characteristics of the adolescent period, began to behave differently. Tasting the freedom of physical development, it became enthusiastic, proud, and seemingly fearless. Adolescent humanity began to experiment and soon discovered many laws of nature it had not discovered before, and a sense of power never before imagined arose. In the charged atmosphere of scientific discoveries and technological innovations, concomitant with the emergence of the physical and mental prowess of the adolescent age, religion—humanity's main fortress for spiritual matters—was neglected and almost forgotten. Its force weakened markedly as a result. Established world religions, whether Judeo-Christian, Muslim, Buddhist, Hindu or other, failed to perceive the significance of this remarkable new phase in the collective life of humankind

The Psychology of Spirituality

and became, for all practical purposes, irrelevant and ineffectual.

With newly found capacities and the removal of many restraints, adolescent humanity began to feel nearly omnipotent. This proved to be a deadly combination. First, God was driven out of the minds and hearts of humanity. Next, instinctual, animalistic, and self-centred tendencies began to predominate. The fruits of science were soon abused, and instruments of mass destruction were created. The forces of love, kindness, and mercy were too often defeated in the struggle for material development and consumption. Frequently, force took the place of love. Information replaced wisdom. Wealth became synonymous with happiness. The earth was shattered into many little centres of self-interest.

Consequently, human knowledge became limited to the physical world, and the laws of the material were applied to the spiritual. The futility of such an undertaking is now clearly before us, as we behold our world divided, dispirited, burdened with injustice, inequality, mistrust, war, hunger, disease, immorality, and death. The world is now seriously ill with the disease of materialism.

Mature Humanity

The answer to this dilemma is not for humanity to discard science but rather to increase our knowledge of the spiritual and the divine. As we do this, we will gradually replace our prevalent adolescent attitude with the thinking and knowledge of the mature (adult) phase of our collective existence. In the adult phase, a balance among scientific, artistic, and spiritual forms of knowledge will be achieved, and the objectives of our lives will become more universal. We will lose our self-centredness and be able to use human knowledge for the service of humanity and the affirmation of life. To achieve maturity, self-knowledge is required.

Self-knowledge

The central aim of all human knowledge is self-knowledge, which, in its most complete and profound form, is the same as the knowledge of God.[3] This is so, not because we are God or a part of God, but because we have been created in the image of God. We cannot then understand God without understanding ourselves, nor can we understand ourselves without understanding God.* Alienation from one is alienation from both. Marx believed the major diseases of humanity were self-alienation and alienation from the environment.[4] While knowledge of the environment gives us insight into the physical world and when applied to ourselves makes us knowledgeable about the physiological, biological, pathological, chemical, and physical aspects of our bodies, it sheds no light on the spiritual dimension of our being. Knowledge of the spiritual requires connection with the Source of spirituality. Having rejected our spiritual dimension, or, having understood it in a very limited and elementary fashion, we have in fact become strangers to our own selves.

All knowledge is acquired through the powers of the mind. We can train ourselves in the use of our minds and greatly enhance our powers of imagination, modes of thinking, approaches to understanding and comprehending realities, and abilities to store and recall information. However, only when all our efforts to acquire knowledge are brought into harmony with our capacities to love and to will, do they gain their greatest significance, thereby creating a condition of inner unity.

II Love

Love is an active force of attraction to beauty, unity, and growth. We human beings are continuously attracted, consciously and unconsciously, to whatever we perceive to be beautiful, to cause closeness, intimacy, and unity, and to nurture our growth and development. However, because our perceptions are not always accurate, we frequently also become attracted to individuals, conditions, or ideas that are not beautiful, cause disunity or inhibit growth. The quality of love, therefore, is closely related to the quality of the object of our love. An example will help to make these points clearer.

---

*While God in His essence is unknowable, we obtain certain knowledge of God through the attributes of God and His Manifestations such as Buddha, Christ, Bahá'u'lláh.

Love and War

As far as we know, there have always been wars of one type or another in human societies. Some wars have been necessary to fight an evil and as such, a necessary evil themselves. War has been used to redress injustice and to discourage greater acts of destruction. Viewed in this light, war has been considered a social duty. Of course, there have always been those who have chosen war to achieve personal glory and gratification. Such people choose war as an object of their love. They do so because they perceive war to have an intrinsic beauty, to be a cause of harmony, and to foster progress. These sentiments are usually expressed in the glorification of war, the handsome figure of the warrior, the beautifully crafted uniforms and military instruments, and in military strategies. Much of the literature of bygone ages glorifies war and describes its beauty. There is also much rhetoric about the value of war, how it safeguards cultures and civilizations, brings people together, and causes a higher level of harmonious and unified patriotism. Lovers of war also claim that war is the cause of growth and development because it adds to scientific knowledge and technology, helps sluggish economies, and allows for the victory of good over evil.

It is a demonstrable fact that wars are anything but beautiful, unifying, or life-enhancing. While there are some limited and just wars, such as those fought against the Hitlers of history, even those wars, however necessary they may have been, nevertheless brought with them much ugliness, disunity, and destruction. Yet despite these facts and because of its faulty understanding of the nature of war, humanity continues to have a love affair with war.

To the thoughtful person, war and love are totally irreconcilable. As to the nature of war, who can argue with the assertion that war is death and love is life, war is cruelty and love is kindness, war is separation and love is unity, war is ugliness and love is beauty, war is stagnation and love is growth?

The Activity of Love

Of all definitions of love, I find the following most illuminating: Love is an active force of attraction. We may ask, what is the activity of love and from where does its power come? The main activity of love is creation. Love creates life, nurtures and enhances growth and development, and creates unity and harmony. These activities of love are present in every aspect of humanity's life. It is love that creates families, rears children, feeds the hungry, cares for the sick, finds shelter for the homeless, binds the wounds of the injured, removes strangeness and prejudice, and causes unity and togetherness. These are only some of the activities of love, and they are all creative.

Many people believe that love is blind, that it happens to you without volition. Such a view of love is accurate only in the initial stage of love when the powers of yearning and attraction dim the light of reason and make us behave as mindless fanatics in the face of logical evidence put before us by those not touched by the force of love. However, the fact remains that love is an inherent capacity we all possess, and we must foster its growth and development. The definition of love as an active force means that it cannot be stagnant, passive, or undirected. Love must be filled with vitality and life, must direct our actions, and be enlightened and purposeful. However, love is more than an active force of attraction. What ultimately determines the nature of love is not only its force of attraction but also its object of attraction.

Love and Attraction

It is not enough to be attracted; *what* we are attracted to is even more important. A healthy love is attracted to beauty, unity, and growth. We do not fully understand beauty. Our first thought about beauty is usually the physical attribute of a person, or a thing, or an idea, but we soon begin to appreciate other, more profound aspects of beauty. We then see beauty as an aspect of all creation—this world, this life, this universe. We realize that both the outer universe and the universe within us are beautiful, desirable, pleasurable, enjoyable, and fulfilling. But while beauty exists in all creation, we must be able to appreciate it. Not infrequently we fail to discern beauty and instead see ugliness and are repulsed. Love helps us see beauty and cherish it.

In everyday life we encounter examples of how love helps us to see beauty and cherish it. Our ability to see the unique beauty of our spouse, child, or friend—a beauty that is not seen by others, is the most powerful example that beauty is in the eye of the beholder. We alone see beauty. However, if others were willing to put themselves in our place and attempted to look at our diseased or disfigured spouse, child, or friend, and were willing to learn of our history and our lives together, what we have shared and experienced, and the way we have made one another's lives meaningful, then they would also be able to see the beauty of these people. We should remember that beauty is not only in the eye of the beholder; it is also there for us to behold.

Unity is another object of the attraction of love. Love is an active force of attraction to unity. Inherent in all human beings is a desire for intimacy and union. Life begins with the intimacy of the union of husband and wife, and then continues with the intimate bond between parents and child. As the child grows and becomes aware of its independence and separation from its parents, the mother in particular, it is banished from the paradise of union to the land of separation. From then on, we constantly yearn for the return of that intimacy. We fall in love, create marriages, have children of our own, build cities and nations, and now are moving towards creating a united world, all because in our innermost being we yearn for intimacy and union.

Love is also an active force of attraction to growth. Love is a cause of life, growth is a sign of life, and they are wholly interrelated. We cannot grow without love, and when we love we grow. Growth is painful, as is love. Both require discipline, delay of gratification, rejection of self-centredness, and giving of oneself. Neither love nor growth are possible in the context of lazy irresponsibility, instant gratification, indulgence, or selfishness. No wonder many people misunderstand love and seek as their love objects those people, ideas, or things that pamper them and allow for fleeting satisfaction. Such love relationships are doomed from the start. They are not truly based on love but on ignorance and self-centredness, the opposites of the very essence of love, enlightenment, and universality.

III Will

Human will refers to our freedom to choose between good and

evil, between action and inaction, and to determine the direction and quality of our lives. Our freedom is not absolute however. We have no choice with respect to family, for example, or the need for sleep, or accident and misfortune, or the process of aging. We have no choice about death. Our fundamental freedom may be exercised in regard to the choices we make to determine both the direction and the quality of our lives.

In psychotherapy there is a tendency to reject the primacy of the role of will and to place much greater importance on forces that are beyond the reach of our volition such as instincts, drives, the unconscious, and childhood experiences. Many schools of thought in psychology share the opinion that human behaviour is completely determined and that freedom of choice is merely a wish. At the other end of the spectrum lies the notion that human beings are totally free, from which arises the school of thought that sees freedom of action in almost every respect. The truth lies somewhere between these two extremes.

An example may help us understand the role of will in life. In many respects, life is like sailing. To sail we need a boat (the body) and a sailor (the soul with its power of will). The boat must be seaworthy. The wind provides the motive power for the boat. The sailor determines the direction and destination of the journey. Notably, the presence or absence of wind is not decided by the sailor. In the same way, we have no choice about the conditions of our birth, the hereditary endowments we receive, or fail to receive, the basic talents and capacities with which we are born, and our childhood experiences. Once the sailing has begun, however, the sailor is in control and can either make informed decisions or sail without adequate knowledge of the position and the circumstances of the boat. In the same way, we can use our will in an enlightened and loving way, or live a life of ignorance, close-mindedness, and selfishness.

Our will gives us motivation, the courage to act, and the wherewithal to be creative. The signs of human will are present from the earliest days of life. In the human infant we see many indications of will. Some children refuse to be breastfed. Some are assertive in their communications, while others are totally passive. Parents frequently remark on the differences between their children from the time of their birth or even before. One significant aspect of these differences is the way the powers of will are expressed. At that early age, will is greatly influenced and controlled by the child's instincts. However, as the child grows, the ability to decide and to make choices also increases. This is particularly so if parents help their children recognize and develop their capacity to choose.

As it was true about our capacities of knowledge and love, so it is that the human will can be either abused or creatively employed to improve the quality of life. We can choose to do good or evil. We have a choice between war and peace, love and hate.

Though we have freedom of will, not infrequently we are afraid of it. We may also abuse or abdicate our will. When we are afraid to choose, we tend to blame someone else, whether it be our neighbours, our enemies, or God. We abuse our will by committing destructive acts, and we abdicate our will by refusing to act when action is needed. In fact, most of our difficulties are related to the abuse of our capacities of knowledge, love, and will, or result from a discordance among them. The secret of avoiding anxiety and stress is to achieve unity of the three capacities of knowledge, love, and will. Inner peace is achieved when and as we use these united capacities in a creative, life-endowing, growth-inducing, and universal manner. This is one aspect of a spiritual lifestyle.

To summarize; knowledge, love, and will are attributes of the soul. These three qualities are totally interrelated. Their harmonious functioning is the very basis of the inner peace, tranquillity, and strength we all seek and for which we all yearn.

Knowledge, love, and will have special, unique, and enormous powers. Knowledge has the power of discovering and demonstrating the realities of all things. It works like the sun, under whose rays the qualities of everything become obvious and understandable. Knowledge likewise gives us the power to discover realities. Love, in its turn, has the very remarkable power of attraction, that force which brings people, things, and ideas together. Indeed, what makes the physical world function is the power of attraction among the various parts of the atom. What makes families and societies work together is also the power of attraction. The same is true of ideas and views of the world. Attraction is the power of love and the thing that makes its activities possible. Will, the third attribute of the human soul, also has its own power: the power to choose, to decide, and to act. Finally, whenever we speak of love or knowledge or will, we should remember that they are ultimately most effective if employed together.

This psychological union has its counterpart in the spiritual realm of existence. When, in its upward march of evolution, humanity reached the level of conscious knowledge and learned of its choices between good and evil, the primal unity between God and humans was replaced by a new phase in which our spiritual growth became our personal responsibility. We were then aware and mature enough to be held justly responsible for our acts. This freedom was a gift of God to humanity. Yet, we have rejected it with vehemence. We yearn to return to the era of childhood ignorance, when we had neither choice nor responsibility, when there was also no perceptible difference between us and the animals. Now that we are aware, have knowledge, and realize that we have a choice, we find life difficult.

We protest and say that if God is loving why does God allow so many people to starve? But we must also ask, now that we have enough food in this world and the means to transport it, why do we allow so many people to die of hunger? We may ask, why does a just God allow so much disease in this world? But we could just as easily ask, why do we? It is in our power to cure or prevent most diseases because they are caused by various infections, by manufactured chemical substances, or are the result of our lifestyles. Malnutrition and mass starvation in one segment of humanity and overindulgence and wasteful living in another part is an imbalance that humanity should no longer accept. The main question is, how long will we yearn to return to the primal state of union, which is of course impossible? Our challenge is to enter our collective age of maturity and create a spiritually enlightened and scientifically progressive union through love, knowledge, and will—the forces of our soul.

Primary Human Concerns

●

Human life is an exciting panorama of unique cultures, differing lifestyles, and divergent concepts about our nature and the purpose of life. While some communities have had the opportunity to attain a relatively high level of economic and technological advancement, others, with people of equal capacity, have had to spend much more time on the task of providing the basic necessities of life. In both cases, however, individual human beings universally share three primary concerns: concerns about self, relationships, and time.

CONCERNS ABOUT SELF

Self-awareness is a uniquely human quality. It is through the power of self-awareness that we engage in self-evaluation, self-appreciation, self-consciousness, self-centredness, and self-denial. Self-awareness helps us to define and identify ourselves as unique beings and to shape our lives according to our concepts and views about our nature. Freud's narcissistic formulation, Erikson's concept of the identity crisis, and Frankl's search for meaning all have their genesis in human self-awareness.

The Psychology of Spirituality

As expressions of self-awareness, our concerns revolve around whether we are tired or rested, hungry or satiated, sexually dissatisfied or satisfied, professionally successful or unsuccessful, financially poor or rich, intellectually passive or active, and artistically dull or gifted. We define ourselves in terms of our relative physical attractiveness, intellectual acumen, social desirability and power, and the ethical, moral, and spiritual values we uphold. In brief, we spend much time and energy on issues and concerns related to ourselves, because concern about self is a primary and universal phenomenon.

CONCERNS ABOUT RELATIONSHIPS

Concerns about relationships come second only to concerns about self in importance and frequency. The statement, "No man is an island," is poignant. It refers to the basic need of every individual to be acknowledged, appreciated, and understood by others. We need not only to understand ourselves but we need also to be understood by others. Our search for identity and uniqueness is only meaningful when it is either in comparison to or in connection with others. For example, a married woman in one part of the world introduces herself as the mother of Ali (her son); while another is known as Mrs. Jones; a third has hyphenated her own and her husband's surnames; and a fourth keeps the name of her parents after marriage. Each of these individuals is defining herself in the light of her self-concept, the nature of a major relationship in her life, and the customs and expectations of her society.

Types of Relationships

Four basic kinds of relationships can be identified: containing, complementary, competitive, and cooperative relationships.

In a *containing relationship* the life of one person is totally (or to a very large extent) contained within the life of the other person. As a result, the contained person does not have the freedom or opportunity to live an independent and self-directed life. While under some circumstances, as in infancy, such a relationship is extremely valuable and necessary, under most other conditions it proves to be unhealthy and very limiting for both parties involved.

Examples of a containing relationship include: the mother-fetus relationship, some forms of marriage in which one individual (usually the wife) is completely contained within the life of the other, the life of a child contained within the overbearing and limiting life of an overprotective parent or family, and finally, the life of groups of people held within limits by an authoritarian power such as the state or a religious institution. From these examples it is clear that this kind of relationship, although quite common, is indeed a very primitive one, useful only at the biological level (infancy).

Examples of a *complementary relationship* include the parent-child relationship, employer-employee relationship, and teacher-student relationship. Under these circumstances the individuals involved have specific roles, needs, and capacities. In a state of harmonious relationship, the needs of one person are satisfied by the capacities or actions of another, and as a result, a complementary type of relationship is formed. Here again, as with the containing type of relationship, either a healthy or unhealthy form of relationship can develop. For example, parents, employers, or teachers may take advantage of their superior powers or abilities in the relationship. Alternatively, these powers and abilities can be used to create an atmosphere of trust and growth that allows the other person to mature and develop. Under most circumstances the outcome of such a process of growth is that the complementary relationship eventually gives way to other forms of relationships.

Competitive relationships are widespread today. These relationships are characterized by an ongoing struggle between those involved, as can be observed in many marriages, in work and school settings, and between siblings, adolescents, families, nations, and races. Competitive relationships are the hallmark of adolescence, and their prevalence today is one proof that humanity, in its evolution towards maturity, has moved beyond childhood and arrived at the age of adolescence. Competitive relationships are intense, demanding, excessive, and prone to inconsistency. These are relationships that cannot last forever, and they are not conducive to a productive, harmonious, and predominantly conflict-free lifestyle. Competition is one of the main reasons why many contemporary marriages are in a state of conflict and disharmony, nations are at loggerheads, and societies are disunited and at war.

The natural, healthy process of development in a relationship involves an evolution from competition towards cooperation. A *cooperative relationship* is the sign of maturity and is characterized by harmony, mutuality, moderation, and encouragement. The participants in this type of relationship are able to transcend self-centredness and self-doubt and relate to others from a position of self-knowledge and self-giving. There are both considerable similarities and basic differences between cooperative and complementary relationships.

The similarity between complementary and cooperative relationships exists because they both require harmony, understanding, and willingness to cooperate on the part of the parties involved. However, while people do not necessarily relate on an equal basis in complementary relationships, in cooperative relationships equality is essential. In complementary relationships one party is often in a position of giving (e.g., parent, teacher) while the other is in a position of receiving (e.g., child, student). However, in a cooperative type of relationship the parties must be able and willing to give as well as receive. A fleeting glimpse at history clearly shows that humanity has always yearned to achieve this level of relationship. In the contemporary world many individuals consciously pursue the goal of achieving it.

Yet the fact remains that human relationships are seriously troubled. Despite our best efforts we find ourselves at odds not only with our own selves but also with almost everyone else with whom we come in contact. Parents and children do not agree; husbands and wives are disunited; workers and their employers are in constant struggle; and races and nations are in a state of mistrust, hostility, and war. Somehow we have failed to improve our relationships despite the fact that we have paid a great deal of attention to them, discovered much about their dynamics, and made great attempts to use our knowledge to improve them. The reasons for this failure are many, but ultimately they are due to the fact that we have severed our relationship with our true selves. Once we re-establish this relationship, we will become more in touch with ourselves, will acquire qualities of the age of maturity, and consequently will be able to relate to each other in a cooperative and unifying manner.

CONCERNS ABOUT TIME

Time is the context in which our concerns about self and relationships take shape. Gradually over time we traverse the stages of childhood and adolescence and begin our adult life. We become aware of change in ourselves; first getting bigger, stronger, and more capable, and then growing gradually weaker, less capable but wiser. Time affords us the opportunity to grow, to learn about relationships, and to experience unions and losses. It reminds us of our beginnings and the direction of our journey through life. It is within the framework of time that we both celebrate and dread birthdays and are simultaneously fascinated and frightened by death.

While our concerns with self and relationships are usually conscious, our preoccupation with time is often beneath the surface of our awareness and in some respects, buried within the depths of our unconscious. Because of this, we tend to underestimate the role of our thoughts and feelings about time and their effect on our daily behaviour and activities. Time is an inescapable element in our journey through life and its stages of infancy, childhood, adolescence, adulthood, old age, and death. Time is always with us.

Concerns about time, relationships, and self are the primary concerns in life. They are most obvious to us when we are conflicted, anxious, or unhappy. Ultimately we have to deal with these concerns to the best of our abilities, and this takes us back to the previous discussion of our fundamental qualities of knowledge, love, and will. These human qualities have their fullest expression in the context of our concerns about self, relationships, and time. It is their integration with one another that creates all forms of human behaviour and lifestyle, and motivates us to continue our journey through life, even though it is often difficult and laden with misery.

Knowledge, love, and will are developmental, cumulative, and unlimited in their scope, intensity, depth, and duration. These characteristics last as long as our reality lasts, and they have the capacity to be expressed in healthy, growing, creative, and life-affirming ways or in unhealthy, stagnant, boring, and destructive ones. The dynamics of these cardinal human capacities of knowledge, love, and will, whether expressed positively or negatively, become most dramatically obvious when they are studied in the framework of the three major human concerns about self, relationships, and time. And that is what we are going to look at in the next section.

Integration

You have already noticed the value I have placed on unity, harmony, or integration. Disintegration and dysfunction may, for simplicity's sake, be understood as the lack of this most positive of all values. Let us now examine how the three main human capacities (knowledge, love, and will) integrate or mesh with the three main concerns: self, relationships, and time.

The dynamics of everyday life usually takes place habitually and without deep contemplation on the part of most of us. In fact, the simple process of everyday life is very complicated and very majestic. Every moment of life is rich with awesome and far-reaching potentialities. It calls into action our powers of knowledge, love, and will. It focuses our attention on ourselves, the world around us, and the fact that our life is passing by. It offers us new opportunities and fills us with sorrow about those we have lost. Every moment of life is a mysterious and glorious moment, if we were to understand its significance and the requisites for its fulfillment. Therefore, to understand better how our lives evolve and how we become who we are, we must take into consideration all aspects of our lives: the biological, the psychosocial, and the spiritual.

Our biological and psychosocial dimensions express themselves in the form of needs for security and survival, desire for gratification and happiness, and motivation to work in order to fulfill our needs and desires. In other words, the biological and psychosocial dimensions constitute the primary human concerns already described.

The spiritual dimension of human reality, however, encompasses both the Main Human Powers (MHP) of knowledge, love, and will, and the Primary Human Concerns (PHC) about self, others, and time. The task before us now is to examine the relationship between these Powers and Concerns, both under healthy and pathological conditions and along a developmental continuum. Figure 1 provides us with a helpful overview of these points. Each situation is shown in its healthy form and in three stages of development. For example, under healthy conditions, the human capacity to know and the human concern about time are expressed differently in each of three main stages of life. During childhood and adolescence, our knowledge about time is mostly about the present, while later in life we become acutely aware of our mortality, and in a more mature state we embark upon the serious task of understanding our immortality.

Primary Human Concerns	Main Human Powers		
	Knowledge	*Love*	*Will*
Self	· Self-experience · Self-discovery · Self-knowledge	· Self-preoccupation · Self-acceptance · Self-growth (development)	· Self-control · Self-confidence · Self-responsibility[a]
Relationships	· Sameness of people · Uniqueness of people · Oneness of people	· Acceptance of others · Empathy with others · Unity	· Competition · Cooperation and Equality · *Movasat*[b]
Time	· Present (here and now) · Mortality · Immortality	· Primary union · Separation · Secondary union	· Desire · Decision · Action

Figure 1: An integrated schema of the Main Human Powers and the Primary Human Concerns under healthy circumstances.

a. It should be noted that in each section three hierarchical levels of development are identified. Thus, for example, self-experience is the most basic level of knowledge about one's self, while self-knowledge is the most advanced level of the same process.

b. *Movasat* is an Arabic word that describes the highest level of maturity in human relationships, a condition in which individuals would prefer others over themselves without any hesitation or hope for reward, and as the natural expression of their being. *Movasat* has a similar but broader connotation than altruism, which denotes unselfish concern for the welfare of others.

Integration of Knowledge, Love and Will and Concerns about Self

●

THE INTEGRATION OF KNOWLEDGE AND CONCERNS ABOUT SELF

Primary Human Concerns	Main Human Powers		
	Knowledge	*Love*	*Will*
Self	· Self-experience · Self-discovery · Self-knowledge	· Self-preoccupation · Self-acceptance · Self-growth (development)	· Self-control · Self-confidence · Self-responsibility

The integration of self and knowedge takes place in three stages of self-experience, self-discovery, and self-knowledge. During childhood we are totally self-centred, and consequently the beginnings of our capacity to know lie in our becoming aware of ourselves. This initial self-awareness begins in the child in the form of *self-experience*, which is at first related to our biological functioning and the experiences of pain and pleasure.

Gradually we become more aware of our emotions and thoughts. This increased self-awareness begins to give the child the courage to experiment and discover, entering the process of *self-discovery*.

During childhood and adolescence, biological and psychosocial dimensions play a very important role, but in order for the child to develop an integrated and whole personality the spiritual dimension also needs to be considered. This integration results in the acquisition of the third and most advanced stage—*self-knowledge*. It is through self-knowledge that we become aware of the fundamental nobility of our being, begin to validate the spiritual nature of our reality, and give meaning and purpose to our lives. Without self-knowledge life becomes anxiety-ridden, confusing, frightening, and painful. This is why people who have not had the opportunity for healthy and integrated development with respect to their self-knowledge, become confused about themselves, the nature of their reality, and the purpose of their existence. Without an adequate knowledge of these important issues, we become anxious, distressed, and psychosocially and physically unhealthy. The link between the disorders of knowledge and these unhealthy conditions is stress, which has physical, psychological, and spiritual causes. Stress, therefore, is a sign that we need to increase our self-knowledge. However, self-knowledge does not take place in a vacuum. It is a condition that requires involvement with other people and a willingness to become less self-centred and more giving to others. It follows that development of true self-knowledge is only possible in the context of relationships, not in isolation.

INTEGRATION OF LOVE AND CONCERNS ABOUT SELF

Primary Human Concerns	Main Human Powers		
	Knowledge	*Love*	*Will*
Self	· Self-experience · Self-discovery · Self-knowledge	· Self-preoccupation · Self-acceptance · Self-growth (development)	· Self-control · Self-confidence · Self-responsibility

The earliest stage of the relationship between love and self is *self-preoccupation*, followed by *self-acceptance*, and finally *self-growth*. *Self-preoccupation* is natural in children. The child begins life selfish by nature and can only understand self-interest. This type of love is closely related to children's views of themselves as basically weak, dependent, and open to danger on the one hand, and omnipotent and powerful on the other. This condition, however, does not always automatically disappear as the child grows older. We find that individuals with a high level of self-preoccupation and self-interest hold the same views of themselves.

Under healthy circumstances, most people move from self-preoccupation to *self-acceptance*, a quality that requires a higher level of emotional and intellectual maturity. At this level, we perceive ourselves to be both acceptable to ourselves and to others. We learn to have a more realistic view of our capacities, assets, and liabilities, and we learn to see the same qualities in others. It is during this stage of development that many people decide to adopt a routine and organized mode of life and begin to create a relatively small, homogeneous, and seemingly safe circle of relatives, friends, and acquaintances. Under these circumstances the individual's creativity, curiosity, and love for new horizons of knowledge and new forms of experience are to an appreciable degree sacrificed in favour of safeguarding the protective cocoon they have created. Some people live their whole lives in such a state and dull their senses, thoughts, and feelings with the help of drugs and alcohol, preoccupation with trivialities, accumulation of objects and material things, and occasional excitation through sensual and physical excesses.

Others find such a lifestyle unrewarding. They become distressed, either embarking on a process of further growth or else becoming unhappy and distraught. A healthy self-love requires growth in an integrated and comprehensive manner. The individual needs to grow physically and thus remain healthy; to grow intellectually and thus become knowledgeable and informed; to grow emotionally, and thus be able to deal adequately with both the joys and sorrows of life; and to grow spiritually, thus making life meaningful, creative, and enlightened. Such a growth process is demanding and painful. When we reach the stage of maturity, when we embark upon that journey, we have begun the process of *self-growth*.

Integration of Will and Concerns about Self

Primary Human Concerns	Main Human Powers		
	Knowledge	*Love*	*Will*
Self	· Self-experience · Self-discovery · Self-knowledge	· Self-preoccupation · Self-acceptance · Self-growth (development)	· Self-control · Self-confidence · Self-responsibility

The human will first appears in the form of *self-control*, then *self-confidence*, and as it matures it will finally manifest itself in the form of a deep sense of *personal responsibility*. Although these qualities are present to some degree from childhood, they become most developed when our willpower has also developed and grown.

The growth of our will is seen clearly when we study its development from childhood. Children make demands, refuse approaches and offerings, and show interest or withdraw from circumstances with such a force that they evidently possess a capacity that is uniquely theirs. This capacity—human will—must traverse several stages of growth in order to become a mature and healthy tool for the fulfillment of a person's objectives towards success in life. Under healthy conditions children gradually learn to use their willpower for *self-control*. Initially, this control is aimed at the biophysiological aspects of a child's functioning—bowel control, walking, and motor coordination. These elementary forms of self-control are augmented gradually by emotional, social, and intellectual self-control. This is a process through which the person learns to become a "civilized" member of society.

The civilizing process can be quite distressful, especially in those circumstances and environments in which the wishes, needs, and objectives of the individual and those of society are in opposition. This disharmonious situation often results in aggravation, frustration, anger, and even violence. Under reasonable and healthy circumstances, however, the individual not only achieves some measure of self-control but also begins to acquire *self-confidence*. Healthy individuals control and direct their activities with self-assurance and consequently are able to develop those unique aspects and characteristics that render their efforts interesting and attractive. People who lack self-confidence tend to underestimate their capacities and to overestimate their shortcomings. Such individuals live a life of shame, fear, isolation, and dissatisfaction. They often seek psychiatric help with a host of symptoms that, in reality, are indications of this lack of self-confidence. Conversely, self-confidence can be abused and turned into arrogance, pride, and insensitivity. These qualities are characteristics of an immature, juvenile personality, causing considerable harm to the individual's personal life and interpersonal relationships.

A healthy integration of self and will requires that self-confidence eventually give way to *personal (self-) responsibility* At this level people live and function with a profound sense of duty and responsibility to themselves and others. At the core of this is the crucial issue of preservation of the nobility and the integrity of oneself and others. In contemporary society many people avoid responsibility and find every available excuse to absolve themselves from accountability for their actions. Nowhere is this more clearly apparent than in the realm of human thoughts, feelings, and actions. The phenomenal efforts aimed at proving humans to be animals, subject only to the strict rules of their genetic endowments and instinctual drives is just one example of this tendency to avoid responsibility. Ultimately, all individuals must accept the fact that, unless incapacitated, their actions are their own responsibility.

At this point it will be useful to present two case studies as examples which demonstrate the unhealthy conditions we encounter when the development of the *self* has not fully taken place in the context of the human powers of knowledge, love, and will.

Case One: William

William, a twenty-six-year-old man married to a woman ten years his senior, was bewildered by his wife's anger and resentment. She considered him to be self-centred, cowardly, and unaccepting of any major responsibility in his life. William was puzzled by these accusations. He had a university education, worked as a computer programmer, and was both confident and responsible at his job and in sports. Aside from his job most of William's time was spent in body-building. Through his physical activities and training, he

The Psychology of Spirituality

CASE STUDY

gathered a number of male and female friends who admired his body and his "easy-going" personality. When asked what were his greatest areas of disagreement with his wife, he stated that he wanted to live an easy life, that he was not a "reader," and did not like to "think and talk about heavy things such as the right way to rear children." He stated that he saw nothing wrong with the way he related to their two children. Many nights he played with them, and he felt that "it was not abnormal" that when they were "horsing around the children would get hurt and cry." Also he did not see why his wife was so angry at him for spending so much time bodybuilding. He considered it "very important to be physically healthy." In addition he stated that a number of women he knew admired his body. He added that he refused to accept the criticism of not being responsible because he felt that his wife should shoulder the responsibilities for the care of their children, their home, and their finances, while he should work and do his physical activities.

His wife, a journalist by profession, worked full-time and saw all these issues from a higher level of integration and growth than he did. Soon after these disagreements surfaced, William began an affair with a twenty-year-old "easygoing" girl who "agreed" with his philosophy of life.

This is a good description of an individual whose self-knowledge is predominantly based on awareness related to his physical development, whose love shows itself in the form of self-preoccupation and the quest for instant gratification, and whose sense of responsibility aside from that of his job has not yet developed. William's self-centred and limited view of himself and his capacities contributed to his choice of a lifestyle that did not allow for higher levels of growth, maturity, self-awareness, and self-knowledge, and which prevented establishing lasting and intimate interpersonal relationships. Individuals like William usually have short-term materialistic objectives that often result in disillusionment and lack of fulfillment. Their relationships are usually self-indulgent and short-lived.

Case Two: Rosanna

Rosanna, a highly educated and well-read person, was quite unhappy because of much confusion and doubt about her intellectual abilities. She had much difficulty accepting herself and was very self-critical and self-rejecting. She had an incredible lack of self-confidence.

Rosanna's problems were clear examples of the main disorders that occur with respect to the development of self vis-à-vis knowledge, love, and will. Her difficulties in respect to self-knowledge were so strong that she avoided all opportunities for self-discovery and self-awareness, including her main areas of interest—literature, poetry, and writing. She also considered herself to be unlovable and was extremely anxious in her interpersonal relationships. These relationships were usually unsuccessful because of her self-critical attitudes. Although she was very hard-working and driven, she could not fulfill her potential because of her lack of self-confidence. Her therapy focused on helping her to develop along the lines of self-knowledge, self-love, and self-responsibility.

After one year of psychotherapy, Rosanna displayed a remarkable change in all these areas. She gradually improved her level of self-knowledge, began to see herself in a positive manner, and did not hesitate to present herself as a knowledgeable and capable individual. She started to write, publish, and teach at a university. Her capacity for self-acceptance increased, and she embarked on a painful but rewarding journey of self-growth. Several years later, she had made such marked changes in her life that it was very difficult to imagine that for almost forty years she had lived a limited, unfulfilled, and stagnant existence.

Integration of Knowledge, Love, and Will and Concerns about Relationships

●

INTEGRATION OF KNOWLEDGE AND CONCERN FOR OTHERS (RELATIONSHIPS)

Primary Human Concerns	Main Human Powers		
	Knowledge	*Love*	*Will*
Relationships	· Sameness of people · Uniqueness of people · Oneness of people	· Acceptance of others · Empathy with others · Unity	· Competition · Cooperation and Equality · *Movasat*

After concerns about self, the next category of human concerns are those related to relationships. Once again, these concerns are more specifically apparent in the framework of the human characteristics of knowledge, love, and will. The integration of our capacity to know and our ongoing concern about relationships determines how we see other people.

As children we initially tend to view others as the same as ourselves, and we strive to become the same as others. This quest for sameness creates a sense of security and belonging. The reasoning is that if we are the same, and feel, think, and wish in the same manner, then we will be accepted and loved by others. While this interest in sameness is a natural aspect of childhood and adolescence, it is not limited to this age group. As adults, many of us attempt to imitate others in the hope that we will be more readily accepted. However, by imitation we not only fail to achieve acceptance but also lose our uniqueness and individuality in the process. As we mature, we gradually begin to appreciate the uniqueness of every person.

It is a fact that all human beings are created unique. No two individuals are identical[*] in the same way that no two snowflakes are identical. This diversity is a testimony to the infinite richness of creation. It is one of the main sources of the overwhelming beauty of the created world. This sense of uniqueness should not be considered total and complete, and must eventually be supplemented by a feeling of oneness with all people, so that isolation and estrangement are not allowed to settle in and fester.

The undue emphasis on individualism so common in the Western world underscores the uniqueness of every individual but places this uniqueness in the context of a competitive environment of mistrust and isolation. On the contrary, the concept of the oneness of people refers to the fact that people are unique yet one. They are unique in their individuality and one in their humanness. Under unhealthy circumstances, people are not viewed as unique but rather as different and inferior or abnormal, an attitude that results in the development of fear and prejudice. Such a view is certainly not conducive to the healthy growth of the individual. In such an environment, the experience and acceptance of the oneness of all people becomes impossible.

From this brief description it should be clear that at the root of many current social problems lies a lack of true knowledge about ourselves and others as well as an ignorance of the evolving dynamics of the *sameness*, the *uniqueness*, and the *oneness* of all people. These constitute the main points of consideration in human relationships. At the level of sameness we have empathy for one another, while uniqueness allows us to become objective and realistic about each

---

[*]Identical twins are, of course, genetically the same. Nevertheless, they are different in respect to the time and conditions of their birth, and their environment, which can never be exactly the same.

specific situation. Finally, through understanding the oneness of all people we arrive at a capacity for empathy and cooperation.

INTEGRATION OF LOVE AND CONCERN FOR OTHERS (RELATIONSHIPS)

Primary Human Concerns	Main Human Powers		
	Knowledge	*Love*	*Will*
Relationships	· Sameness of people · Uniqueness of people · Oneness of people	· Acceptance of others · Empathy with others · Unity	· Competition · Cooperation and Equality · *Movasat*

Our love for others needs to be characterized by the qualities of *acceptance, empathy,* and *unity*. Every child's first challenge is to accept others with trust and confidence. This is the beginning of love for others. The child learns to do so through the experience of parental acceptance. Self-acceptance develops slowly but surely through being accepted by others who enter the child's life. Acceptance of others, as we all know, is obviously not an easy task and continues to challenge us throughout life. Examples of nonacceptance or intolerance are rampant in world societies and are the basis of individual mistrust and suspicion as well as racial, religious, nationalistic, and all other forms of social prejudice.

At one level, these conditions belong to the disorders of the self and at another level to the disorders of society. Acceptance of others becomes possible only when the person develops *empathy* for others. This is the second stage in the development of love relationships. At this level, a person is aware of both the sameness and uniqueness of others and is able to identify with their joys and sorrows. At the heart of many interpersonal relationships, we find an inability to see others as we see ourselves—noble and good.

In healthy, integrated growth, our love for others contains not only acceptance and empathy but also realization and appreciation of human *unity*. The experience of unity allows us to be fully aware of others, attuned to their hopes and despairs, responsive to their needs and circumstances, and prepared to offer assistance and self-sacrifice as required. Such a relationship is like the relationship of the various organs and parts of the human body. The human body can function in a healthy manner only when there exists total harmony and unity among all its component parts. Such is also the condition of the body of humanity. It follows then that the ultimate level of love for others is the recognition and unqualified acceptance of the unity of all human beings.

INTEGRATION OF WILL AND CONCERN FOR OTHERS (RELATIONSHIPS)

Primary Human Concerns	Main Human Powers		
	Knowledge	*Love*	*Will*
Relationships	· Sameness of people · Uniqueness of people · Oneness of people	· Acceptance of others · Empathy with others · Unity	· Competition · Cooperation and Equality · *Movasat*

The effects of human will are most obvious in the context of relationships. Initially, relationships are *competitive* in nature. Children tend to show their will in relationships with others by comparing themselves to others and trying to better them. This tendency is, of course, rooted in children's lack of self-confidence and their feelings of inferiority. Competitive behaviour is the hallmark of childhood and adolescent stages of development. Yet, these traits are also frequently encountered among adults. This is especially true today when humanity is collectively in the final phase of its age of adolescence.

Under healthy circumstances competition gradually gives way to *cooperation* and *equality*. It is the power of the human will that helps a cooperative person communicate with and serve others in an effective manner. It is important to note that many current marital and interpersonal difficulties are due to the unwillingness and, at times, the inability of people to achieve harmonious and cooperative ways of communicating. The proclivity towards individualism greatly hinders the capacity for cooperative relationships. To develop our capacity to cooperate, we must move from individualism to the level of unity, discarding competitive types of relationships.

Cooperation and equality, although signs of maturity, are nevertheless not the ultimate stages in the healthy use of human will in our relationships. There is yet another stage—the spiritual approach to human relationships. Spiritual individuals not only are able to relate in a cooperative and equal way but are also able and willing to prefer others over themselves (*movasat*). This quality of *movasat* or altruism may seem unrealistic within the framework of contemporary competitive societies. Nonetheless, the general direction of the development of humanity is towards ever greater levels of maturity, equality, and integration, all of which encourage *movasat*.

To illustrate the points described above, I will present two cases that clarify key issues concerning the development of interpersonal relationships, as related to the human powers of knowledge, love, and will.

Case One: Bruno

CASE STUDY

Bruno spoke about his fear and agony while serving in the United States Armed Forces in Japan. He had felt a considerable degree of isolation and loneliness, having been homesick for his family and friends. In recounting his experiences in Japan he said, "Doc, the most disturbing thing of all was to walk the streets of Tokyo and see all those strange foreigners, those Japanese!" Here Bruno was speaking from the perspective of an individual who sees differences, rather than similarities, strangeness rather than uniqueness, and separation rather than unity. In the case of Bruno, we are dealing with the absence of integration of the concern for human relationships and the capacity for understanding and knowledge of the noble reality of all people. Furthermore, this absence of awareness contributed to Bruno's inability to accept other people unconditionally and made it difficult, if not impossible, for him to empathize with others. Consequently, he felt lonely, isolated, and, of course, not united with others. To assist Bruno we had to begin from his childhood, when, as the son of an Italian immigrant, he was subject to rejection and ridicule. Consequently, he grew up setting himself apart and seeing others as strangers in relation to himself. He had not learned to trust others and now had to do so in the context of therapy, first by accepting himself, then by accepting others—a process that took several years to complete.

Case Two: Peter and Patricia

When I inquired of Peter and Patricia why they had so suddenly and violently separated, causing considerable confusion, pain, and unhappiness for themselves and their children, they provided the following account.

They had been married for thirteen years. For the first three years of their marriage, they lived separate lives but under the same roof. Both continued their jobs, had separate bank accounts, shared equally in the household expenses, and equally divided all the responsibilities involved in their life together.

Peter then decided to return to university to obtain a doctorate, upon which decision there followed years of resentment and anger on Patricia's part, as she became solely responsible for all the household chores and the care of their two children born during Peter's doctoral studies. Patricia felt cheated, ignored, and unloved, while Peter felt totally bewildered because he was going to school and working at the same time "for the family." When he finished his doctorate, it was Patricia's turn to return to school to obtain her master's degree. Now it was Peter who resented the additional work and responsibility placed on his shoulders. Both Peter and Patricia silently, and probably unconsciously, kept a mental record of who had done what and when, who had sacrificed more, who had given more, and who had shown a higher level of love and consideration.

By the time Patricia had finished her studies, both she and Peter felt equally resentful and rejected. Each competed with the other in all aspects of the relationship. They saw no true equality or cooperation in their marriage, and they were complete strangers to the notion of altruism. The relationship was no longer viable because of the intensity and depth of their competition and because of their unwillingness to see merit in deeper cooperation and service to one another. Their solution was to separate, an act that dramatically reduced their opportunities to achieve higher levels of cooperation and unity within the framework of their family and the participation of their children.

The Fundamentals

CASE STUDY

In fact, in families where the parents are gradually able to transcend the competitive stage of relationship and begin to cooperate with each other, children tend to have a much easier time with respect to such issues as sibling rivalry and adolescent rebellion. Furthermore, cooperative parents, while concentrating on raising and educating their children and enhancing their own individual and marital development, also have much greater opportunity to acquire the quality of altruism and tend to focus on each other's growth in a reciprocal and harmonious way. But for Peter and Patricia this was not possible. They knew how to compete and how to cooperate, but they did not consider the possibility of relating by giving the other's needs preference over one's own needs without resentment or anger. *Movasat* did not exist within their perspectives on life and relationships.

Integration of Knowledge, Love, and Will and Concerns about Time

●

INTEGRATION OF KNOWLEDGE AND CONCERNS ABOUT TIME

Primary Human Concerns	Main Human Powers		
	Knowledge	*Love*	*Will*
Time	· Present (here and now) · Mortality · Immortality	· Primary union · Separation · Secondary union	· Desire · Decision · Action

Time plays an extremely important role in our approach to life and its tasks. There are three major areas of concern with respect to time: the *present, mortality,* and *immortality.* During childhood we are basically aware of the present. Children, because of their self-centredness, needs, and vulnerabilities, are very concerned about the immediate conditions of life and tend not to think of the future or the past unless they are forced to do so, and forced they are. The first incident of separation from the mother forces the child both to remember the time of union, which was in the past, and to imagine the time of reunion, which is in the future.

It is this awareness of the past and the future that brings both apprehension and hope to the child. If the separation is sudden, dramatic, or prolonged, it can result in considerable fear and even panic in a child thus making the child highly sensitive to all subsequent separations and losses. We find the consequences of this type of trauma at the root of many psychiatric disorders.

The natural, healthy result of gradual separation from a love object is a realization that all relationships are temporary and that, in fact, this life is temporary. In other words, we gradually become aware of our *mortality*. Such an awareness causes much anxiety, an anxiety that is usually pushed into the depths of our unconscious and kept away from the realms of awareness. Despite this heroic effort, we cannot avoid the fact of our mortality, and we have no choice but to face our fears of nothingness, annihilation, and death. It is this awareness of mortality that causes most of the anxieties of contemporary materialistic humanity.

Within the framework of a spiritual approach to life, the sense of the present and the fear of mortality are superseded by the awareness of *immortality*—the immortality of our spiritual reality. It is this knowledge that decreases the fear of death and allows us to deal with separation and loss in a more realistic, mature way. Within the framework of immortality, the past, present, and future become integrated into a sense of timelessness, opportunity, and the imperative. People with an awareness of the immortality of their being can become active creators and actors in the arena of life and can take full responsibility and joy in shaping their journey of existence.

INTEGRATION OF LOVE AND CONCERN ABOUT TIME

Primary Human Concerns	Main Human Powers		
	Knowledge	*Love*	*Will*
Time	· Present (here and now) · Mortality · Immortality	· Primary union · Separation · Secondary union	· Desire · Decision · Action

Like all other aspects of human life, love is developmental in its nature and therefore closely related to the passage of time. In infancy, love, which is the bond between the child and the mother, is a union that has not yet been subject to separation. It is a *primary union*, independent of the dimension of time. Because time is ever present in our lives, this primary union becomes subject to the changes and chances of life, and we begin to experience *separation* from the object of our love. This separation is painful and can be traumatic. But the separation is always and inevitably necessary. It provides us with the opportunity for self-discovery, self-acceptance, growth, acquisition of empathy, and realization of the uniqueness of ourselves and others.

For many people, this phase of separation is extremely frightening; the fear is especially profound when the separation is in the form of either rejection or death. Usually the phase of separation is temporary, and love manifests itself again in the form of yet another union, a union strengthened by the experience of separation and what we learn about ourselves as a result of this separation. We experience the joys of this reunion and the benefits of a more mature *secondary union* in all forms of love: between ourselves and our children, spouses, other human beings, and ultimately God.

INTEGRATION OF WILL AND CONCERN ABOUT TIME

Primary Human Concerns	Main Human Powers		
	Knowledge	*Love*	*Will*
Time	· Present (here and now) · Mortality · Immortality	· Primary union · Separation · Secondary union	· Desire · Decision · Action

To understand the developmental stages of will, we must focus on the human qualities of *desire, decision-making,* and *action.* These three qualities are different stages of the development of the role of will in our lives. In childhood, human will shows itself through *desires* and needs that cannot wait and must be gratified on the spot. Society's rampant desire for instant gratification is one clear example of the immature level of growth of will in many people. It is also an indication of current attitudes about the meaning and purpose of life—attitudes that suggest one's only objective is to enjoy oneself, to gratify one's desires, and to avoid anything painful or unpleasant. These views and conditions notwithstanding, the fact remains that with the passage of time, and under healthy conditions, the human will transcends the level of desires, and we begin to make *decisions* involving delay in gratification and even foregoing gratification altogether. Such a mature use of human will is at the core of human progress and development.

Ultimately, decisions must be made and put into *action*—actions that not only fulfill human desires but also bring the fruits of human knowledge and love into reality. Thus, the relationship between *desire, decision,* and *action* is developmental. In the earlier stages of personality development, desires are predominant and powerful whereas the capacities of the individual to decide and act are limited. However, as people mature, their capacities for decision-making and action increase. Through the passage of time, and because of the increasing powers of knowledge and love, a mature person is willing and able to choose between various desires and to put into action only those that are conducive to the enhancement of the quality of life and relationships.

Human experience in respect to time is not easy to understand. The following case studies involve the issues of mortality, death, love, desires, decisions, actions, and their roles in our lives.

Case One: Timothy

CASE STUDY

For the past two years Timothy had been extremely preoccupied with death; indeed, he was very fearful of it. He was now thirty-eight years old, and until five years earlier he did not even think about such "depressing and negative issues as death." He, his wife, and their only child, Heather, age eight, had been living from day to day, enjoying their lives in the framework of the present. They had little concern for the future. They were financially comfortable and professionally satisfied. Then their daughter became ill with leukemia. The horror and agony of this event was immense, and as a result Timothy became extremely fearful, angry, and sad.

Fortunately, Heather responded quite well to the treatment of her cancer and began to improve considerably. While his daughter and wife reacted to this improvement with relief, Timothy continued to worry and feel extremely fearful and anxious to such an extent that he could no longer think about the daily aspects of his life. He had been confronted with the question of mortality. The fear of death and annihilation had begun to haunt him. He had not been able to free himself from this fear which, interestingly enough, became worse when his daughter was pronounced so improved as to no longer require treatment.

Timothy's case demonstrates the process of the emergence of awareness of time and its role in one's life. Prior to the onset of his child's illness, Timothy had been virtually indifferent to time. For him time was the disjointed moments of the present. He had lived his life without much consideration for the passage of time and the future. This approach to time was particularly easy for him because most of his immediate basic needs for food, shelter, clothing, security, work, leisure, and companionship were satisfied.

Under such circumstances a person risks becoming oblivious to the passage of time and the need for awareness of one's existence in the context of a lifetime with a past, a present, and a future. His daughter's illness forced Timothy to look at the question of mortality, but he was disinclined to move beyond this level to ponder the issue of immortality. As a result, his profound fear immobilized him. It was in the context of therapy that the issue of the immortality of the human reality had to be investigated and understood. The first step in this process was reflection on the possibility of the imminent death of his daughter.

It was inconceivable for him to imagine the nonexistence of a reality such as Heather, and he had to answer her questions about death. Heather wanted to know about death and after death. Timothy and his wife did not know how to respond to her questions and began to scramble for answers. It was in this process that they experienced an awareness similar to that described earlier in the cases of Carol and Dawn.

Case Two: Justin

A dramatic case representing the processes of primary union and reunion was observed in Justin, a five-year-old boy who actively searched for a means of killing himself in order to join his deceased

CASE STUDY mother. His mother had gone to the hospital to deliver a baby, but she had died in delivery and never returned home. The child, bewildered and in shock, asked for his mother and, when told that she "had gone to heaven" he yearned for reunion with her through his own death.

Justin's main relationship had always been with his mother. She was his primary object of love and union, the primary person through whom all other relationships, including his own relationship with himself, acquired their meaning and significance. Gradually through childhood and adolescence, children develop a capacity to see themselves independently of their parents and eventually find it possible to separate from them. For Justin, however, these processes of individuation and separation were aborted due to the sudden and untimely death of his mother. In his mind, the only solution was to die in order to become reunited with his mother who, he was told, lived in "heaven." In providing therapy for such a child there is need for strengthening the bonds of love between the child and another significant adult or adults, helping the child to grieve over the loss of a parent, and providing the child with a better understanding of the meaning and nature of death.

In my work with children facing either their own death or the death of a parent, sibling, or another close individual, I use the womb analogy described earlier to provide these children with a better understanding of the concept of death and its relationship to life. Analogies are powerful instruments of education because each person understands the concepts according to his or her own level of growth and maturity. In addition, an analogy can be simplified or elaborated upon according to the age, intellect, and emotional capacities of the individuals involved.

Case Three: Susan and John

Disorders in the development of love within the context of time are also quite frequently observed in the marital relationship. On many occasions in the clinical setting we encounter couples who are distraught about a decline in their love relationship. They report noticing that one or both have become very preoccupied with themselves, or their children, and consequently are devoting far less time and energy to the marital relationship. This change in the nature of the relationship is often perceived to be a sign of the decline of commitment and love in marriage, while in reality, it is the middle phase (the phase of separation or individuation) of the development of love in the context of time. The same dynamics are applicable to the processes of the separation of adolescents from their families, which end the primary union and pave the way for the reestablishment of the relationship with the parents, this time at a higher level of maturity—the phase of secondary union or reunion. The case of Susan and John depicts various stages in the development of love.

They came to me because of a serious crisis in their marriage. For some time, John had been involved with another woman and had concluded that he was no longer sure about his marriage. Consequently, he had decided to leave Susan and to live with his girlfriend. This sudden decision to move out of the house caused considerable unhappiness and shock for Susan, who seemed to be totally unaware of what had been happening until a few months before their separation.

The couple had met in their late teens. At the time, both were away from home, quite insecure, needing someone to allay their fears and confusion. In such circumstances, they were attracted to one another. John had never actually lived on his own and was fearful of living alone. Susan, likewise, was very insecure, especially since she had come from a very unstable home. They "fell in love," a love that manifested itself primarily in gratification of some of their basic needs—dependency, companionship, and, above all, the need for a person who would validate their experiences of themselves, give them a feeling of worth and a realization that they were indeed likable and lovable. In the face of these extreme emotional needs, the fact that they were, to some extent, able to satisfy each other's needs was a major motivation for marriage.

As the years passed, their married life fell into a routine of working, looking after the necessities of life, establishing themselves professionally, and other such issues. The couple had no children. Further evaluation revealed that John had a low tolerance for frustration and a strong desire for instant gratification. Susan's predominant characteristic was her tremendous need for security. Consequently, she focused all her attention on ensuring that they were secure both financially and professionally. She was quite unhappy

The Psychology of Spirituality

CASE STUDY

with her husband because he had not been able to hold down a job. Frequently, he had lost jobs because of his inability or unwillingness to face demanding and problematic conditions in his workplace.

Further evaluation of this marriage showed that the initial powerful force of attraction was their mutual need for companionship and escape from their fear of loneliness. However, once married, their need for companionship and their fear of being alone were satisfied, and each began to have new needs that they did not share. In essence, they lived two separate lives while sharing living quarters. During these years, they basically avoided the painful realities that confronted them, and consequently John pursued the route of gratification while Susan became involved in attempts to gain security. During the course of the first interview, John stated that as far as he was concerned, the most enjoyable lifestyle was a sort of "serial monogamy," meaning he preferred to establish relatively short-term, intense relationships with women who would satisfy him. When these conditions changed, he would establish a new relationship with another woman who would be willing and able to satisfy his needs.

The concept of growth was totally absent from this couple's life during their married years; they became aware of its absence only when they were confronted during the course of therapy with the processes of development in love relationships.

Case Four: Julianna

"I cannot finish any of my projects," said Juliana, a very intelligent nineteen-year-old woman. She went on to say that despite her considerable desire and heartfelt decision to pursue her studies at school, finish her projects at home, and attend to her various responsibilities, when it came to action she failed herself and did not accomplish anything. This had been her habit for a long time. She usually had been able to avoid her indulgent parents' criticism. Gradually, however, she had become aware of the passage of time and the widening gap between her accomplishments and those of her peers. This alarmed her and motivated her to seek help.

Juliana's dilemma was a typical one, which we can all occasionally see in ourselves and those close to us in varying degrees of severity. At the core of the dilemma is a disorder of will, demonstrating itself in the fact that the person desires to be active and fruitful, frequently makes a decision to act, but fails to do so. Juliana demonstrated her disorder of will in the course of therapy. She discontinued therapy after only three interviews because she decided to leave for a vacation and then move to live closer to a newly found boyfriend. She also had many elaborate plans for her education, none of which moved beyond the level of desire.

Once again, Juliana failed to finish a task. This time the task was that of psychotherapy aimed at helping her to overcome her inability to use her power of will in a healthy manner. One may wonder what would be the eventual life history of such an individual. Although prediction of the course of individual cases is neither possible nor appropriate, evaluation of clinical trends is both necessary and very informative. My clinical observation of such cases indicates two possible outcomes. To the first group belong those who, because of the unhealthy use of their will, continue a life without purpose, direction, or creativity. Such individuals tend to feel dissatisfied, bored, dependent on others, and fearful of assuming responsibilities. The second group tends to live a life of indecision and purposelessness until eventually, in response to certain life crises, they suddenly discover their potential to take initiative and begin to use their powers of knowledge, love, and will to overcome the crises and challenges of life. This discovery may come about with or without the benefit of a therapeutic experience, but in either case the individual is headed towards considerable change, usually of a positive nature.

◇ ◇ ◇

In the preceding pages I have described the relationship between our powers to know, love, and will, and our fundamental concerns about ourselves, others, and time. Our lives are a continuous process of progression and evolution along the axes of knowledge, love, and will. Major psychological disorders occur when this process suffers or comes to a halt. Accordingly, various psychological disorders can be studied not merely in the light of their symptoms but rather with respect to the presence or absence, and also the severity, of one or more of the three disorders of knowledge, love, and will.

PART FOUR

When Things Go Wrong

Adversity is the first path to truth.
Lord Byron, *Don Juan*

On the Purpose of Life and the Process of Healing

●

Is there a purpose to life? This is a universal question. It can be answered in the singular or plural. People say the purpose of life is love or freedom or justice or happiness or success or power, or just about anything. Many see no singular purpose except in a sort of package: to have food and shelter, family or friends to love and be loved, a meaningful and well-paid job, good times, and, if possible, no illness or death. Still others choose specific purposes such as knowledge, service, growth, or creativity. Most people do not usually spend much time thinking about the purpose of their lives. Even when the issue is raised, many respond with either puzzlement and confusion, or else they reject the question as irrelevant.

Regardless of our opinions about the purpose of life, we are always dealing with various challenges, difficulties, and opportunities in our lives. A fundamental aspect of our humanness is that we are aware. It is our self-awareness that compels us to be concerned about ourselves, our relationships, and the passage of our lives. These are existential concerns. In other words, because we are alive and aware, we have no choice but to think about these issues. Even when we try to avoid them, they still nag at us and demand our attention.

Over the years I have observed that by far the greatest percentage of people who seek psychiatric or psychological counselling and even medical help, do so because of their unhappiness or puzzlement about some fundamental aspect of their lives. People usually come to a health professional with a complaint such as depression, anxiety, physical symptoms, marriage and family problems, loneliness and relationship difficulties, sexual matters, problems with the law, drug and alcohol problems, and a variety of fears, compulsions, and bothersome habits. Some have little interest or energy for life. Others are in constant struggle with their lives. Still others dread their lives.

The normal tendency among health professionals is to focus on the patient's symptoms and to deal with each of them separately. This unsatisfactory approach is probably one of the main shortcomings of modern medicine.

In the context of our materialistic times, the human being is perceived as an object rather than a person. Because this object is extremely complex, modern medicine has divided it into its component organs and parts, and has developed specialties that concern themselves only with a specific part of the human body. Specialists usually become so focused in their area of expertise they disregard the fact that they are indeed dealing with a *human* being. Of the many criticisms of modern medicine, the most valid is that it has lost its soul.

Modern medicine has developed into a highly mechanized, inhuman system. Members of the health professions no longer perceive themselves to be healers. They are technicians of the body and the psyche. To be a healer, one needs, first and foremost, to be in touch with the humanness present in all of us. The healer sees life, purpose, beauty, poetry, and the divine in the individual. The healer imparts strength, hope, and love for life, and helps the patient use all the available capacities and opportunities to regain health. To the healer, disease is important because it has taken away health. The healer aims at restoring health and at preventing disease.

To become a healer, one must come in touch with the powers of life, purify the mind with a positive attitude, and set the heart on that which causes health. The process of healing requires love—a love so pure and unconditional that it will cause profound calmness, serenity, assurance, and inner peace, all of which are necessary to cure the disease. The healer also needs to strengthen the will and the resolve of the patient so that the patient will be able to face all the challenges of ill health with determination and optimism.

Study of these issues is not included in the curricula of medical schools; nor are these topics, generally speaking, taught at universities and colleges. These are spiritual matters that are held to have no place in the strongholds of materialistic civilization—the universities. The closest some university courses get to these issues is in the ethics, religion, or philosophy departments. But even these studies are limited in scope because they use the limited mechanistic definition of the scientific method. While there is no doubt that the scientific method is the best instrument for the advancement of knowledge, there is also no doubt that the parameters of the scientific method, originally established for the study of physics and chemistry and other physical sciences, need to be greatly modified and expanded to meet the requirements for the study of the spiritual dimension of human life.

Earlier it was shown that knowledge, love, and will are the central spiritual powers of the human being. The main problems of life can, therefore, be classified as disorders of knowledge, love, and will. The powers of the soul (knowledge, love, and will), of course have a profound effect on the physical body and vice versa. That is why we cannot consider any human problem to be solely physical or psychological. While some disorders are primarily physical, they also affect our psychological condition; and while other disorders are primarily psychological, they also affect the body to a greater or lesser degree. Here we confine ourselves to the psychological disorders of knowledge, love, and will.

Disorders of Knowledge

●

Our knowledge can be broadly divided into three groups: self-knowledge, knowledge of the world (both the physical environment and other people), and knowledge of reality. Self-knowledge begins in the first days of life. As children, we interact with our parents and our environment, and receive certain responses. These responses and life experiences have a profound impact on the growing child and are retained in our memory. As we grow up, most of these memories leave our conscious awareness and become a part of our habitual approaches to life circumstances as well as our unconscious. In addition to the lessons learned from our environment, we also learn from our internal experiences. The more elementary of these experiences are hunger, pain, and sexual drives, all of which give us a certain awareness and motivate us to behave in specific ways. We also learn through our minds by observing different situations in our environment, by experimenting, and by reaching logical conclusions. Our emotions give us yet another kind of self-knowledge. When we feel happy, sad, angry, calm, or fearful, we are provided with opportunities to reflect on these feelings, find the reasons for them, find the ways of dealing with them and, in the process, learn more about ourselves. Self-knowledge can also occur as a result of sudden flashes of insight. This is inspiration. We also have intuitive knowledge.

Our knowledge is, of course, not limited to self-knowledge. As we grow up, we develop knowledge about other people, nature, and the universe. Our self-knowledge, combined with our knowledge of the world, helps us form our approach to life. If we think of ourselves as weak and vulnerable and the world as a dangerous place, we live differently than if we feel courageous and think of the world as a place of opportunity.

These differences are important because they tell us something about our understanding of reality. Is the world really dangerous or safe? Under what circumstances is it safe? Are human beings basically peaceful? Is human nature aggressive? Can we trust others? What about evil? Does evil really exist? These and other similar issues are at the core of our desire to know and understand reality and are closely related to a healthy development of our lives. However, when our views about ourselves, our world, and reality are inadequate or incorrect, then we are faced with a disorder of knowledge, and our life becomes burdened with misconceptions, fears, and anxieties.

In psychotherapy, the therapist tries to help patients to gain an understanding into the nature of their own thoughts and feelings about themselves, the world, and reality. This is called insight. The therapist also tries to help the patient gradually find a way to bring these views into closer accord with what is perceived to be reality. Many therapists, for example, aim at strengthening the ego boundaries of their patients and helping them to bring their behaviour into conformity with the norms of society. But what if the society itself is not healthy?

The daughter of a well-known politician was once brought to the hospital because she had attempted suicide. Evaluation of the family showed that it was a very authoritarian and rigid household. The parents were extremely concerned—not about their daughter but, rather, about her behaviour. They demanded that she behave in certain very rigid, predetermined ways and not befriend young people of the "wrong" race or social status. The parents were excessively concerned about appearances and had defined a very limited life for their daughter.

The daughter, however, was young, enthusiastic, and full of universal hopes and ideals. She wanted to be friends with all kinds of people. It did not matter to her whether they were rich or poor, black or white, of her own nationality or from another part of the world. For the parents, reality was a world divided into two camps, good and bad. They, of course, belonged to the good camp and wanted their daughter to shun the other camp. For the daughter, the world was one, filled with many different people and races, all beautiful and interesting.

Here the clash between the parents and the daughter was over their respective definitions of the reality of the world of humanity. So the question of reality is extremely important. Our awareness of reality is directly related to our efforts to search for reality. In other words, as we mature and develop more wisdom and experience, we become more aware of the realities of existence and more open to new concepts and ideas.

Life, in and of itself, is a school in which we learn about many things. Some people go through the school of life participating fully in all its aspects; others participate in this school only marginally; and still others stop learning. This is our choice, but if we do not learn from life, we will lead lives of misery, isolation, and ignorance.

Now let us examine the relationship between our inner development and our understanding of reality. Psychological observations show that, in the early months of life, children do not make a distinction between themselves and the world they inhabit. For them all is one. This primal perception of oneness is, of course, soon shattered. The child begins to have experiences that force recognition of the separation existing between self and the world. The face of reality, therefore, changes, taking on myriad forms in people, places, and events. In early childhood, our understanding of both ourselves and our world is quite limited and elementary. It may be likened to the perception our early ancestors had of both themselves and the universe. When we look back at those ideas, they emerge as superficial and superstitious. At the time, though, these represented the highest levels of understanding about reality attained by people. For example, we now know that the earth is not flat, but, for our ancestors, that was reality and the highest level of their understanding of the shape and place of the earth in the universe.

The same principle applies to spiritual issues. Love is a good example. Love is a spiritual reality. For the child love means receiving care, attention, and nurturing from adults. The reality of love, according to the understanding of a child, is to receive. For the parent, the reality of love is to give. For the husband and wife, the reality of love is both to give and receive. For a highly mature and spiritual person, love is unconditional. Our perception of the reality of love is therefore relative rather than absolute.

This is true of all realities, whether physical or spiritual. As we grow, we understand more. The fundamental disorder of knowledge emerges when we think that we possess absolute and ultimate knowledge of reality. If this disorder of knowledge existed in science, scientific development would cease. There would be no new discoveries or breakthroughs in knowledge. Such a way of thinking is absurd. How could anyone possibly claim to know everything about anything? It is the relativity of our understanding of physical reality that allows us to seek more knowledge.

Why should the same not be true about spiritual knowledge? Why should the same not be true of love, will, and wisdom, our views of morality, and our understanding of the spiritual dimension of human nature, and of the reality of religion? All of these facets of spiritual reality are relative, not absolute. They are relative in relation to our ability to understand them. They are equally relative in our ability to incorporate them into our individual and collective lives. In our time the major societal disorder of knowledge is the insistence on the part of various religions and ideologies that they each are in sole possession of the absolute truth. But how can absolute truth be so diverse and divergent? How can absolute truth be understood by our limited minds? And how can humanity possibly continue to evolve spiritually if the absolute truth has already been disclosed and has become the source of hatred, disunity, and destruction among the followers of various religions and ideologies? These are among the most challenging questions now facing humanity with respect to our understanding of reality.

While science is marching ahead to attain ever higher understanding of physical reality, religions, by their insistence on their doctrines of absolute truth, are lagging behind dangerously. But science without the benefit of the universal spiritual realities will become a source of destruction. In fact, it has already become so. Likewise, religion without the benefit of the logical and scientific will stagnate and become mere superstition. This, too, has already taken place.

The basic challenge before us, therefore, is to free spiritual reality from the chains of absolutism, which results in division and conflict, and begin to study it in the context of the relativity of all human knowledge, whether physical or spiritual in nature. We must also realize that truth is one and cannot be fragmented. Science and religion are basically one. Both describe the essential connections that proceed from the realities of things.[1] Science shows us the interrelationship among realities of the material world. The same may be said of religion, which, in its pure form, is simply a demonstration of spiritual connections that exist between our minds and hearts and actions. There is also a fundamental unity connecting us all. The whole of humanity is affected by whatever each of us thinks, loves, and does.

These issues become more easily understood if we discuss them as they apply to an actual case. I will do this by describing disorders of knowledge in a case that deals with psychological difficulties related to a person's misconceptions about being inherently "bad."

"I AM BAD": A CASE OF FAULTY SELF-KNOWLEDGE

CASE STUDY

Mary was thirty-three years old when I first saw her for psychotherapy. At that time she was quite distraught with her life and had made a very serious suicide attempt. She was totally unhappy with her marriage. Although she was very close to her three children, she derived very little consolation from this fact. She was haunted by recurring nightmares of considerable intensity that left her frightened and shaky for days. Above all, Mary was paralyzed by a profound sense of "badness." She believed that she was "evil." She was so afraid and ashamed of her self-image, her thoughts, and her feelings that she found it impossible to talk about them in any coherent manner.

Mary's interview sessions were consequently characterized by very long periods of silence, frequent episodes of fear, anxiety, and tears, and her firm belief that she deserved punishment for her evil thoughts and feelings. It took two years for Mary to gain enough trust to be able to talk, however briefly, about her childhood and adolescent years, which were marked by considerable rejection and mistreatment by her parents and others responsible for her care in the boarding schools she had attended. She was brought up in a wealthy, upperclass family. Both of her parents were demanding,

CASE STUDY

cold, and critical. Worst of all, they spent little time with her, leaving her in the care of nannies and placing her in strict religious boarding schools. From early adolescence they involved her in psychotherapy, and at the time of her first interview with me, she had already had twelve years of psychotherapy, psychoanalysis, and treatment with major and minor tranquilizers and antidepressants. During this time she had received various conflicting diagnoses from her therapists.

The emphasis of my work with Mary was to deal with her faulty self-perception as being "inherently bad and evil." My efforts initially proceeded without much result until I decided to focus exclusively on her positive qualities and to avoid discussion of her problems, symptoms, fears, and other psychological disorders.

The decision to focus on her positive qualities was in keeping with the concepts of the psychology of spirituality that ultimately the most important and powerful forces in the life of each human being are the creative, life-affirming, and positive qualities that the person possesses. Any healthy change in one's behaviour and lifestyle requires identification and enrichment of these positive capacities and abilities. In fact, pathological processes often become less devastating in their effects if we develop our potentialities and assets. To do so, we need a knowledge of these assets. Under unhealthy conditions such as those Mary experienced, people quite often become so preoccupied with their problems that they overlook or even deny their actual abilities. This was indeed true in Mary's case. During the course of therapy, the first area of self-knowledge to improve was knowledge about her positive abilities and creative capacities. From all her years of therapy, she had become fully aware of her "problems" and was almost totally convinced that these problems were her reality.

By concentrating on her positive qualities and assets, it gradually emerged that Mary was a highly artistic, sensitive, and gifted person. She played piano extremely well, wrote sensitive poetry, and had a facility for dance. She had never shared these qualities with others. She had stopped playing piano, had withdrawn from her ballet classes, had refused to show her poetry to anyone, and felt ashamed because of her belief in her own "badness." It was the adjustment of focus on her positive qualities that gradually resulted in progress and improvement in Mary. She became more communicative, more optimistic, and more relaxed. Her relationship with her husband and children improved, and she began to work with considerable success. Her nightmares continued to bother her nonetheless, and she was still greatly affected by her feelings of badness.

These latter feelings, although extensively analyzed and well understood by Mary, were persistent not only because of what had occurred in the past but also because of her faulty understanding of her own nature. In the course of many years of treatment, Mary had been able to understand the root causes of her childhood fears, anxieties, and anger. Gradually, she had reestablished her relationship with her parents and by now had far less conflict with them than she ever previously had. Her insights were both intellectual and emotional, and she was aware of her feelings as well as her thoughts. Her level of motivation to live a fulfilling, productive life was high. She received adequate support from her family. But in spite of all this, she continued to be unhappy and miserable because she perceived herself to be "bad." This faulty self-knowledge also caused Mary to have a poor self-image, which in turn made it difficult for her to trust herself or others and ultimately made her pessimistic about the future. Her concerns were, respectively, about self, others, and time.

The treatment plan for Mary was based on these facts. The first goal was to help her gain an understanding of the positive nature of her own self. As we did so, she gradually began to speak about her conflicted feelings and her profound sense of badness for experiencing some degree of pleasure from sexual activities.*

She also began to speak of her ideas about life, shared her poetry, and divulged her inner quest for a greater degree of knowledge on the one hand and spiritual enlightenment on the other. It was around this time that she also reported that for the first time in a long time she had been able to pray. This was a significant event because the return to prayer signalled the return of her sense of worth and the fact that she was "good" enough to commune with God and be accepted by God. Her years of strict and abusive upbringing in the convent had, on the one hand, made her a devout

---

*She recounted that while in the boarding school she was sexually stimulated and molested by the nuns and priests who were in charge of her.

The Psychology of Spirituality

CASE STUDY

Catholic and on the other hand, caused her to be very resentful, angry, and fearful about God. As she gradually began to modify her views of herself and was able to perceive herself as a basically good and creative being, she was also able to separate her history of abuse from the fundamental nobility of her being. Consequently, she was able to pray again. To her relief, the nightmares also disappeared around this time. It was then that she was able to accept herself as not being "bad" but possibly "good." The misconception about the true nature of her own reality was gradually corrected. A new level of self-knowledge and consequently self-acceptance emerged. This important development had its roots in the gradual correction of her disorder of knowledge about herself.

Disorders of Love

●

Disorders of love occur with respect to the two main aspects of love: its nature and its object. Disorders of the nature of love refer to the intensity of love and the level of maturity of the person involved.

Human love may be either intense and deep, or half-hearted and superficial. An intense, profound love has certain qualities such as creativity, vitality, and joy of life, while a half-hearted, superficial love has a quality of shallowness, fear, and sorrow. In clinical work we encounter this latter type of love in children and adults who themselves have been deprived of love, especially in their formative years. Rejection, separation, and loss are universal experiences and cause us doubt and anxiety about our love relationships with others.

When we are rejected by someone we love, we not only feel very angry and sad but also experience a profound sense of doubt about our own lovability. Likewise, when we experience separation and loss, our views about our capacity to love and be loved are greatly challenged and not infrequently adversely affected. Therefore, two very common forms of disorders of love are the insecurity about our capacity to love and the insecurity to be loved. These usually arise in relation to experiences of loss, separation, and rejection.

Another group of love disorders are those encountered as a result of a lag in the overall maturation of the person, where the capacity to love is inadequately developed. Under healthy circumstances love goes through various stages of growth, beginning at a self-centred level, traversing stages of competition and cooperation, and finally arriving at the level of an unconditional love.

These stages are each distinct and hierarchical in nature, having a cumulative quality. In other words, at each level we are capable of sharing love at that given level as well as at all lower levels. A person who has matured to the stage of cooperative love is capable of both receiving and giving love, and sharing that love with others. At the same time, however, under appropriate conditions that person will compete to show more love (as in the celebration of birthdays, anniversaries, etc.). Such a person is also able to receive love (as in times of illness and need) or give love (as in the case of a parent or teacher). Disorders of love are seen in people who give but cannot receive love, who receive but are unable to give love, or those who tend to compete in the love relationship with respect both to giving and to receiving love. The main characteristics of the love relationship at each stage of its development are outlined in figure 2.

The third and final major category of the disorder of love is related to the love object. For human love to take place, there must be a love object. In other words, we need to have a person, an idea, or a thing as the object of our quest, wish, desire, and attention so that our love can show itself. The quality and character of our love is greatly influenced by the nature of our love object. Human love is only as pure, tender, meaningful, enlightened, and eternal as its love object. If people develop a love of war, then their love can never be pure, tender, meaningful, or enlightened. If they choose to love fame, wealth, or power, they will have a love experience in keeping with the characteristics of these love objects.

In psychotherapy, therefore, we need to determine both the level of maturity of love and its object. In this context, the psychotherapist does not hesitate to ask such difficult questions as why and who or what the person loves. Likewise, the clients need to answer, with equal candour and depth, such troublesome questions as why they are loved, why they should be loved, how they are loved, and who loves them. All these issues need careful attention from both the client and the therapist. The following two case histories are examples of a disorder of love in respect to the issue of a love object

When Things Go Wrong

Stages of Development	Characteristics
Self-centred Love	• Self-love is almost indistinguishable from selfishness. • Individuals love in order to prove to themselves and to others their own ability to love. • Love is one directional either primarily giving or receiving with little ability to do both. • This type of love is only healthy in childhood.
Competitive Love	• Self-love has the quality of ambivalence, i.e., individuals both love and hate themselves. • Individuals love others in order to prove themselves more capable of loving than other people, or to prove that they are loved less or more than others. • Love relationship is competitive, and the lovers tend to have an explosive, argumentative, and erratic realtionship. • This is the most common type of love relationship in adolesence.
Cooperative Love	• Self-love has the quality of self-acceptance. • Individuals love others in order to fulfill their equally felt and understood need to love and be loved. • Love relationship is cooperative in nature, and lovers tend to share, give, and receive and to allow themselves to love and to be loved as appropriate. • This type of love is the one that most adults need, especially in the framework of marriage and friendship.
Unconditional Love	• Self-love has the quality of selflessness. • Individuals love others unconditionally in the same way that the sun shines over all unconditionally. • Love relationship is universal and all embracing in its scope. The individual is a lover of humanity. • This type of love is the most advanced love, as seen in the lives of the prophets, saints, and those who love free from prejudice and exclusiveness.

Figure 2: Developmental stages of love and their characteristics

and a disorder of love as related to the person's understanding of the nature of love.

CASE STUDY

DAVID: A CASE OF A DISORDER OF "LOVE OBJECT"

David was thirty-nine years old when he requested assistance because of an inability to finish his doctoral thesis. At that time he was a professor at a well-established North American university and was considered a world-class authority in his field of specialization. More important, his thesis topic was in the area in which he had long been acknowledged as an expert. At the time of his first interview, he had already been working on his thesis for more than four years and had only to write the remaining one-third to finish. The members of his thesis committee had assured him of the high quality of what he had already produced and had stated that the thesis, once completed at the same level of quality, would be accepted without problem. In addition, David himself was quite aware of his own expertise and did not doubt his ability to finish the thesis in an acceptable manner.

Nonetheless, David's awareness of his own abilities, the fact that the deadline for finishing his thesis was fast approaching, and the threat that not having a Ph.D. would jeopardize his academic reputation and progress, were not sufficient reasons to induce him to finish the thesis. Whenever he attempted to work, he experienced considerable anxiety and panic, resorting to alcohol and tranquilizers to calm himself. In a state of drunkenness and stupor, he would be unable to continue his work and would abandon it for that day.

To solve this problem he had sought psychotherapy, and over four years a number of psychologists and psychiatrists had treated him with analytic therapy, behaviour therapy, and various tranquilizers and antidepressants. As a result of these treatments, he had acquired considerable insight into the dynamics of his behaviour. He had learned that he feared success, had a very poor self-image, wanted to be dependent on others (especially a mother substitute), harboured much anger against his parents (particularly his father), and did not want to give his father the pleasure of seeing him succeed. He further informed me that on different occasions he had been diagnosed as depressed and treated with antidepressants. He had been diagnosed as having an anxiety disorder and that he needed relaxation and tranquilizing medication. He had been diagnosed as phobic and treated with a behaviour therapy program. He had accepted some of these explanations while rejecting others and had tried all modalities of therapy in search of a cure. Further evaluation revealed that David was happily married, had several healthy, well-functioning children, and that financially he was under no stress. His own overall health was good apart from the fact that he drank and smoked excessively.

CASE STUDY

I began my work with David with three premises: that finishing the thesis was not the main problem; that the nature of the basic difficulty was yet unknown; and finally, that, whatever his basic problem proved to be, there was no reason to believe that David would not be able to deal with it and overcome it. Three months later David was awarded his Ph.D. On the afternoon of that same day he began to drink, ostensibly to celebrate, but as time passed he became more agitated and depressed. The following morning he came for a therapy session, half-drunk, tearful, acutely sad, dishevelled, and asked, "Now what?"

He then told a "secret." He said that as a child he grew up in a ghetto in a European country. His parents were poor, uneducated, and lower class. He received little guidance or encouragement to shape his life or to plan for the future. Nonetheless, he decided to choose the highest goals he could imagine. These goals were to become educated, to become world famous in his field, to hold a position as a professor at a university, to marry, have children, live a life of relative abundance and comfort, and, finally, to earn a Ph.D., which would be the crowning achievement of his life.

At the time of this crisis, all objectives of his life with the exception of earning a Ph.D. had been accomplished. He was now faced with two alternatives: either to not finish his thesis and thus prolong his quest for the ultimate objective and love of his life, or to choose the other more frightening alternative of finishing his thesis, thereby losing the main purpose and love of his life. Further therapy showed that the fear of a lack of purpose and love had prevented him from finishing his Ph.D. Now that he had his degree and this last, most important purpose and love of his life had been accomplished, he had become acutely distraught by the emptiness, purposelessness, and lovelessness of his life.

The Psychology of Spirituality

CASE STUDY

In further discussion of the issue, he stated that as far as he was concerned human life was limited to this plane of existence; that the highest level of accomplishment was intellectual development; and that with death all but intellectual contributions become nonexistent. However, he had gradually realized that intellectual achievements were also temporary because the continual discovery of new facts would eventually render most of his contributions unimportant or irrelevant.

The challenge before David, therefore, was a spiritual challenge, a challenge involving the meaning and the purpose of life, of nonexistence and eternity. David's quandary about the purposelessness and meaninglessness of life brought into focus by the importance that he had placed on obtaining a Ph.D. is best understood when we consider the primary human concerns (self, relationships, and time) and the fundamental human powers. David's primary concerns were about self and time. Obtaining a doctoral degree had long been seen as his ultimate achievement as a human being. Now that this objective was fulfilled, he began to worry about the future. He dreaded that the future would be empty and bereft of striving and of "love."

Striving is the essential component in the life of any human being. It is a form of love; it is a quest for more of whatever may be the object of our quest at the time. Every human being has the quality of striving or questing, which is an aspect of the capacity to love. When we are in love—and people are always in love—we desire, strive, and quest for an object, a person, or an idea. Human love is simultaneously a combination of profound feelings of striving and attraction as well as knowledge that we are attracted to a specific object, person, or idea. The quality of human love depends on the degree of the quest and the nature of the object of the quest. In David's case the ultimate object of his quest was an academic degree beyond which he dreaded life without any quest, striving, and love.

In psychotherapy, it was first brought to David's attention that the thesis was not the main issue or problem. Furthermore, I assured him that he had underestimated his capacity to deal with the challenges of his life and that there was no reason to believe he would not be able to deal successfully with these challenges. David responded by completing his thesis. He then began to evaluate his feelings and thoughts, and he became aware of the "disorder of love" from which he was suffering. He had chosen as an object of his love a goal well within the reach of his abilities. Therefore, his life had a limited objective in keeping with the limited nature of his love object, i.e., the academic degree.

The major task for David was to reevaluate his life plan altogether. He had to look into the future and decide on the nature and course of his life to come. These were spiritual undertakings that, in the past, David had been unwilling to consider or face. Once he became fully aware of the processes involved and understood the logical issues underlying the need for living a spiritual life, he had no difficulty embarking upon this new approach. When he stopped therapy, David was in the process of enlarging and expanding his view of himself and his life objectives, and of understanding the intellectual, emotional, and spiritual aspects of his being. He could accomplish most of these tasks by himself, and therefore there was no need for him to continue therapy.

JANE: "LOVE MEANS NO PAIN"

Jane, a twenty-four-year-old, single university graduate, sought psychiatric consultation primarily because she was not happy in her personal life, interpersonal relationships, and work. In her personal life the two most disturbing issues were her inability to mourn the recent loss of her father and to establish a direction in her life. In her interpersonal relationships she was puzzled by the fact that despite her total involvement with her male friends, these relationships usually lasted for a relatively short period of time. Finally, she was dissatisfied in her work with both the nature and the level of her activities and accomplishments. She was working as a secretary at the time but felt that she had much greater capacity and ability.

Jane was very intelligent; she had graduated with good marks from university and had never had any problems with her intellectual or artistic pursuits. She also had never exerted herself to pursue higher goals and objectives than those opportunities that automatically presented themselves. Jane was not only quite intelligent and gifted but also strikingly beautiful. She possessed qualities very attractive to others.

There was no scarcity of individuals interested in establishing friendships and close relationships with Jane. She was fully aware of

The Psychology of Spirituality

CASE STUDY

this fact and seemed to have a realistic attitude towards herself. At her job Jane was offered several opportunities for advancement, but in spite of all this she was unhappy and felt neither loved nor lovable.

Jane was born in an upper-middle class family, had several younger and older siblings, and had a close relationship with both parents but especially her father. There were no traumatic experiences and no major losses or deprivations that could be considered traumatic enough to account for her present difficulties. She had had a very comfortable childhood, had many friends, socialized easily, and experienced no major difficulties during her adolescent years. She had never used drugs and drank only occasionally and minimally. She had no history of promiscuity.

Although Jane was fully aware of the need to mourn her father's death and had reviewed the circumstances of his death on several occasions, she had not been able to cry or allow herself to feel the pain of loss and separation. This inability to experience pain and suffering was also present in other aspects of her life. Jane avoided pain and suffering at all costs. She had been fortunate to be physically healthy and emotionally well taken care of, and therefore she had little experience with either physical or emotional pain and discomfort. Moreover, she felt that it was absolutely unnecessary to suffer.

A closer look at her life experiences showed that throughout her childhood and adolescent years she had been provided not only with what she needed but also with whatever she wanted. She had been protected from experiencing mental and physical discomforts and had lived a life of instant gratification. She had a deeply rooted belief that pain and suffering were bad. The price that Jane paid for this type of upbringing and lifestyle was that she could not tolerate the pain of growth. She found the give and take of intimate relationships and their demands painful. As soon as a relationship reached a level that required commitment and delay of gratification, requiring her to respond to the demands of another person, she lost interest in the relationship and eventually left it.

The same dynamics were present with respect to her work. After two years of working as a secretary where she had been liked, admired, fussed over, and praised by a large number of people who worked in the office, she finally had applied for a job that placed her at a more advanced position and required individual initiative and creativity. In the new position she had to be on her own and was given a free hand at her work. A few months after this promotion she was so unhappy that she decided to resign. The unhappiness was not due to her inability to work well at the new job. In fact, she discharged her responsibilities quite well, but the new job deprived her of the gratification she received from the praise and attention of her previous superiors and in addition put demands on her. It required her to plan, to move away from the satisfaction of immediate results, to learn to delay desires, and to experience the pain of growth.

In essence, Jane was suffering from a disorder of love in respect to the nature of love and the dynamics of growth. She stated that as far as she was concerned pain and suffering were bad, and the purpose of life was to avoid pain and experience only happiness. She had great difficulty in changing her views and finally decided to terminate her therapy.

It should be mentioned that some four years earlier she had sought psychotherapy but had stopped when treatment proved to be difficult and demanding. Once again after eight months of treatment she had reached the same impasse.

The desire for instant gratification, combined with the inability to tolerate pain and suffering causes unhappiness because it creates a life with insufficient and unsatisfactory growth, a life devoid of creativity, excitement, and fulfillment. Added to this is the nonexistence of a lasting purpose and meaning in life. These conditions are not exclusive to Jane. She is typical of many young people who have been reared during the past few decades. Abundant material opportunities and wealth, combined with an almost total disregard for the spiritual needs of the individual in the post-war industrialized world, have resulted in the emergence of a special type of family which can best be described as indulgent. Such a family constantly seeks pleasure, especially of the sensual, physical, and material type, and avoids pain and discomfort, even that which is required for growth and development. Members of these families develop a tacit agreement that the most important issue among them is their comfort and the gratification of their desires. Children reared in such families receive much attention to their physical needs and material wants. Their desires are immediately satisfied. They are protected from the realistic pressures and challenges of life. They are seldom given the opportunity to talk about

CASE STUDY

serious issues such as the purpose of life, the meaning of death, or even the fact that death occurs. Family misfortunes, disagreements between parents, financial difficulties, career changes and setbacks, illnesses and other important challenges facing the parents are hidden from the children. These children are reared in a fool's paradise. They are brought up to believe in make-believe, to think that there is no limit to the resources required to satisfy all their material and physical needs, that there is no such thing as separation, loss, or death, and that happiness is achievable through possessing material objects. Once they reach the age of adolescence and maturity, these children are suddenly faced with the realities of life, its demands, and the effort that it requires of them. They feel betrayed, angry, and fearful. Consequently, they act with a variety of unhealthy responses to the normal challenges of life.

Jane's behaviour is one such response. There are other types of responses, but they are all destructive and unhealthy, and usually of an aggressive and violent nature. From the perspective of the psychology of spirituality, Jane not only suffered from a set of misconceptions about life, growth, and pain but also equated gratification with love, the absence of pain as an indication she was loved, and an easy relationship as a sign that she was "in love." These misconceptions about love caused her to live a superficial and empty life. She needed to review her views on these issues and above all to realize that allowing oneself to experience the pain of growth is an act of love. Although Jane's therapy was stopped at this point, she had nevertheless become aware on an intellectual level of the requirements for growth and love, both of which are accompanied by some experience of pain. It was hoped that these insights would be of some benefit to her in the future. In an evaluation several years later, Jane informed me that she had been able at last to mourn the death of her father, to alter her views about the pain of growth and love, to work at a very demanding job, and to establish a serious love relationship, marry, and have children. She stated that the crazy notion that "love is painful" never left her alone. She could not forget it, nor was she able to disregard its frequent occurrence in her own life. She finally had to look at these issues with more care, and this was the beginning of change in her.

Disorders of Will

●

To complete this review of major psychospiritual disorders, we now look at the issue of will. Human motivation has its roots in our knowledge and love, as well as in our will. It is our will that gives us power to act and to be creative.

Many contemporary psychotherapeutic systems tend to reject the primacy of the role of will in human behaviour. They place much greater importance on the unconscious processes that are, by definition, beyond the reach of human will. By doing so, these systems invest the therapist with considerable power and authority, while at the same time they deprive individual patients or clients of their fundamental ability to choose, act, and be creative. The result of this orientation is to render the therapeutic process ambiguous, mysterious, unidirectional (from therapist to client but not vice versa), and even at times, irrational. In fact, all individuals are responsible for their decisions, actions, and behaviour when their mental and reasoning faculties are not impaired.

The view that behaviour is solely or primarily due to genetic, instinctual, and biological factors, childhood experiences, and environmental influences does not take into account the creative capacity of the individual. We humans are creative beings. We create our own unique personalities, selfhood, and lifestyles. We are created in the image of our Creator, and as such we are ourselves creators. Of all that we create, the creation of our lives is the most dramatic and important achievement.

Whenever we are denied this creative dimension, we become like machines or animals, we lose our humanness, our opportunity to choose, to decide, to experiment, and to experience the joy of accuracy and the pain of mistake. In the contemporary world, most people are reared to disbelieve in their own creative capacities and their power to choose the direction and nature of their lives. People with this kind of orientation develop a negative self-image, are fearful and uncertain, and are apologetic, hesitant, and pessimistic.

Disorders of will are usually combined with the disorders of knowledge and love. The following case history clarifies some of the main issues about the disorders of will and their relationship with the disorders of knowledge and love.

CASE STUDY

IN QUEST OF POWER AND SUCCESS: THE CASE OF JOSEPH

Joseph was seen in therapy because he had been suffering from depression for ten years, and a recent relocation to the city required the services of a new psychiatrist. He was in his late fifties, worked as a director of a large and highly regarded international consulting agency, and was well respected by his colleagues and well known for his publications and professional activities. He was married, had three children, and his family circumstances and relations were quite healthy and satisfactory.

His depression was characterized by long periods of low interest in life, depressed mood, pessimism, considerable anger, difficulty in handling criticism, especially by those in authority, and a high level of agitation and anxiety. In the course of the past twenty years, he had received intensive psychotherapy from a number of psychoanalysts and psychiatrists, as well as drug therapy and pastoral therapy, all with some measure of success. But the fact remained that with all of these therapies Joseph had never been fully free from his emotional distress and had often felt depressed and agitated. To alleviate his problems, sometime earlier he had begun drinking heavily and was consequently suffering from a number of medical complications of alcohol abuse.

CASE STUDY

Joseph was born in a missionary family. His father was an authoritarian, a severe and emotionally rigid man who lived a life characterized by emotional and intellectual rigidity and excessive control, highly competitive behaviour, and fascination with and fear of power. Joseph himself displayed all of these characteristics.

These are the classical characteristics of an authoritarian personality. Such individuals are usually quite successful in those aspects of their lives which are dependent on individual initiative, power struggle, and personal and professional dominance, yet very inadequate in the realms of feelings and interpersonal relationships. On both accounts Joseph matched the prototype. The authoritarian type suffers from three main disorders of the human psyche: disorders of knowledge, disorders of love, and disorders of will. The most striking aspect of the disorder of knowledge in an authoritarian personality is the dichotomous view of creation. An authoritarian individual sees dichotomies everywhere: men and women, power and weakness, love and hate, friends and enemies, rich and poor, to name but a few. From this perspective, life is perceived in black and white; there is little room for integration, flexibility, creativity, and change. The alternate solutions to problems are few in number and either good or bad, acceptable or unacceptable, and above all respectable or unworthy in the eyes of those in position of authority and power. This limited and narrow approach to life impoverishes the ideas, insights, and perspectives of authoritarian individuals and makes it especially difficult for them to be open to new approaches, views, and philosophies, which are prerequisites for human growth, creativity, and fulfillment.

Disorders of knowledge occur in degrees, and in Joseph they were moderate in their intensity. As a very intelligent person with a highly trained mind and one who had many contacts with people of prominence on both national and international levels, Joseph had been exposed to many new ideas and perspectives, and had the opportunity to learn about different cultures and ideologies. Because of these circumstances, he was, at one level, open-minded and internationally aware, but at the level of personal perspectives on life and its purpose and meaning, he had basically adopted his parents' views on these issues with only minor modifications. The clearest example of this fact was Joseph's perspective on the role of power and competition in human relationships. Power for him was

CASE STUDY

the most important force in human relationships, and his therapy had to bring this matter to his attention. He had to be encouraged and helped gradually to alter his perspective about the necessity, wisdom, or desirability of power struggle as the main approach to interpersonal relationships.

The issue of power orientation is not merely an indication of a disorder of knowledge but, more important, it is a sign of a disorder of love. The authoritarian person loves through power. In other words, an authoritarian person has much difficulty in showing love, affection, and warmth in an open and unconditional way. The authoritarian considers these qualities as signs of weakness. Finally, power orientation is a clear disorder of will. It is here that human will is used in the service of power and much abuse is sanctioned.

Authoritarian individuals, by seeking power to obtain security and isolating themselves to promote an identity, live in a constant state of fear and anger. They are afraid of strangers, of those more powerful than they, and of those who seek their power. This constant fear is accompanied by feelings of resentment, anger, and in many cases, outright hatred of others who, in their opinion, are the causes of their fears. Thus these fearful and resentful people are constantly on guard not to convey the existence of any tender feelings in themselves. Love, compassion, the need for warmth, closeness, and kindness are perceived as signs of weakness. Authoritarian individuals cannot risk showing any weakness and so in this respect their emotional lives are extremely limited. Likewise, it is impossible for them even to admit to themselves their own fears. The only emotion that authoritarian individuals allow themselves to experience is the feeling of anger. Their families, people close to them, and those in authority, are the only individuals in the world whom they feel they can possibly depend upon. Thus they will not openly express their feelings of anger towards them. The only recourse for them is to project these feelings onto outsiders, strangers, and those who are weaker. Here we are dealing with the authoritarian's unavoidable case of prejudice. At the family level, warm and tender feelings (essential for the development of the marriage and emotional growth of the child(ren)) are either missing in the authoritarian family or are bestowed, based on the condition that the child conforms to and obeys the parental wishes and desires. Children, therefore, thirst for love and warmth, but at the same time have much difficulty accepting them. Gradually some of these children follow in the footsteps of their parents, begin to seek power, and become aggressive and competitive. Furthermore, they become fearful of emotional and intimate relationships.[2]

Joseph found showing his love or allowing people's love to reach him almost impossible. A person who lives a rigid life with fear of loving and being loved usually develops feelings of boredom, loneliness, hopelessness, and meaninglessness, and, in time, may become clinically depressed. The symptoms of depression in Joseph, no doubt, were closely related to the disorders of knowledge and love. In addition to the disorders of knowledge and love, there was very strong evidence that above all Joseph suffered from a disorder of will.

The psychodynamics of the authoritarian personality are such that they require excessive use of will to enforce one's power upon those in an inferior position and to conform to the wishes of those in a superior position of authority. To do this requires a well-disciplined and unwavering will. While such a quality is very useful and, in fact, essential for all successful human endeavours, it is also very unproductive and even unhealthy when it is used in excess and for the wrong purpose.

Such was the case with Joseph. In his interpersonal relationships he showed love, courtesy, and care as long as the people involved conformed to his wishes, were his inferiors, or else approved of him and his efforts if they were his superiors. Consequently, both at home and particularly at work, he had often been involved in bitter power struggles and had experienced many angry and rejecting exchanges with others. In fact, this excessive and unhealthy use of will and power had made it necessary for him to change his job many times and had resulted in his frequently feeling rejected.

Psychotherapy aimed at helping Joseph to become aware of the characteristics and dynamics of his disorders of knowledge, love, and will. Those disorders had affected his life profoundly and caused him to suffer from an ongoing condition of disappointment, conflict, and depression. Treatment focused on both the past and the present. All these dynamics were reviewed at some length. Progressively, he was encouraged to modify his dichotomous view of life, his power-oriented approach to love, and his excessive and unhealthy use of his will. In addition, he was encouraged to focus

CASE STUDY: on the future, which brought him face to face with the issue of death and other spiritual questions he usually avoided. After one and a half years of therapy, Joseph became free from depression for the first time in ten years.

Freedom and Human Will

●

To understand the nature of human will and its disorders better, we need to look at the question of freedom. When people speak of freedom, they are usually referring to either personal or social freedoms. Personal freedom deals with our choice of actions. The general view is that adults should be free to do whatever they want to do, as long as this action does not hurt someone else. Therefore, such issues as the choice of food, drinks, drugs, dress, or anything personal, should be entirely a matter of personal preference.

It is generally felt that if someone wishes to drink alcohol or take drugs they should feel free to do so, as long as this action does not harm others. In practice, however, we know that the situation is not so simple. When a person drinks alcohol, the very act of drinking has ramifications beyond that person's life. If the drinking is heavy, the effects are obvious. The person could cause an accident, become an alcoholic, or develop a chronic illness. All of these developments affect not only the life of the drinker but also the lives of many other people at home, work, and in the community. Indeed, even when we drink moderately or minimally, we strike a blow to our free will. It is a well-established fact that alcohol, once consumed, reaches the brain cells quickly and affects the brain function to a remarkable degree. Alcohol, in fact, immediately removes our freedom, and from that moment on we are, to varying degrees, under its influence. Our will has begun to suffer.

Another common view of freedom is in respect to our social rights and privileges such as the freedom of speech, the freedom to assemble, and the freedom to participate in the democratic process. The United Nations Charter of Rights, the American Bill of Rights and the Canadian Charter of Human Rights are noteworthy examples of attempts made by humanity to protect and safeguard the freedom and rights of citizens. However, the question of freedom is broader in its scope and deeper in its significance. Freedom, like all other human conditions, is developmental. There is a hierarchy of freedom. Elsewhere, I have discussed the issue of freedom, and identified three stages in its development—freedom from the limitations of physical needs and environmental threats, freedom from the oppression of other human beings, and freedom from selfishness and egotism.*

In our world today millions of people are slaves to hunger, disease, drought, and severe climatic changes. Likewise, a large portion of humanity is subject to the tyranny and aggression of their fellow human beings. Even in countries where economic and social conditions could allow for freedom from these types of human suffering, many people still live in circumstances where survival becomes the main or even sole preoccupation of the individual. The homeless in New York City, the street children in urban America, the illegal immigrants, and the refugees in countries of Europe and North America, the socially segregated and wronged North American native peoples, Inuit, blacks, and Hispanics are just a few examples of people who do not have the necessary freedom to evolve and grow, to actualize their potential, and to demonstrate their capacities. And this in the wealthiest and most democratic countries of the world. The same is true for all the victims of poverty, prejudice, and violence. These people do not have true freedom. Social freedom depends on equality, justice, unity, and peace.

These social conditions are lacking not because we are unaware of their significance, but because we have not yet achieved the third and still higher form of freedom: freedom from selfishness

---

*. H. B. Danesh, M. D., *Unity: The Creative Foundation of Peace* (Ottawa, Toronto: Bahá'í Studies Publications and Fitzhenry-Whiteside), 1986.

and egotism. This type of freedom applies both to the individual and society, and it calls for victory over our animal heritage. It calls for the spiritualization of our lives; to become other-directed rather than self-centred; to be generous and self-sacrificing instead of selfish and egotistical. We need to be able to postpone the gratification of our needs, to see ourselves as members of the body of humanity, to refrain from the much valued but highly destructive competitive practices of our society, and to prefer others over ourselves, or at least to treat others as we ourselves wish to be treated. In short, spiritual freedom demands that we abandon our materialistic values and adopt in their stead those universal values based on the nobility of every human being, equality of all people, unity of humanity, sanctity of life, reality of the human spirit, and purposefulness of human existence. Freedom from selfishness and egotism is not possible if we focus only on its psychological roots. We must also study the spiritual causes of selfishness and egotism.

Psychological causes of selfishness and egotism are related to our experiences of abandonment, rejection, deprivation, and other traumatic life experiences that make us prone to mistrust ourselves and others and to become unduly self-preoccupied and self-reliant. However, because it is impossible for us to be fully independent, we are always, to a degree, dependent on others. It is a part of human nature to be dependent on others. We need each other for all the important aspects of our lives. We need to love and to be loved, to share ideas and to learn from each other, to do things for others and to receive appreciation for what we do. For us to be someone, we need someone to recognize us. Clearly, it is psychologically healthier to be other-directed rather than self-centred. But psychology, particularly in its contemporary materialistic framework, encourages self-centredness. It calls for the relaxation of attitudes with respect to our instinctual needs and encourages the pursuit of personal happiness, gratification, and self-interest. It also justifies much of our self-centred behaviour by offering psychological explanations for this behaviour. It is not uncommon to encounter people who say, "I'm selfish because my parents didn't have much time for me when I was little." It is as though an explanation for selfishness renders it healthy.

It is here that the importance of applying spiritual principles to the issue of selfishness and egotism becomes obvious. To be spiritual is to be universal. Spirituality frees us from the limitations of the competitive, animal-like life. It connects us with all humanity, all creation, our past, present, and future. It places us within a cosmic ecology of life, knowledge, and love. It allows us to see our own welfare in the well-being of others, our joy in the happiness of all, and our sorrows in the grief of others. A spiritual lifestyle, by its very nature, frees us from limiting, self-centred preoccupations. When we begin to free ourselves from our selfishness and egotism, then we become much more able to defend the rights of the poor, the downtrodden, and the weak in our midst. This is the higher form of freedom that we all need.

The whole of humanity is now poised for a fundamental change. The current universal conditions of injustice and lack of true freedom cannot continue. The choice of change is either towards chaos or towards a spiritual civilization. The disorder of will occurs when we use our will in selfish pursuits rather than more universal objectives. The interesting aspect of universal pursuits is that they contain in themselves the best interests of the individual as well.

Human will, at its highest level of maturity, functions in harmony with the other two spiritual attributes of soul—love and knowledge. The greater the harmony among our capacities of knowledge, love, and will, the greater is the measure of our inner peace. When these capacities are used in the context of truth, unity, and service, a spiritual life has begun.

In Part Five we will see how we can acquire a spiritual attitude and outlook. We will show that to do so we need to replace our current adolescent ways of thinking and behaving with those of a mature stage of life.

PART FIVE

From

Adolescence

To

Maturity

*When I was a child,
I spake as a child,
I understood as a child,
I thought as a child:
but when I became a man,
I put away childish things.*

1 Corinthians 13:11

The gifts and blessings of the period of youth, although timely and sufficient during the adolescence of mankind, are now incapable of meeting the requirements of its maturity.

'Abdu'l-Bahá

From Adolescence to Adulthood

•

So far, we have shown that at the core of our humanness are three powers: to know, to love, and to will. These are powers of the human soul shared by all people in all cultures regardless of their specific temperaments, talents, or conditions. We have further shown that human capacities to know, love, and will need to be nurtured and developed in a healthy way. Otherwise, they can be abused, causing considerable destruction in the individual and in the collective life of humanity. Finally, we reviewed some of the clinical expressions of the disorders of knowledge, love, and will as they pertain to our personal lives, interpersonal relationships, and our contributions to society.

We now need to identify those dynamics and processes that will allow optimal and healthy development of the human capacities of knowledge, love, and will. What should the healthy outcome of human knowledge be, and how can this be achieved? Can we develop and use our capacity to love, so that it will be free from prejudice, isolation, fanaticism, and self-centredness? How is self-love translated into universal love, and what is the outcome of such a process? How can we use human will in a healthy way? How can we prevent the enormous abuses that take place routinely at all levels and strata of human life? What are the fruits of healthy development of human will? In short, how can we develop our capacities to know, love, and will, in a healthy way?

The remaining sections of this book address these questions with particular attention to the dynamics of the spiritualization of both the individual and society. Through them, we can see our way towards the development of an integrated and full life. In this section I will explain how as we put behind us our collective childhood and adolescent ages, at least three basic developments will act in synergy. First, our capacities of knowledge, love, and will, as a consequence of our transition to adulthood and the acquisition of new spiritual insights, will express themselves according to the spiritual principles of truth, unity, and service. Second, these spiritual principles will create new levels of consciousness, universal in their scope and powerful in their impact, which in turn will further accelerate the rate of our evolution and impel us to use our mental and emotional capacities to a fuller extent. Finally, the emergence of higher levels of consciousness and the introduction of the spiritual principles of truth, unity, and service, once fully integrated with those spiritual practices, will dramatically alter our lifestyles, both at the individual and collective levels and will pave the way for the creation of a spiritual civilization and the establishment of a new world order.

The process of becoming an integrated person is very exciting and not necessarily very difficult. What is difficult, however, is the mental and attitudinal shift that we need to make. This is a paradigm shift of the utmost importance. We need to see ourselves as integrated spiritual beings before we can start the task of becoming so. This section, therefore, is dedicated to the requirements and dynamics of achieving this new mindset—the spiritual mindset.

KNOWLEDGE AND TRUTH

The human capacity to know is an all-encompassing capacity. It includes the capacity to know of both the physical world (through application of scientific principles to study of the world of nature) and of the metaphysical realities of consciousness and spirituality (through our understanding of human nature and human relationships in the context of ethical and spiritual teachings appropriate to the coming of age of humanity.)

In all these forms of knowing, the human soul is always in search of truth. We human beings want and need to know the truth about everything. We can say that at one level both human nature and the purpose of human life are intimately connected with the process of active search for truth. A mature human being both needs to search for truth and must search for truth. Otherwise, the unique human capacity to know will not move much beyond the primitive stages that we share with the animals. At this level, both the human and the animal capacity to know are limited to knowing how to survive, gain pleasure, and avoid pain.

In fact, in certain respects, animals are superior to humans. Some animals have stronger and more acute sight, hearing, taste, smell, touch, instincts, and physical abilities, all of which are important for survival, gratification, and pain avoidance. The hallmark of humanness is to be able to transcend the survival and pain/pleasure instincts and to embark on a journey of consciousness, truth-seeking, and enlightenment. The human capacity to know is essential for the accomplishment of this objective, and its ultimate and noble outcome is the discovery of truth in all its forms and expressions. However, it should be noted that our understanding of truth will always remain relative and not absolute. At any given time, we discover scientific and spiritual truths only partially, according to the level of our individual growth and collective evolution. Therefore, our search for truth will never stop.

In everyday life, knowledge and truth come to prominence in such seemingly unrelated matters as truthfulness, trustworthiness, faithfulness, fidelity, loyalty, and honesty as well as scientific truth, creative integrity, and spiritual purity. These matters are all based on the fundamental issue of truth. We human beings are by nature drawn to truth and need truth to trust and to be able to function in life. We therefore need to know about not only how the world functions but also how people function. Once we understand the laws of nature and know the cause of such natural conditions as disease, famine, and earthquake, we are then better able to deal with them and to do something about them. The knowledge of these realities empowers us to discover, innovate, and change our life situations. The same applies to truth in our personal and interpersonal life.

Truthfulness and its many variations such as trustworthiness

The Psychology of Spirituality

and faithfulness are essential aspects of human life. Without them our life energies will be spent fighting dishonesty, suspicion, and disloyalty. These qualities are not only moral and ethical in their nature, they are also essential components of a healthy, integrated lifestyle. This is so because truth, in all its variations, is an indispensable aspect of being human—being capable of knowing, understanding, and discovering truth.

The following two vignettes demonstrate the important role of knowledge and truth in our personal and interpersonal life.

CASE STUDY

Interview One: Jan

Jan is a twenty-eight-year-old nurse who is married and the mother of a three-year-old son.

Therapist: How are you today?

Jan: I don't know. I guess the same.

Therapist: The same as what?

Jan: The same as always. You know.

Therapist: No, I don't know.

Jan: I don't know how I feel, what I think, and why I do what I do. I don't know anything. And besides, what is there to know? I go to work every day, and everybody says I'm a good nurse. I love my son and take good care of him. And I do the best I can as a wife.

Therapist: You sound either desperate or depressed.

Jan: Well I am, and I'm not. I am desperate because I go through the routine of life, but I don't know for what purpose. Depressed, I'm not. We've already gone over this. I sleep well, eat well, don't have suicidal thoughts or crying spells, and there are no financial, health, or job stresses that can explain my desperation. And we've tried antidepressants. They just make me feel dopey and gain weight. I'm not depressed. I simply don't know what this life is all about. You tell me. What is your life all about? Tell me what to do, and I will do it.

Therapist: But then you'll be living my life, not yours.

Jan: So, I must get to know myself. That's a tall order.

● *From Adolescence to Maturity*

Interview Two

CASE STUDY

The interviewees are a married couple in their mid-thirties.
Therapist: How are things?
Wife: I feel so humiliated and angry. I had always trusted him, never questioned his honesty. And now this.
Husband: But I've stopped seeing her. I haven't seen her for four weeks. And I've been helping with the kids. What else do you want?
Wife: So now I owe you something for spending a few lousy minutes with the kids.
Husband: I didn't mean it that way. I want everything to go back to the old ways.
Wife: That's impossible.
Husband: But why?
Wife: For one thing, I no longer trust you. I don't know when you are lying and when you are telling the truth. After the deceit, nothing is the same.

LOVE AND UNITY

As noted before, love, among other things, is the human power of attraction. By nature we human beings are attracted to that which is beautiful and pleasurable. This power of attraction lies at the very core of our relationships. When we fall in love with someone, it is because we find them attractive and pleasant to be with. In fact, when most people speak of love, they describe two powerful forces: attraction and gratification. People usually fall in love because they find their beloved attractive and also able to gratify some of their immediate and important needs. In the romantic phase of love (which is the first phase), we are usually attracted to the more obvious qualities of the other person. Our attraction then becomes very powerful when, in addition, we find that the person to whom we are attracted can also fulfill some of our desires and needs. A love relationship becomes particularly powerful when both mutual attraction and mutual gratification of needs are present. It is then that the lovers are consumed with one another. No moment goes by without their thinking about each other, wanting to be together, and dreading the time of separation.

This passionate and intense initial phase usually does not last because as lovers spend more time together and begin to know each other better, they discover aspects of one another that they find unattractive. Besides, their powers of will begin to clash. They do not always agree. Not every matter is equally important to them. Their priorities are different. Their objectives do not match. Their needs begin to change, and what they initially found to be attractive, they now find to be the opposite. A crisis of love sets in whereby each feels discouraged, frustrated, and disillusioned. Above all, each begins to imagine that their love has come to an end. They conclude that their love is dead, and they may begin to look for new love. During this phase some couples tend to argue and fight, while others choose to avoid each other in an atmosphere of cold anger. During this phase the couple also blame each other for their miseries. They withold their affection from one another, and not infrequently, one or both of them begin to seek new friends, hoping to start new romantic love relationships. In other words, they abandon the second and most difficult phase of love and return to a new love relationship in its first phase—the romantic phase.

While the second phase is the most painful, it is also most conducive to personal growth. It is a phase that tests not only our love but also our powers of understanding and will. How accurate is our knowledge of the other person? How truthful are we with ourselves? Could it be that as a result of this love relationship we have discovered we are selfish and do not wish to admit it? Could it also be that we are insecure and that is why we cannot relate on an equal basis? That we are prone to hide our shortcomings, and do not wish to admit this? That we are jealous, and to hide our jealousy we project our lack of trust in ourselves on the other person? During the second phase of a love relationship, these and other painful, yet highly valuable, questions emerge. They are the fruits of self-knowledge achieved in the process of loving another human being. Because these insights are painful, those involved often blame each other for their difficulties and may even initiate the breakup of their relationship.

If we are willing to understand ourselves and our loved ones further, and if we are willing to use our power of will to help

From Adolescence to Maturity

ourselves to grow and become more integrated, then we will arrive in the third phase of the love relationship—the phase of enlightened love or unity. In this phase our love is strengthened by a much higher degree of self-knowledge and knowledge of each other. We become more aware of each other's strengths and shortcomings. We develop greater sensitivity to each other's needs and capacities. We grow more patient with one another, and we no longer need to compete. We are willing to encourage each other, to see each other from the perspective of oneness, to recognize one another's positive qualities and to assist one another to evolve and grow. This kind of love relationship is enlightened, wilful, and tender. It is an expression of the unity of two souls.

Unity and love are totally interrelated. Unity is the expression of universal love; love of one for many and many for one, all seeing in each other the unique beauty that is theirs. To put it differently, love unites people. Through the process of attraction, enlightenment, and cooperation, we realize that we are at once, similar and different. We are similar with respect to our humanness and different with respect to the unique ways we express our humanness. This uniqueness attracts us to each other, and this similarity keeps us together. Unity therefore is the expression of love at an unconditional and universal level.

However, because we have not yet learned to love in a mature manner and create marriages and relationships on the basis of equality, many of our love relationships sour and instead of achieving unity, result in separation and estrangement.[1] The following two vignettes give us a glimpse of this process.

Interview Three: Carl

CASE STUDY

Carl is a forty-five-year-old married man. He and his wife have four children.
Therapist: How are you?
Carl: Things are rough. I'm totally confused.
Therapist: What about?
Carl: I'm confused about what I should do. I miss my lover very much. She doesn't want to see me. She says she loves me, but doesn't want to do anything with me as long as I'm married.

The Psychology of Spirituality

CASE STUDY

I don't know whether or not I love my wife. She tells me she loves me, but I don't feel it.

Therapist: What do you mean?

Carl: The way she loves me is not the way I want her to love me. You know what I mean?

Therapist: Tell me.

Carl: I mean, she loves me by taking care of me, our house and our children. When I'm sick, she's there. She's such a good person. But her love is different from Maryanne's. Maryanne loves me with passion. My wife doesn't.

Therapist: Was there ever passion between you and your wife?

Carl: At the beginning of our marriage we had so much fun. We were passionate. But then the kids came along, and everything changed.

Therapist: What about the kids?

Carl: Oh, I love them so much. I can't imagine living without them. They are what keeps me in this marriage.

Therapist: What else do you love?

Carl: Maryanne, and my wife in a different way, my parents, family members, some friends.

Therapist: How about your job?

Carl: Oh, I don't love my job.

Therapist: But you spend a lot of time on your job. You work overtime, and on the weekends. You do it with passion. You're dedicated to it. You're spending long hours at the construction site.

Carl: Okay. I love my job.

Therapist: Do you love yourself?

Carl: I don't think I'm selfish or something. But I guess I love myself. These days I hate myself.

Therapist: What else do you love?

Carl: I don't know. Should I love someone else? It seems there are many different kinds of love, some more important than others.

Therapist: Yes there are different types of love relationships, but more important, there are different stages of love. And it seems that you take your love so far and no further.

Carl: What do you mean? I don't understand.

Therapist: It seems that your wishes come first.

From Adolescence to Maturity

CASE STUDY

Carl: You mean that I put myself ahead of others?
Therapist: Yes. And consequently, as soon as your desires are not met, you leave. You don't give your love a chance to evolve and create a state of unity between you and the other person. When love does not evolve into unity, it sours.
Carl: I need to think about this.

Interview Four

The couple are in their late twenties. They have no children.

Therapist: You both look very upset. (The wife begins to cry. The husband fidgets in his seat and avoids looking at his wife.) What's going on?
Wife: Ask him.
Husband: It is the same old thing. She got upset about nothing.
Wife: Nothing? Threatening me and coming at me with a broomstick is nothing? Forcing me to go around town in the middle of the night to find drug pushers is nothing?
Husband: I wanted to be with you.
Wife: I don't want to be with you when you do those things.
Husband: I'm doing nothing wrong. I needed some drugs for the party. Wasn't anything hard, a little hash. You just don't understand. I thought that you loved me.
Wife: You think loving you means that I should do what you want me to do.
Husband: (Angry) I'm not asking for much. The house is untidy, and you took the whole afternoon off to be with your friends. I don't even know who you were with.
Wife: You know perfectly well that I was with Julia and Sandy. We had a couple of drinks. But I don't understand how it's related to love.
Husband: I feel you love me when you do what I want you to do.
Wife: And what about me?
Husband: I work. I work hard, and all I expect is a happy time at home.
Wife: I work hard too, and in addition I have to do all the house work and everything else. If this is love, I don't want it.

WILL AND SERVICE

Love and knowledge ultimately need to be expressed in deeds which require our power of will. Human will, however, can be abused in various ways. It can become extremely rigid and inflexible, unresponsive to the ever-changing circumstances of life and the ever-increasing level of our knowledge. This extreme rigidity of will is found in military leaders, dictatorships, and authoritarian families, organizations, and societies. Rigidity has a profoundly negative impact on people who are subject to it. It not infrequently results in destruction and violence. Unfortunately, in the course of history and even in our world today such individuals with a highly rigid, strong, and intractable will are viewed with awe and respect. Not infrequently they are identified as ideal leaders. It is interesting to note that according to the Bible, eventually "the meek shall inherit the earth," not the rigid authoritarian leaders.

The opposite extreme of rigid and inflexible will is the paralysis of will, which is usually the hallmark of victims of oppression who, in response to tyrannical leaders (in society) or spouses and parents (in the family), have become too frightened to act, to use their knowledge, or to express their feelings. The healthy expression of will is dependent upon the development of adequate self-knowledge and positive self-love. It is in these situations that we eventually come to have open minds, open hearts, and free will—a will free to act in an enlightened and loving manner. In a spiritual lifestyle, the outcome of human will is service.

The concept of service requires clarification. To begin with, service does not mean subservience to others and blind obedience. Second, to be of service requires that we be just, relate to others from a position of equality, avoid egotism and arrogance, be considerate, and if required, prefer the well-being of others and society over our own wishes and desires.

The idea of giving priority to the well-being of others is not based on some unattainable utopian ideology. Rather, it is based on the objective truths that humanity is a single organism and that all people are the constituent members of this organism. As we approach our age of collective maturity, these truths will become more entrenched in our ways of thinking, and we will eventually achieve such a high degree of oneness, harmony, collaboration,

From Adolescence to Maturity

cooperation, and sensitivity between each of us and and the rest of humanity, that the well-being of one will become identical with the well-being of all, and the pain of one will be the pain of all. It is at this stage that we truly acquire the capacity to use our will in the service of others.

When human will is used in an unhealthy way, the outcome is destruction. The following vignettes provide examples of this destructive process.

Interview Five: Sandy

CASE STUDY

Sandy is thirty years of age, a university graduate, a computer analyst.

Sandy: I don't see the use in coming here. Nothing has changed. I've been coming here for two months, week in and week out.

Therapist: What do you want to change?

Sandy: My life. It's no good the way it is. At home we don't communicate. At work I find myself isolated. There's too much pressure.

Therapist: Surely you could change the situation if you wished.

Sandy: How?

Therapist: By changing your approach to your life, by changing your ways. But if you decide to do this, you must be prepared for hard work. You must be willing to get to know yourself. To love yourself in a healthy manner. To relate to other people as you wish them to relate to you. It's all in your hands. No one else can do it for you.

Sandy: It sounds hard. It's no fun.

Therapist: It is hard. Looking at ourselves is painful. Postponing our desires is also painful. You have a decision to make. You have to do the job. I will be here, but the bulk of the work has to be done by you.

Sandy: It's too hard, and I see no value in suffering. I think I'll call it quits.

Therapist: Well think about it, and if you change your mind let me know.

The Psychology of Spirituality

CASE STUDY

(Five months later)

Therapist: What's brought you back?

Sandy: I've decided I can no longer live the way I've been living for a long time. Nothing's changed. Possibly things are worse.

Therapist: But remember, trying to get to know yourself, and changing some of your ways is difficult and painful.

Sandy: I know. This time I think I have a stronger will.

Interview Six

This exchange is between the chief executive officer (CEO) of a company and a consultant.

CEO: Something has changed in our company, and we don't know what it is. The symptoms are all there. Sick leaves and absenteeism are the highest they've ever been. By 4:30 everyone is gone. At coffee breaks and lunch time, people are scattered in and out of the building. There is no spirit of closeness. There is a lot of gossip and backstabbing. Our production and our profits are down. Everything is down.

Consultant: Was the situation ever different?

CEO: Oh yes, last year. Everything was the opposite. People were happy, worked hard, and there was lots of socializing and good camaraderie.

Consultant: What's changed?

CEO: Nothing that I can identify. If anything, last year was much more difficult. Last year, our employees decided, on their own, to spearhead a major food drive for the poor. You should have been here. For a whole year people were involved in this thing. All kinds of phone calls would come in to the office. Meetings were held during the day and in the evening. Lots of people were doing their work after hours because during the day they were soliciting food, talking on the radio, giving interviews to the reporters. It was a madhouse. Mind you, the drive was extremely successful, and everybody who participated was very happy. But the management was worried. This year we informed the employees that this kind of activity doesn't belong here.

●*From Adolescence to Maturity*

CASE STUDY

Consultant: How were the production and profits last year?
CEO: Last year we had one of our best years, and because of the improving economic climate we thought this year would be our best yet. This was actually the reason we said no to another food drive. Because we thought it would be too much for the staff.
Consultant: But with this decision you took the spirit of service out of your workplace, and with it the will to work.

✧ ✧ ✧

Let us further review these vignettes in the light of the capacities of knowledge, love, and will, and the qualities of truth, unity, and service. In these case studies, we have respectively two examples each of disorders of knowledge, love, and will.

In Interview One, the twenty-eight-year-old nurse is simply not accustomed to searching for meaning and enlightenment. She has learned to be a good mother, worker, wife. But her life is barren. There is no enlightenment, no search, no questions, simply a vague sense of desperation. Search for knowledge is an essential dimension of being human, and it is missing in her life.

Interview Two also deals with knowledge, but in a different sense. In this case the wife no longer knows whether or not she can trust her husband. His extramarital affair has shattered her confidence in him. Here we are dealing with yet another important aspect of the human quest for knowledge, that is, the need for truth and truthfulness.

Both the forty-five-year-old man in Interview Three and the younger person in Interview Four perceive love in a limited and self-centred way. For them, love is almost synonymous with gratification and enjoyment. There is little awareness that a mature love requires both giving and receiving, that love is painful, and that in its mature and healthy form, love allows for growth and creativity and will ultimately result in the achievement of a state of unity.

Interviews Five and Six deal with the issue of human will and its effects on our deeds. In Interview Five, the computer analyst is unwilling to go through the necessary steps for self-knowledge and growth, both of which are painful. She opts instead for the status quo, doing nothing. But her situation continues to deteriorate, so she decides to return for help. This healthy exercise of will may very well be the key to resolving her life crises.

Interview Six depicts a very important factor in human motivation. Whenever there is a purpose and a meaning in our lives, whenever we are able to share and have an experience of unity, and whenever our actions result in service to others, we are highly motivated, and we experience those rare occasions in which our thoughts (knowledge), feelings (love), and actions (will) are in a condition of synergy. It is this synergy that results in inner peace and a sense of joy.

From this description it is clear that the prerequisite for healthy personality development is a code of conduct that will allow us to acquire knowledge, enlightenment, and wisdom; to develop a mature, tested capacity to love; and to engender the courage and wisdom to act in a creative, life-affirming way.

These are obviously ethical issues. For many, the introduction of ethics into psychology is problematic. Such opponents argue that psychology is the science of human behaviour and that science and ethics do not mix. Through the science of psychology, they say, we learn why people behave as they do and feel as they feel, and then all we have to do is to correct the behaviour and modify the feeling. Behaviour can be modified, they state, either through insight into the causes and dynamics of the behaviour, or through behaviour modification by means of reward and punishment. Feelings, likewise, can be corrected either through understanding their causes or by finding chemical and physical means to change them. They conclude that there is no need for ethics. Ethics belong to religion, and religion is a thing of the past.

On the surface this is a good argument, but it is fundamentally wrong. To begin with, no human endeavour, scientific or otherwise, is value free. All human activities are performed within the framework of the tripartite capacities to know, love, and will. In their very essence these capacities call for certain outcomes that throughout history have been identified as being ethical in nature. The ultimate outcome of the process of knowing is truth, of love is unity, and of will is service. Truth, unity, and service are the qualities of a mature, integrated person and of a truly humane civilization. They are also ethical in nature. To understand these points better, let us look at the issues of truth, unity, and service more closely.

Towards a Universal Code of Ethics

●

We are now in a position to identify a universal code of ethics based on our capacities of knowledge, love, and will. As stated, these are the capacities of the human soul, and when they are developed in the framework of spiritual and scientific principles, their outcomes are respectively, Truth, Unity, and Service.

Truth

Philosophers have made many attempts to define truth. The objective here is not to engage in a philosophical exploration of truth but rather to take a practical look at the role of truth in everyday life.

Independent search for truth is a part of our human nature. We constantly want to know. We try to the best of our ability to find the truth about everything. Of all truths, the most important are those related to ourselves. Who am I? What is the reality at the core of my being? Am I a body or soul, or am I a body and soul? What kind of a person am I? Am I courageous, truthful, faithful, trustworthy, honest? What is the purpose of my life? All these and other related questions need to be taken seriously. We human beings *need* to know about these truths. However, our understanding of them is both limited and relative. We will never be able to understand them fully. The search for truth is a lifelong quest. All people, under all conditions, to varying degrees, consciously or subconsciously, are searching for answers to these questions related to the nature of and the reason for their existence.

The crucial quality needed for a successful approach to these questions is truthfulness with oneself. We can, if we choose, lie to others. But we cannot lie to ourselves. We can delude ourselves, make ourselves believe untruths, and rationalize what is clearly false. But in all these attempts, at some level, we are aware that truth is being hidden. Truth is similar to light. When truth shines, it shows the reality of ourselves. That is why we are afraid of truth, and at the same time we are in need of truth.

Being truthful with oneself paves the way for a truthful relationship with others. At the root of most interpersonal difficulties lies our ignorance of each other and consequently our misunderstanding of one another. At the social level this misunderstanding and ignorance cause prejudices of all kinds. At the interpersonal level, it complicates human communications and causes feelings of hurt, resentment, and anger. So we need not only to understand ourselves but also to understand each other. We need to find the truth about each other. We need to communicate honestly and truthfully. We need to fulfill our promises so that our trust is not broken and a false impression is not given.

As we can see, the issue of truth is far from being solely philosophical. In everyday life, husband and wife must be able to be truthful with each other if their marriage is to thrive and be strong. Children need to trust their parents which, in turn, requires the parents to be truthful with their children. Employees and employers, teachers and students, people and their governments, nations and other nations, all need to be truthful with one another if they wish to have a trustworthy relationship. In all interpersonal and international interactions, truth is indispensable. Without it, all human relationships suffer. This is the condition of our world today. Husbands and wives, parents and children, governments and their people, and various nations—none trusts each other. None tells each other the truth. All suffer. We need truth not merely as a code of ethics but because it is an indispensable aspect of a healthy human life and human society.

From Adolescence to Maturity

UNITY

Closely related to truth is unity. Unity refers to oneness, and oneness is the quality of truth. Truth is oneness and oneness is truth.

Unity is also closely related to love. It is impossible to be united without love or to love without recognition of our fundamental unity. In our personal relationships, the question of unity is interwoven with love. Lovers yearn to be together, to be united. When lovers are separated, they suffer, but not infrequently they also suffer when they are together. This happens because we have not yet learned to be united. Love alone does not guarantee a good and joyful relationship. In fact, not infrequently love relationships are painful and unhappy. However, if the lovers become united, they will have a much happier and less painful love relationship. To achieve unity we need to recognize that while we are separate human beings, we are also one. We live in a highly individualistic society, and consequently separation and distinction between people are encouraged. Competition is regarded as essential for personal development and accomplishment, and attempts at establishing unity are viewed with suspicion and doubt.

In our world today, the concept of unity is very foreign. Some see unity to mean sameness, and as such the concept is unappealing. Others see unity as a process that ultimately results in domination of one person or group over others. These types of unity are totally unacceptable. For when I speak of unity, I mean a condition that is the opposite of the above conceptions of unity.

Unity here means that at the core of their being, humans are one and that together they make up an integrated whole—humanity. More specifically, all human beings are composed of the same elements of matter. All human beings possess the same three capacities: to know, love, and will. All human beings go through the same life processes of conception, birth, growth, and death. We are the same with respect to all the major questions of life and death. But we are also unique. Each of us looks different; thinks, feels and acts differently; and lives a unique life.

The challenge of unity is to maintain the rich diversity of humanity and at the same time to see the fundamental oneness of all people and their interdependence with each other and with the world of nature. In our universe, everything is related to every-

The Psychology of Spirituality

thing else, and all things influence every other thing. Changes in one affect the whole. Unity, therefore, requires us to see that "the earth is but one country, and mankind its citizens."[2] It requires us to care for the welfare of all people regardless of their nationality, race, creed, class, or their other unique characteristics. Unity demands that we develop a world consciousness. It calls for actions that are universal and all-encompassing in scope and just and fair in their application. Once again we see that unity is more than an aspect of a code of ethics that can be discarded at will. It is evident that human life and civilization cannot continue without the achievement of unity. The era of separation has come to an end. The inescapable need of the modern world is unity.

SERVICE

Service is the third element of the universal code of ethics emerging as a result of the evolution of humanity and its coming of age. As we enter the era of our collective age of maturity, we realize that the standards of behaviour acceptable during childhood and adolescent periods of human social evolution are no longer suitable.

In a mature society, competition must give way to the personal pursuit of excellence and cooperation. Self-centredness needs to be replaced with concern and love for others. Relationships based on power and domination have to be abandoned in favour of cooperation and equality. Authoritarian modes of behaviour have to be discarded and dictatorial methods of government replaced with true democracy and meaningful, free participation of all citizens. These and other changes necessary for the collective growth of humanity are only possible through certain specific individual and societal alterations.

What is required at the individual level is service, not because we wish to be seen as "good people," but because without service no one can grow. We humans are a part of that cosmic ecology of life and consciousness which permeates the whole universe. We are also the conscience of this universe.[3] As far as we know, we human beings are the only beings in our immediate universe who possess the ability to decide, to choose, to go the way of evil or good. We

● *From Adolescence to Maturity*

can both destroy and create. We can act greedily or generously and be selfish or of service. We have the fate of our world in our collective hands. We can either compete and destroy each other, or cooperate and be of service to one another. Service is an indispensable aspect of human life. It is a part of human nature in its sublime and mature state.

In our contemporary adolescent world, the idea of service is suspect. To understand the concept of service better, we should distinguish it from charity. Service is an act of generosity and assistance from an equal to an equal, while charity is giving from one who has to one who does not have. In an integrated lifestyle charity will give way to service. A reciprocal relationship develops. Each person both gives and receives as well as teaches and learns at the same time. In the act of service we sacrifice our egotism, establish our equality with everyone else, and replace our individualism with unity.

In the next section I will briefly review the structure and function of the human brain and its role in the development of human consciousness and evolution. Study of these issues is important because if indeed our consciousness (soul) is the product of our brain, and if our brain is programmed to follow the instinctual route, then all our efforts to create a spiritual lifestyle will fail. If we are by nature attracted to untruth, individualism, and self-interest, then all our efforts to live a life of truth, unity, and service will fail. We have to accept that our lives, such as they are, will continue to be a constant struggle for survival, and we will remain the highly neurotic victims of an oppressive and materialistic civilization. However, if we are by nature spiritual, then our attempts at applying spiritual principles to our lives will succeed. We will be able to create a peaceful, united, and just world civilization. We will succeed in our attempts to decrease the conflicts, tensions, and aggravations that inflict our lives. And we will, at last, enter our age of maturity—the era of spiritual civilization.

No serious observer of the human scene today can deny the absolute necessity for the application of principles of truth, unity, and service to contemporary human life. Our world today is so confused by conflicting ideas, interests, and practices that unless people are allowed to investigate truth for themselves, unite with each other in the pursuit of their common goals, and create a world of justice and mutual cooperation and service, the world situation will rapidly move towards destruction and extinction. What follows, although addressed to the individual, is applicable to human societies as well.

The Brain, Consciousness, and Spirituality

●

The ultimate aim of many human endeavours is to decrease tension, to achieve calmness and peace of mind, to release the energies of mind and body from the demands of psychological and interpersonal conflicts, and ultimately to achieve happiness. The secret of human happiness lies in the attainment of unity—unity between what we think, feel, and do, and unity with all other human beings. Unfortunately, most frequently the quest for happiness, and therefore the need for unity, is replaced with the pursuit of pleasure, which somehow justifies and legitimizes most of our actions, particularly if they are aimed at the gratification of our self-centred desires. It is not unusual to encounter people who engage in extramarital affairs and leave their marriage and family, exclaiming "I needed affection of which my spouse deprived me." This is ultimately an act of self-gratification. Here the far-reaching negative effects of such behaviour on everyone involved are totally ignored, and a serious condition of inner and interpersonal conflict is created. We also frequently encounter people who have beaten or injured other people and who excuse themselves by saying, "That person made me angry," as though this justifies their violent behaviour.

The main characteristic of all these types of behaviour is that they give the instinctual primacy over the spiritual. In other words, these people consider human instincts to be more important and more powerful than all their other human capacities such as the capacities to know, love, and will. But in reality these powers are infinitely greater than instincts. The whole objective of an integrated life and spiritual psychology is to put human instincts in the framework of knowledge, love, and will, and to apply the principles of truth, unity, and service to them. By doing so we will discover that we can survive without needing to be self-centred, can succeed without needing to exercise power over others, and can be happy by participating in the joys of others. The whole objective is transformation from an animal-like life to a uniquely human life.

At the core of all therapeutic endeavours should be this objective—a transformation that is in reality a transcendence. Transcendence here refers to the spiritualization of our more primitive interests and concerns that are related to the earlier stages of our evolution. By understanding the structure and functions of our brain, we can see the course of our evolution and how transcendence is possible.

THE BRAIN AND ITS FUNCTIONS: A SUMMARY

The human brain is one of the most complex structures in the universe. It is composed of fifteen billion neurons, almost equal to the number of stars in the Milky Way. Research on the brain helps us to understand it in terms of three functioning units: alertness, information processing, and action. These units are not locations in the brain; rather, they are processes that are the outcome of the work of the brain as a whole. Of all beings possessing brains, the human brain is the most complex and advanced. In evolutionary terms, the human brain is composed of at least three brains: the reptilian brain, the paleomammalian brain, and the neomammalian brain.[4] Paul Maclean, Director of the Laboratory of Brain Evolution and Behavior of the National Institute of Mental Health in the United States, has been particularly interested in the work of the reptilian part of the human brain. His special interest is in respect to our emotions. He believes that humans have inherited ancient forms of animal mentation called paleopsychic processes.

From this perspective we can identify three brains, which according to MacLean, "amount to three interconnected biological computers, each having its own intelligence, its own subjectivity, its own sense of time and space, and its own memory and other functions."[5] The most primitive of these brains is the reptilian brain or the brain stem, which has functions of self-preservation and survival of the species. A number of scientists believe such behaviour as establishing territory, growling, foraging, hoarding, as well as greeting and formation of social groups are among the functions of the reptilian brain.[6]

Humans in general display this type of reptile-like behaviour, and some human beings actually live according to these tendencies. From these observations we may conclude that through the process of their evolution, humans were at one time living a life similar to that of reptiles. This, however, does not mean that we should continue to live like reptiles and should abandon our efforts to transcend our reptile-like tendencies. If we had neither evolved nor possessed a more developed brain as well as a consciousness and understanding uniquely human, then of course we would have been reptiles and acted as such and been considered "normal" by other superior beings who could think, analyze, and reach conclusions. But the fact is that we are humans, and we can decide whether or not we wish to follow our reptile-like tendencies. This is at the core of the problem of contemporary research.

It is a fact that conclusions reached by researchers cannot be separated from their worldview and understanding of reality. No matter how detached or objective a brain researcher is, the conclusions reached by the researcher are still coloured by that person's views about human nature and the workings of the world. Let us consider the following statement by MacLean:

> Except for altruistic behavior and most aspects of parental behavior, it is remarkable how many behavior patterns seen in reptiles are also found in human beings.[7]

One may ask what is left when we take away altruistic and parental behaviour. We have already excluded the human capacity to be conscious, to know, love, will, sacrifice, create, imagine, experience the pain of separation and the joy of reunion, sing, behold beauty, write poetry, learn principles of mercy, justice, growth, and unity. If we remove all of these, what else is left? Probably some type of reptilian behaviour. We may also ask why this is so surprising. Of course, we humans do also have the functions of self-preservation and survival of the species, and as such we are similar to reptiles. MacLean says that certain human behaviour, such as ritualism, awe of authority, and social pecking orders, may possibly be related to our reptilian brain. This may be so. These types of behaviour are clearly destructive, and no longer contribute to the development of either the individual or society.

The task before humanity is to use our uniquely human capacities of mind and consciousness to modify these archaic and destructive tendencies that are the remnants of our evolutionary past. The way this change takes place is not yet clear. Could it be that our consciousness (soul) affects the evolution of our brain, and, if so, how? Aside from the powers of our mind, what else affects our collective maturation? Could it be that the spiritual teachings of religions play a significant and primary role in the evolution of human consciousness? These are questions that concern the psychology of spirituality and which need to be studied more fully. But let us first continue our review of the brain's functions.

The Limbic System

Below the cortex is the limbic system, which is also called the mammalian brain. All mammals have the limbic system, the main work of which is to help to maintain homeostasis: constancy and stability of the internal environment. In addition, the limbic system controls our emotions. The limbic system not only performs the "keeping alive" functions but also conditions many of the operations of the brain. For example, the hypothalamus, which is an important part of the limbic structure, regulates eating, drinking, sleeping, waking, body temperature, heart rate, hormones, sex, emotions, and balance. These are survival activities, and all are regulated by a part of the system the size of a pea—the hypothalamus.

Because humans and mammals both have a limbic system, it is therefore not surprising that researchers find many similarities between humans and animals with respect to some basic aspects of our daily living. In this respect the role of emotions is particularly important. We have not yet developed much knowledge about the working of our emotions, nor have we learned ways of dealing with our emotions in a creative and constructive manner.

Most research on the brain with respect to emotions revolves around stimulation of those centres in the brain that either cause anger and fear or bring pleasure and excitement. These emotions are shared between humans and animals. Many people respond to emotions as though there is nothing they could or should do to modify them. For example, in our contemporary world behavioural scientists and lay people alike believe that emotions should be expressed and that desire for pleasure should be fulfilled. They blithely ignore that humanity, throughout its history, has concluded that these emotions need to be controlled and that careless handling of them can be a cause of difficulty in society. An uncontrolled expression of our anger may cause pain, suffering, and even death. Our uncontrolled pursuit of pleasure likewise causes both social and personal problems. Consequently, there has always been a confrontational relationship between those who call for freedom of emotions and others who advocate their control. These confrontations have usually taken place in the arenas of public good and personal rights, freedom and order, and science and religion. In our world today these battlefields are scenes of considerable activity, but nowhere is the war as fierce as that between science and religion. It seems that religion is losing ground and the era of complete legitimization of the reptilian and mammalian lifestyles for people is at hand.

If and when this happens with all its related consequences, we may even return to our prehistoric life. A good example of the struggle between science and religion is expressed by Edward O. Wilson, professor of zoology at Harvard University and author of *Sociobiology: The New Synthesis*. Wilson, according to Richard Restak, author of *The Brain: The Last Frontier*, believes that "our deepest and, in some sense, our most human values are physically determined and, hence, explainable as 'our overwhelming predisposition to register certain facial expressions when we are sad or angry or perhaps even sexually aroused'."[8]

Let us study the above statement carefully. Wilson speaks of "our deepest, and in some sense, our most human values" and then goes on to define these as sadness, anger, and sexual arousal. He further explains that these "deepest" and "most human values" are physically determined because of "our overwhelming predisposition to register certain facial expressions." We may ask why sadness, anger, and sexual arousal are defined as deepest human values? They are, in reality, natural responses to conditions of deprivation, threat, and stimulation that humans share with animals. How is it that these emotions are described as human values? What makes these emotions possessors of values in humans, is not that we, like animals, simply have these emotions, but rather that through our unique human nature we have the capacity and tendency to elevate these biologically rooted emotions to the spiritual realm of creativity, meaning, and purpose. Thus, sadness in humans becomes closely connected to love, union, and separation. Anger is aimed at injustice, poverty, and ignorance, and sexuality becomes a vehicle for the expression of the human soul's longing for union and creativity. It is at this level that these emotions assume the status of uniquely human values.

But what about our facial expressions, which Wilson considers the proof that human values are physically determined? As noted before, the expression of human reality in life is through our body. Both our biological and spiritual qualities manifest themselves through expressions, movements, and actions of the body, hence through our facial and other bodily expressions. However, the fact that our body is the vehicle of expression of our emotions (and also our thoughts and values) does not negate the fact that we have a choice about how to use our emotions. A spiritual person would use anger for the cause of justice rather than for self-centred or unjust actions. Sex here becomes a sublime act of togetherness rather than a depraved rapist's attack, and sadness becomes intimately related to meaning and love rather than a sense of meaninglessness and confusion. Under these circumstances, facial expressions are of secondary significance.

This issue is of such crucial importance that it justifies more attention. Let us return to Wilson, who wrote in *Sociobiology*:

> ...self knowledge is contained and shaped by the emotional control centers in the hypothalamus and limbic systems of the brain. These centers flood our consciousness with all the emotions—hate, love, guilt, fear and others—that are consulted by ethical philosophers who wish to intuit the standards of good and evil. What, we are then compelled to ask, made the hypothalamus and limbic systems? They

evolved by natural selection. That simple biologic statement must be pursued in order to explain ethics and ethical philosophy.[9]

Here is a good example of the battle of science and religion, with science on the attack. Let us examine this statement. It begins by a reference to self-knowledge, which is not defined. "Self-knowledge" here is under scrutiny because it is a uniquely human phenomenon. At least we know of no other species that possesses self-knowledge, and we also know that we humans have self-knowledge. Because the aim of evolution scientists (among others) is to prove that humans are mere animals and nothing more, if self-knowledge is discredited, their task becomes much easier.

The statement says that "self-knowledge is contained and shaped by the emotional control centers...." On the surface this point seems valid. Many times our self-knowledge is affected by our emotions. It is not, however, created by emotions. Self-knowledge has a distinct reality that may be affected by our emotions. In fact, it is the truth of the converse statement—that our emotions are contained and shaped by our self-knowledge—which even allows Wilson's remark to sound reasonable.

The history of civilization, which comprises the social and spiritual evolution of humanity, is the living example of the effects of self-knowledge on our emotions. It shows that emotions have been used for constructive endeavours, but there is also ample historical evidence of our failure to use them positively. It is the latter situation that is of greatest concern. How can we develop our self-knowledge so that it results in the victory of the spiritual over the instinctual? This is at the core of being human—transcending our instinctual heritage and embarking upon an era of true freedom, freedom from the bondage of our animal-like tendencies.

Wilson's statement then goes on to say that the emotional control centres in the hypothalamus and limbic system flood our consciousness with all the emotions, and by doing so, contain and shape our self-knowledge. We may well ask what consciousness is. Is it identical to self-knowledge? Where does it originate? How does consciousness flooded by emotions shape self-knowledge? Is this not one of the crucial differences between animals and humans, that animals have emotions but no consciousness of or control over these emotions, while humans have these emotions and know that they have a choice about the manner of their expression?

Wilson basically indicates that the hypothalamus (part of our limbic system) is the site of our emotions and that these emotions affect our consciousness. This is true. It is also true that according to the theory of evolution the hypothalamus and limbic system have evolved over millions of years.

However, none of these observations deal with the central issues—the origins of self-knowledge and consciousness. Here we may ask what is the force of evolution? Is it natural selection alone? What about the pull of human consciousness that constantly challenges our brain to evolve and function at ever-higher levels? While evolution theory seeks explanations for behaviour in terms of its adaptive evolutionary value over millions of years, spiritual psychology seeks to explain human behaviour in terms of our species' response to the evolutionary powers of the mind (or soul). In other words, human evolution has been and continues to be a combination of biological evolution and spiritual evolution. While we have more specific knowledge about our biological evolution, we have just barely begun to study and research our spiritual evolution. The relationship between biological and spiritual evolution becomes particularly clear when we study the cortex. But before we review the work of the cortex, one final note needs to be made.

Restak noted in a discussion with Edward O. Wilson that according to Wilson, love joins hate, aggression, fear, etc., through the limbic system. Restak noted that if this is the case is it not better to overcome the biological constraints imposed by our own limbic systems. Wilson replies: "Although we can overcome the biological constraints imposed by our own limbic system, we are forced to do so at great economic and social cost in terms of time, energy, and resources." Wilson then goes on to say, for example, how difficult it would be to ignore our "meat-eating" evolutionary program and become vegetarians, or how trying it will be to "ignore people's biological differences" by wanting to create equality between women and men. He feels the same is true about aggression. It costs a lot to bring about peace because "peaceful coexistence does not come 'naturally' but exacts a cost in time, effort and money." However, with respect to peace at least Wilson is willing to be "unnatural" and considers peace "important enough to justify these costs." He goes on to say he is "less sure of the wisdom of some other goals."[10]

These perspectives are far from being value-free scientific observations. They are products of minds and hearts closed to spiritual realities and limited by physical similarities between humans and animals. These theories have a seductive nature, because they explain away the need for us to assume responsibility for our violent and destructive behaviour and for our self-indulgent lifestyles. These explanations are also seductive because they are seemingly based on scientific facts. However, as we saw above, they are based on biased materialistic values.

The Cortex

The mammalian brain only appeared in its present form some fifty million years ago. Since then, the growth of the mammalian brain has been noteworthy; nevertheless that remarkable development does not begin to compare to the evolution of the human brain during the past two hundred and fifty thousand years. This development is unique to the brain of *homo sapiens*. Of particular importance are the following facts. Restak writes:

> ...the present level of brain enlargement in most mammals was reached early in evolution and maintained up until the present time. Our brain, in contrast, underwent its greatest growth spurt during the last two hundred and fifty thousand years. Even dolphins, who share with us an increased brain-to-body ratio, possess brains which have not developed much in the past twenty million years. In essence, a dolphin today is about as intelligent as one of its ancestors twenty million years ago.[11]

Restak then goes on to put forward certain cogent questions. He asks: "Why did the human brain develop so rapidly in such a short period of time? What was the stimulus for this growth? How did it fit into the evolutionary scheme of things?" He then notes that "the exponential growth of the human brain during the last two hundred and fifty thousand years is unique in the history of evolution." "Even today," he says, "we lack a satisfactory explanation how it came about."[12]

What, if any, plausible explanation can be given from the perspective of spiritual psychology? The fact that evolution of the brain vastly exceeded the needs of prehistoric humans is unique in the history of evolution. Evolution theory states that evolution takes place through natural selection, and natural selection takes place in a gradual form, step by step. Through the imperatives of survival and growth, the evolving organism is given advantage over others in order that it survive and evolve. In humans the evolution of the brain did not take place in this manner. In fact, the opposite happened. Our species, 250,000 years ago, was provided with an organ (our brain), which we still have not learned how to use completely. This is unique to humans and clearly demonstrates that human evolution did not take place solely along the path of natural selection. This crucial fact was indeed known to the fathers of the theory of evolution, Charles Darwin and A. R. Wallace. In 1869, Wallace wrote to Darwin: "Natural selection could only have endowed the savage with a brain a little superior to that of ape, whereas he possesses one very little inferior to that of an average member of our learned society." Darwin responds: "I hope you have not murdered completely your own and my child."[13] By this, Darwin is referring to their theory of evolution, which postulates the gradual emergence of *homo sapiens* from the apes. The unique evolution of the human brain did then, and still does, pose a fundamental, unanswered question with respect to the true nature of human evolution.

In his quest for an answer, Restak posed this question to Edward O. Wilson. Here is, in part, Wilson's response, as reported by Restak:

> It is entirely within the range of possibility that the brain became so hypertrophied and complex that at some point its most important development was no longer related to the earlier genetic evolution. In other words the influence of culture became predominant over strictly biological considerations....[14]

This explanation is very significant but still inadequate. Either the natural selection theory applies to the human brain, or it does not. From the perspective of spiritual psychology, the natural selection theory can be applied to the biological evolution of humanity, but for spiritual evolution and hence evolution of the human brain, we require a more comprehensive explanation.

Wilson acknowledges that one "cannot of course explain the brain simply on the basis of evolution, and at the same time it is not totally dependent on the cultural environment either."[15] Here we may well ask what the possible explanation for the extraordinary evolution of the human brain could be, aside from the biological and cultural influences.

In this respect it would be useful to remember that in the span of nine months the human fetus traverses similar stages to those that humanity traversed in millions of years in its evolution on this planet. In the same way that in the womb the fetus develops a large and complex brain not for the continuation of its life in the womb, but rather in anticipation of its enormously enhanced consciousness in life in this world; likewise, the prehistoric human may have developed its extraordinary brain in anticipation of, as well as in response to the dawn of an era of greatly enhanced human consciousness. We could postulate that 250,000 years ago our animal-like ancestors began to develop truly distinctive brains on their way to becoming human-like humans.

Jonas Salk, a world reknowned scientist and the discoverer of the polio vaccine, makes a similar observation about the relationship between the process of evolution and the life of the fetus in the womb. He says:

> ...we see that during the nine months of human gestation, ontogeny [the development of a single organism] recapitulates phylogeny [the evolutionary development of a species through time]. As the human fetus develops, its changing form seems to retrace the whole of human evolution from the time we were cosmic dust to the time we were single-celled organisms in the primordial sea to the time we were four-legged, land-dwelling reptiles and beyond, to our current status as large-brained, bipedal mammals. Thus, humans seem to be the sum total of experience since the beginning of the cosmos.[16]

A significant aspect of life in the womb is the development of a large and complex brain, which we may postulate is in anticipation of and in response to the enormously enhanced consciousness in this life. Likewise, the prehistoric human may have developed its extraordinary brain in response to and in anticipation of the dawn of an era of greatly enhanced human consciousness.

In my view, 250,000 years ago our animal-like ancestors began to develop truly distinctive brains on their way to becoming more human as a response to the sudden and powerful appearance of one or more individuals in their midst who possessed a significantly

The Psychology of Spirituality •

higher level of consciousness than the rest of the population. This process is akin to mutation in biological evolution. This theory is not as far-fetched as it may appear at first glance. In fact, there now exists a considerable body of evidence that human thought and consciousness have powerful effects on the brain and alter both the anatomy and physiology of the brain.[17] Furthermore, history shows that all major civilizations came into being after a new paradigm of consciousness was introduced to humanity. A close study of this pattern shows that the essential and universal aspects of these new paradigms of consciousness are those which define human nature, explain the purpose of human life, and put forward standards of morality and ethics in human relationships. These issues are all spiritual in nature. It is not therefore surprising that major civilizations are based on the teachings of the founders of universal religions and "spiritual" philosophers. To the former group belong such figures as Buddha, Moses, Zoroaster, Christ, Muhammad, and Bahá'u'lláh. In the latter category we find Socrates, Plato, and Confucius among others.

Notwithstanding these observations, the question about what caused the human brain to evolve so rapidly requires still further elaboration, and we will return to this theme. However, we should first finish our review of the functions of the brain.

The cortex performs functions that greatly enhance our capacity to adapt and to evolve. It is through the instrumentality of the cortex that we make decisions, organize our world, analyze the complicated conditions we face, produce speech and understand it, and create arts, painting, and music.

The brain has two hemispheres. This is true for the brain of all primates, but only in humans are the two hemispheres specialized for their different functions. This specialization is the most recent development in human evolution. In spite of the extensive research done with respect to the work of the brain's two hemispheres, there is little consensus about their exact functions. Still, from this body of research, we can prepare a list (not complete by any means) of major functions of the brain. These functions have been identified in a series of experimental and clinical studies, and they show that the left hemisphere controls the right side of the body. It controls language and logical activities and is linear in its mode of thinking. The left hemisphere is predominantly involved with analytical logical thinking, especially with respect to verbal and mathematical functions.

The right hemisphere controls the left side of the body as well as spatial and artistic activities. The right hemisphere is involved predominantly with synthesis and has a limited language ability. It is through the properties of the right hemisphere that we orient ourselves in space, create arts and crafts, develop our body image, and recognize faces.

Here it should be mentioned that although left and right hemispheres have certain predominant capacities, nevertheless each hemisphere has the same capacity as the other, although to a lesser or greater degree. Clinical observations have shown that if a child is injured in one hemisphere, the other hemisphere assumes its specific functions.[18] The specialized functions of the right and left hemispheres have interesting implications with respect to our spiritual capacities to know, love, and will.

Love is a spiritual power of special quality. While knowledge and will are active processes, love is a process of attraction. Through love we are attracted to the object of our love. As such, love engages our whole being in pursuit of our beloved and involves our thoughts as well as our will in this undertaking. Therefore, love has a great synthesizing capacity. Its function is holistic, and it nurtures our creative and artistic capacities.

From these observations we may postulate that attention to the powers of the right hemisphere can greatly enhance our capacity to express love. This is a crucial issue at this time in our world. Throughout history humanity has evolved, and its civilization has developed on the wings of knowledge and love. Knowledge, at least knowledge of the physical and natural laws, has given us enormous powers that can be used or abused. Love has been emphasized, not by scientists but by the founders and some followers of the major religions of the world. It seems that great advances of science have helped the left hemisphere to become dominant in the work of the brain. This is not surprising because physical and natural laws are easier to explore. They are accessible to experimentation and study through our senses, and, as such, we have more tangible access to them. But love and other spiritual qualities such as justice, unity, and mercy are not as easily accessible, particularly to humanity in its stages of childhood and adolescence.

The Psychology of Spirituality ●

Now as we approach our collective age of maturity, we will be more able to understand the nature and characteristics of love. By doing so we will actualize more of the potential capacities of the right hemisphere, until a time comes that a balance exists between the hemispheres. The arrival of the era of unity of the spiritual and the scientific will therefore be enhanced by the greater development of the right brain, which in turn will enhance the left brain's own development.

Human Brain and Human Soul: Dynamics of Spiritual Evolution

Having briefly reviewed the function of the human brain we now need to evaluate the implications of these observations. There is no doubt that the human brain is the organ necessary not only for all our survival functions but also for our uniquely human functions of thought, perception, language, reasoning ability, and artistic and creative capacities. Is the brain the primary source of all these capacities, and does it create them as a result of its immense neurological complexity? Or is it the soul that uses the brain as a vehicle of expression, helping it to become more capable and powerful in the process? Was the evolution of the human brain fueled by the responses of the organism to the environment alone, or is it that the brain, directed by the human powers of knowledge, love, and will, became more evolved (advanced) and in turn greatly influenced the environment?

The answer to all these questions seems to be affirmative. In other words, at a certain level of functioning humans respond to and are affected by their environment in a reactive and interactive manner. This is basically true about the "keeping alive" functions of the brain. But when we are talking about "creating anew" functions of the brain, we are dealing with a different hierarchy of functions. Let us consider the following statement by Robert Ornstein, author of *The Psychology of Consciousness:*

> A major difference between organisms' brains is their ability to control the flexibility of action. Consider what happens when a frog is confronted by a fallen tree. The frog has such a specialized sensory system and brain that it probably would not notice the tree unless it hits it. A human can cut it, play seesaw on it, make tables out of it, even make paper for this book. This greater flexibility of action that characterizes the human adaptation is due to a larger brain, and to many, many more cortical cells.[19]

Let us consider this statement and its conclusions. What is meant by flexibility of action? Does flexibility of action involve all human activities? Does this mean that human evolution is simply a process of adaptation at a higher level than animals? While cutting a tree and making a table or paper out of a tree have certain adaptive values, we humans do much more than this with the tree. We make a violin or a guitar from it. We create objects of art out of the tree. We make it a symbol of divinity and reverence. If these activities are indeed all examples of adaptive evolutionary process, then we would gradually see the appearance of these abilities in animals, paralleling the gradual increase in the ratio of brain/body size. The jump from the most advanced animals (with respect to their brain/body ratio) and humans is so enormous that comparisons such as that between the frog and the human border on the ridiculous.

A study of the evolution of the brain shows that over millions of years two sets of functions gradually appeared: "keeping alive" functions which are regulated by the brain stem (the reptilian brain and the mammalian brain) and "creating anew" functions which include such activities as learning, memory, and perception. We share these activities with animals. In addition, however, humans have the capacity to create symbols in the form of language and art, to seek purpose and meaning, and to act with consciousness and awareness. These activities are possible because of the interface of our mind (soul) with our brain. So long as we ignore this fact, we will be faced with the impossible task of trying to contain the vast ocean of human creativity, consciousness, and action in the confining cup of biological evolution.

Let us take another example. Research in decorticated (cortex removed by surgery) cats shows that if they were aggressive before surgery, they remain aggressive after surgery. Likewise, if they were gentle before, they remain gentle after the operation. This is an important finding. It shows that basic emotions such as anger and aggression are instinctual in nature. Animals can change these emotions only to a very limited extent through training that uses the pain/pleasure principles. Human beings also respond in this way and at this level are like animals. But humans can go further. They can control their behaviour and modify it. The essence of humanness is not its natural display of animal-like emotions (such as aggression and fear), but rather its ability to bring these emotions under the control of the powers of the mind (knowledge, love, and will). Thus, human aggressive tendencies can be transformed into human acts of enlightenment, love, and will to fight injustice, prejudice, dictatorships, poverty, disease, and ignorance

Both animals and humans have aggressive qualities, but in animals the aggressive qualities are used to protect themselves from danger, to obtain food, and to defend their territory. Humans also do the same, but humans have the capacity to do more. Thus, we can create a society in which unity reigns and danger is decreased, food is plentiful and all are able to take part in it, and territorial issues are handled in equitable and cooperative ways. Conversely, human beings can do exactly the opposite. They can create a disunited, dangerous, self-centred, and suspicious world.

These are choices we make, and they go beyond the work of the limbic system. No doubt lesions in the limbic system affect our emotional state, but disturbances of the brain are not proof that all human functions originate in the brain. In his book *Beyond Brain*, Stanislav Grof states that "the belief that consciousness is the product of the brain is, of course, not entirely arbitrary."[20] This belief is based on observations that the condition of the brain greatly affects the condition of consciousness. "These observations demonstrate beyond any doubt that there is close connection between consciousness and the brain. However, they do not necessarily prove that consciousness is produced by the brain. The logic of the conclusion that mechanistic science has drawn is highly problematic."[21] Grof then gives the example of the television set. The quality of picture and sound depends on the proper functioning of the various parts of television. A TV technician can rectify a problem, and the sound and picture return. However, through this experiment we cannot conclude that the pictures originated in the television set. "Yet, this is precisely the kind of conclusion mechanistic science has drawn in regard to brain and consciousness."[22]

In *The Mystery of the Mind*, Wilder Penfield, world famous neurosurgeon, reviews the results of his outstanding research on the brain and expresses deep doubt about the mechanistic perspectives, considering consciousness to be a product of the brain. He seriously doubts that consciousness can be explained in terms of cerebral anatomy and physiology.[23] These and similar observations demand a new formulation of human evolution. These facts and observations indicate that human evolution is both biological and spiritual. Human biological evolution basically follows the laws governing evolution of other biological entities. However, as noted before, the evolution of human beings does not follow biological laws alone. Spiritual laws also have their unique impact on human evolution.

BIOLOGICAL EVOLUTION

All creation is subject to the universal laws of evolution. These laws state, among other things, that there is a common origin to all things, that all things change, that this change is towards a higher level of organization and flexibility, and that this process is assisted by unexpected occurrences (mutations), which give a greater capacity for evolution to one or a few members of the same group, thus helping the process of natural selection, which eventually results in the appearance of a more complex and capable species.

The concept of evolution is best known in connection with the work of Charles Robert Darwin (1809-1882) who, in his 1859 book *The Origin of Species*, put forward the view that all living beings, including humans, are descended from the same parent. This view caused considerable conflict between followers of various religions and the scientists who espoused Darwin's theory of evolution, and created a strong controversy that exists even today.

In retrospect, we now possess enough scientific data to see that biological evolution did indeed take place and that humans did not suddenly appear on earth after having been banished from heaven. Study of evolution has shown that biological evolution is only one of at least three evolutions.

Jonas Salk is of the opinion that there is a universal evolution with three phases: the prebiological, biological, and metabiological. By prebiological evolution, Salk means the period between the beginning of our universe to the time when the precursors of life finally emerged on earth. The biological or Darwinian evolution begins when cells as the "units of life" emerged and continues until the appearance of human-like animals. Metabiological evolution begins with the development of the human brain and the capacity to create new forms that would not otherwise exist. Salk gives examples such as buildings, ideas, computers, radio, television, airplanes, nuclear weapons, physics, chemistry, biology, and philosophy and states that "the human mind has altered the rate of evolution in a staggering way."[24] Prebiological evolution is also called physical evolution. Cyril Ponnamperuma, former chief of the chemical evolution branch of NASA's Exobiology Division and professor of chemistry and director of the Laboratory of Chemical Evolution at the University of Maryland, points out that an aspect of the prebiological evolution is chemical evolution:

> Chemical evolution is based on the idea that the building blocks of life were made before life began...the earth is about 4.5 billion years old and we believe the oldest life on earth appeared before 3.8 billion years ago. We have reached that conclusion because of the fossils of living molecules found in 3.8-million-year-old sedimentary rocks at Isua, in Greenland, which are among the oldest known rocks on Earth.[25]

LIFE AND CONSCIOUSNESS

The exact manner in which life appeared is not known. Scientists have made many attempts in the laboratory to duplicate the conditions on earth when life appeared and have particularly focused on the creation of basic organic chemicals, including amino acids. Amino acids are the building blocks of proteins, which are essential for the creation of life. It is now believed "that a primordial soup stocked with organic molecules must have existed on the ancient earth."[26] Scientists are now trying to show that these basic organic molecules probably combined to create larger molecules capable of replication and made of protein and nucleic acid, which is the building block of genes. Scientists hope to create these molecules and therefore create the genetic code and thus life itself.

The situation is not as simple as it seems. In ancient times, there was a concept of "vitalism," which put forward the idea that a life force existed over and above the laws of physics and chemistry operating in the living organism. However, many contemporary scientists believe that all life phenomena could be explained by analysis of their physical and chemical components and interaction, so these scientists discarded the notion of vitalism. "Life force" could not be found through their work, therefore they concluded it did not exist. Only recently have scientists once again begun to look at the issue of "life force."[27]

As Roger Sperry, distinguished brain researcher who shared the 1981 Nobel Prize in medicine and physiology for his famous split-brain studies, observes about these scientists, "the longer, the harder, and deeper they looked, the more convincing it appeared that there are no such things. So it was concluded that all living things are nothing but physiochemical processes in different forms and degrees of complexity." Sperry goes on to say "we biologists had just been searching in the wrong places. You don't look for vital forces among atoms and molecules. You look instead among living things... the special vital forces that distinguish living things from the non-living are emergent, holistic properties, not properties of their physiochemical components. Nor can they be fully explained in mechanistic terms."[28] This seems to summarize the dilemma faced by materialist scientists. The phenomenon of life, and as we later will see, that of consciousness, cannot be fully explained through study of physiochemical components of living organisms alone, nor can it be explained in mechanistic terms. A new component must be added to explain life. This is possible when we take into consideration the issue of metabiological evolution. The main laws of evolution are applicable to all living beings including humans until we are faced with issue of human consciousness.

It is here that the laws of evolution do not conform to facts. What is human consciousness, and where did it come from? Is it produced by the brain, and if so, how? How could an organism like the brain create something that controls the brain itself?

Karl Pribram, distinguished brain researcher, was asked about the precise relationship between the mind and the brain in an interview with a science reporter: "Where exactly does a non-physical mind, or soul, connect with the physical organ?" Pribram responded that this is indeed a problem that has long challenged scientists. This is the problem of "downward causation."[29] By this is meant that mind and consciousness change the patterns of neural processing, they operate on the brain and actually affect the chemical structure of the brain. How is this possible? Roger Sperry notes that

> according to our new views of consciousness, ethical and moral values become a very legitimate part of brain science. They're no longer conceived of as reducible to brain physiology. Instead, we now see that subjective values themselves exert powerful causal influence in brain function and behavior. They are universal determinants in all human decision-making, and they're actually the most powerful causal control forces now shaping world events.[30]

This is an extremely important observation by a distinguished scientist who believes that the most important challenge faced by humanity is to develop a new set of universal values. Sperry observes that the new perspectives on mind-brain relationship have come about as a result of observation that "the higher levels in brain activity control the lower. The higher cerebral properties of mind and consciousness are in command. They call the plays, exerting downward control over the march of nerve-impulse traffic."[31] It is in the light of these observations and findings that Sperry talks about a new model of "mentalism" as opposed to materialism. He calls for a mentalism science to take the place of materialist science, which has rejected the reality, functions, and powers of mind and consciousness.

Pribram expresses similar views:

> For the first time in three hundred years science is admitting spiritual values into its explorations. That's terribly important. If you deny the spiritual part of man's nature, you end up with atom bombs, a technocracy devoid of humanity.[32]

This view is shared by Albert Hofmann, the discoverer of LSD-25: "If you see the wonder of creation, it seems impossible that it was produced by accident. There must be something spiritual behind it, something we name God."[33] These observations pose basically the same question about consciousness as about life. What is the origin of consciousness and why, suddenly, 250,000 years ago, did the prehistoric human develop a brain whose capacity could not be fully used? As we noted before, this development was unique to humans and against the established laws of biological evolution. These laws state that the evolutionary process is a step by step development of those new capacities which the organism is able to use. The exponentially large brain that developed 250,000 years ago in us even today is being only partially used. As such, development of our mind and consciousness still lags behind our biological development. The appearance of the unique human brain and unique human intelligence is the beginning of the third phase of universal evolution described by Salk.

METABIOLOGICAL EVOLUTION

Metabiological evolution is in fact spiritual evolution, a very important aspect of which is the evolution of consciousness. Consciousness here is used to describe such phenomena as intelligence, self-awareness, and mind. The terms all basically refer to the same reality, which is metaphysical and metabiological, and which expresses itself in life through the creation of arts and sciences, the development of values, the emergence of cultures, and the appearance of all phenomena uniquely human. In recent years many scientists have begun to talk about cultural evolution as distinct from biological and chemical evolution. For example, Sperry says that "the so-called Big Three....Consciousness, Free Will, and Values"— were always thorns in the side of materialistic science and were all rejected by that science. The new formulation of science of the mind/brain "makes conscious mental events causal."[34] However, it is interesting to note that scientists such as Sperry believe that the brain generates and creates its own mental programs. These scientists have a very legitimate fear of accepting any concept that cannot be proven through the scientific method. They are, however, quite prepared to admit that the mechanistic method of materialist science, based on the Newtonian World-Machine perspective, is very limited in scope. It cannot understand all realities. It relies primarily on dissection and analysis. It lacks the ability to synthesize, to see the whole, and to accept emergent, nonphysical phenomena such as life and consciousness. Therefore, it tries to explain such phenomena within the framework of the mechanistic and biochemical laws and to create them in the laboratory or computer. It is in the context of this background that the concept of spiritual evolution gains its significance.

Spiritual evolution refers to that process through which consciousness as a spiritual reality has evolved. This process is similar to the development of life as a biological reality and energy as a physical reality. In the same way that life has its own unique characteristics such as growth, replication, and metabolism, consciousness has its own characteristics. It is not composed, is nonmaterial, and is not bound by time and space. However, consciousness, as we experience it, can only occur in the context of the progressive phases of universal evolution (i.e., physical, biological, and spiritual). In other words, for consciousness to appear, the existence of both matter and life are essential.

How the universe began, we really do not know. We have, of course, concepts about the Big Bang and what followed. But what was the origin of the universe remains a mystery. There are only two explanations: the universe came out of nothing; or the universe was created. The first explanation is clearly unscientific. Science teaches us that nothing can be created from nothing. The second explanation requires adoption of a perspective other than the materialistic worldview. This requires, at least at the hypothetical level, consideration that a nonphysical—a spiritual—reality was the primary cause of the universe as we know it.

The concept of spiritual evolution states that the Universal Mind and Consciousness (God), which has existed from the beginning that has no beginning, brought the universe into existence with all its unique characteristics, among them the laws of evolution. Furthermore, the concept of spiritual evolution holds that the Universal Mind and Consciousness has been in the past and continues now and into the future to be intimately involved in this drama of creation and evolution. In other words, what we observe as sudden, unexpected episodes resulting in the three distinctive evolutionary processes, have occurred in response to the Will of this Universal Mind. Therefore, the appearance of life, which is a sudden jump from physical to biological evolution, was due to an impulse from the Universal Mind. To put it in spiritual language,

God breathed the spirit of life into dead (nonliving) matter. God said *be,* and *it* was.[35]

One may argue that this is a farfetched, weird idea. But are we human beings not engaged in the same drama? How was the airplane created? The mind of a person said "be," and it was. Is the same not true of everything that we create and build? Do we not need first to have the idea, the consciousness, and the will? Can anything be created by us without our conscious will?

The act of creation is qualitatively different from the act of evolution. Creation requires conscious volition. Evolution follows a preestablished set of laws. Therefore, it is not at all farfetched to consider the impulses for the original creation of the material universe and the subsequent emergence of life in it to be those of a Universal Mind, which by its very nature is not bound by laws of either physics or biology.

To extend our point, we must therefore apply the same principle to the emergence of consciousness. Let us once again return to the relationship between physical and biological evolution. It is clear that life would not have been possible if there had been no matter to build the body required for life. There are basically two building blocks for all living organisms: the physical components (particularly carbon) and the information components coded in the genes. Both are needed for life to be possible.

The issue of the genetic code is of particular interest. It seems that at this level matter and consciousness meet and make life possible. It is this intricate relationship that impels chemist Cyril Ponnamperuma to exclaim, "In everything there is a certain measure of life."[36] This is so because in everything there is a certain measure of consciousness, albeit a consciousness that is unaware of itself throughout the chain of evolution until it reaches the human level. From the level of subatomic particles and atoms, all the way to the level of galaxies, we observe a purpose and order in existence. Electrons revolve around neutrons; crystals are formed according to a specific design; and stars interact in a logical way. The slightest variation in any of the processes would cause disorder of unimaginable magnitude. But everything follows established laws. As such, we can say that there exists a primitive form of consciousness (purpose and order) that is, however, totally unconscious of its existence. It can only be perceived as such because we are conscious.

The same is true in the domain of biological evolution. Except that here consciousness is much more developed and complex, although unaware of itself. It is at the level of the living organism that we observe truly purposeful and seemingly conscious processes. For example, plant leaves follow light; animals experience pain; and some higher animals display a certain type of intelligence. However, these various types of consciousness are unaware of their own existence. With respect to animal intelligence, the following statement by Pribram is of interest: "I'm tempted to say that humans are as different from nonhuman primates as mammals are from other vertebrates. We're not unique in possessing intelligence, but our kind of intelligence is very, very different."[37]

Biological evolution has demonstrated conclusively that there is a direct relationship between the complexity and size of the central nervous system in general and the brain in particular, and the degree of intelligence that the organism possesses. This observation holds true until we reach the human, when suddenly the unique human brain appears. As noted before, the human brain appeared some three million years ago, and therefore we could date the dawn of spiritual evolution to that time. This is a period when animal-like humans gradually began to be conscious of their own "selves," differentiated themselves from others, developed language, and started to communicate with others who like themselves were conscious of their own consciousness.

For us to understand the nature of spiritual evolution better, it would be useful to define briefly consciousness and to review some contemporary perspectives on consciousness. Pribram observes that

> There are at least three different ways in which the word *consciousness* is used. First, we have states of consciousness, such as sleep or waking or coma, that can pertain to animals as well as humans. Then we use the term to speak of conscious or unconscious processes. If John is in a grouchy mood, you might refer to his 'unconscious problems.' But when a cat hisses, you don't say the cat's unconscious conflicts have determined its behaviour. When we talk about conscious or unconscious processes in human beings, we're talking about degrees of self-awareness. Finally, in addition to the state and process definitions of consciousness, we've got the contents of consciousness—what we pay attention to.[38]

This definition of consciousness is very helpful as it shows the pitfalls of using a word that can mean different things to different people and in different conditions. In the context of spiritual psychology, consciousness refers to the powers of the human mind. The human mind has enormous capacities. In the words of Sperry: "The mind can quickly scan not only the past, but also the projected future consequences of a choice. Its dynamics transcend the time and space of brain physiology."[39]

The relationship between mind and the brain is an ongoing concern for scientists. After a series of split-brain experiments, Sperry observed: "Since each side of the surgically divided [or split] brain is able to sustain its own conscious volitional system...the question arises as to why, in the normal state, we don't perceive of ourselves as a pair of separate left and right persons instead of the single, apparently unified mind and self that we all feel we are." Sperry goes on to say that this is because consciousness is "a higher emergent entity that supersedes the sum of its right and left awareness."[40] This observation and conclusion is similar to the spiritual psychology's concept of soul. We perceive ourselves as a unified whole because of the nature of our soul and its powers of mind—to know, to love, and to will.

Under normal circumstances, the human mind greatly affects the working of the brain. Therefore, when we develop the capacities of our mind and expand our consciousness and self-awareness, we accomplish several tasks. The most obvious of these accomplishments is that in our personal lives we develop a greater degree of integration and wholeness. In addition, through our ideas and deeds we contribute to the process of humanity's collective spiritual evolution. Finally, there is now some interesting scientific evidence that the expansion of consciousness and application of universal perspectives and ethics to our thoughts, feelings, and behaviour have direct effects on the functions and even the anatomy and physiology of the brain.[41]

These findings confirm the central thesis presented in this section: that human evolution is a biopsychospiritual process and that our physical health, emotional stability, and spiritual enlightenment are all major players in the healthy evolution of the human species. It is in this context that the role of religion in human life has to be reevaluated. Here, I am referring to religion as the repository of the ever-progressive moral, ethical, and spiritual principles

From Adolescence to Maturity

appropriate to the needs of humanity as it is entering into its glorious age of collective adulthood.

As we noted before, religion and science are the two halves of human knowledge. One without the other is not sufficient either to answer the questions pertaining to human evolution, or to provide adequate guidelines for establishing a peaceful and enlightened civilization. It is, therefore, essential that we pay particular attention to those issues which allow us to integrate scientific and spiritual principles into practical and easily accessible approaches for development of an integrated and spiritual lifestyle.

In the last part of this book I will highlight those processes that are required for us to achieve both inner and interpersonal unity. I will show that once our capacities to know, love, and will are unified with one another through the spiritual principles of truth, unity, and service, we will achieve a very high level of self-development and integration on the one hand, and interpersonal harmony and cooperation on the other. I will also focus on both the values and shortcomings inherent in the therapeutic process and, finally, will discuss the much neglected area of spiritual lifestyle, including such ancient practices as prayer, meditation, fasting, and sacrifice.

PART SIX

Becoming

An

Integrated

Person

Character is what you are in the dark.
Lord Byron, *Don Juan*

The Challenge of Unity

●

We cannot live an integrated, wholesome, and creative life unless we fuse the biological, psychosocial, and spiritual dimensions of our life into one unified reality. Such an integration has eluded us because both the scientific and spiritual insights at our disposal have been inadequate for its achievement until the middle of the last century. However, now we know enough to achieve such an integration and to take this prodigious step towards self-knowledge.

To live healthy lives, develop harmonious relationships, create happy families, establish progressive societies, and build a peaceful world, we must acquire knowledge of the biological, psychosocial, and spiritual aspects of our reality and integrate them into a wholesome, optimistic, and happy approach to life.

Self-knowledge is not a luxury, but a requirement for humanity's survival. In the past, it was possible for people to be born into a family, remain within the clan, live in a small community, work in a preassigned occupation, and die without much accomplishment beyond having survived under harsh conditions. Even today, masses of humanity are still living under such circumstances. Nevertheless, there is ample evidence that the situation is changing.

The technological advances that have greatly facilitated the movement of people and ideas have removed those barriers that kept people apart and ignorant. The era of isolation has come to an end. This is the age of association and integration. As a result, humanity is awakening to higher degrees of self-knowledge and consciousness.

Consciousness begets change. That is why, when new consciousness is introduced into our lives, for example in the form of a major new world religion, everything changes. The essential factor in this process of change is that we develop a higher level of self-knowledge and at the core of this knowledge is the realization that the human reality is a monumental feat of unity. Life is unity, and unity is life.

LIFE IS UNITY

Life begins through the mysterious unification of matter and consciousness. Through a process unknown to us, nonliving matter, in its elemental forms, is sparked with consciousness, and life is created. From then on, through the forces of evolution, living cells, simple organisms, and ever more complex lifeforms evolve. Central to all life processes is the emergence of ever higher conditions of unity of matter and consciousness until we reach the human species where biological unity attains its zenith and a new stage for the development of higher, nonbiological forms of unity begins.

In a healthy human being, all three dimensions of unity are present and fully operative: the biological, the psychological, and the spiritual. Let us look briefly at each of these dimensions of unity.

THE BIOLOGICAL DIMENSION OF UNITY

Human life is the outcome of the coupling of the body and the mind. As life begins, we learn to understand and experience ourselves in a wholesome and integrated manner. Both our body and our mind define us as the person we are. Neither could, or should, be excluded. We become hungry, we have various desires, we experience happiness, sadness, anger, fear, anxiety, intimacy, and so on. We have thoughts, intuitions, inspirations, hopes, and aspirations, and we make decisions and resolutions. We are all this, and more. We define ourselves in these terms and experience ourselves in these ways. We are diverse, yet we feel one; we are one, yet feel diverse. We are a universe. We have these rich and varied and seemingly contradictory conditions because we are the outcome of a very high level of unity—unity of the body and the soul. Without such unity we are nonexistent.

One of the tragedies of modern science is that it endeavours to reduce all human phenomena to a set of complex biological interactions. It disregards the soul as an independent reality with its own properties, powers, and processes. Indeed, modern science denies the very existence of the soul. The application of the materialistic worldview reduces our human reality to the level of machines, as though we were nothing but machinery.

However, those who try to give primacy to the human soul encounter a different kind of pitfall in denying the fact that our thoughts, feelings, and decisions can only be expressed and experienced through the instrumentality of the biochemical and biological processes that materialistic science considers the sum total of being human. There is no doubt that, in this life, our soul could not function without our body, but it is equally true that our body could not function without our soul. Biological unity—unity of body and soul—is the prerequisite for life and selfhood. The dilemma of the body/soul duality is not resolved either by denying the soul or by ignoring the body. Rather, once the unity of the body and soul is understood, the whole question of duality disappears, and the way is paved for human development to be expressed in ever higher stages of unity.

THE PSYCHOSOCIAL DIMENSION OF UNITY

Humans have a number of instincts that are essential for survival. We share these instincts with animals. These instincts have different functions, all aimed at preserving both the individual human being and the human species. Such instincts as hunger, fight and flight, and sexual desires, serve to ensure that we feed ourselves, defend ourselves in the face of attack, flee from danger, and propagate the human race. It is a fact that we all spend a considerable part of our lives simply to ensure our own survival.

Even when our survival is ensured, when we have enough food, sufficient shelter, easy and affordable access to health care, have two or more children, and are living in safe, peaceful environments, many of us continue, nevertheless, to spend the short days of our lives pursuing more of the same survival tools (i.e., more money, bigger homes, more food, etc.), and acting as though our survival is in danger.

This is due to our ignorance of the law of unity. We do not realize that our survival is not solely dependent on our individual selves. For us to survive, we need each other. As children, we need our parents and other adults. As adults, we need each other. Human beings cannot survive on their own. Yet we behave as though others are our enemies, as though we could live on our own without any help from anyone. Because our concept of unity is still so rudimentary, we have created lifestyles characterized by mistrust of ourselves, of others, and of the future. Consequently, we feel that we have to spend our lives ensuring our survival. At this level of unity, we should make sure that we use our instincts and emotions in a constructive, rather than destructive, manner. A few examples will help to elucidate this point.

The instinct of hunger is given to us so that we will eat. However, if we eat too much, too little, or too poorly, we jeopardize our own health and, ultimately, our survival. Likewise, the fight and flight instincts are potent forces for our protection. However, when everyone carries a gun to protect themselves, when every nation builds tanks and warplanes to protect itself, and when the world becomes a storehouse of enough armaments and bombs to eradicate the entire human race from the face of the earth several times over, then no one is safe. Safety is, rather, the outcome of unity. Our individual existence is dependent upon our collective existence. One is not possible without the other.

Once we have accomplished the unity of instincts, we are then able to pay attention to our feelings and emotions. We can begin to ask ourselves what makes us happy or unhappy, what gives self-assurance, and what causes us to doubt ourselves, what conditions make us fearful or courageous, what brings us anxiety or calmness. These feelings are at the core of human experience. We experience ourselves in these divergent ways and consequently feel conflicted. However, for us to experience emotional unity, we need to reconcile such opposite emotions as happiness and sadness, comfort and suffering, freedom and discipline. There are many such dichotomies about which people feel conflicted. However, these three sets of opposing feelings are sufficient to make the point about emotional unity.

Happiness, above all, is dependent on the condition of our personal and interpersonal unity. If we live a life in which our thoughts, feelings, and actions are harmonious and if we live in unity with others, then we are happy. On the other hand, if we suffer from inner disunity (i.e., disunity between what we think, feel, and do) and if we have interpersonal conflicts, then we are indeed unhappy.

There are two kinds of unhappiness, one resulting from disunity, the other resulting from separation from someone with whom we feel close. In the latter case, happiness and sadness can exist together. For example, I am happy that I have a very good relationship with my wife, while I am sad that I have to travel and be separated from her.

The same dynamics apply to comfort and suffering. We all desire comfort. Pain is difficult to endure. But the experience of pain is essential to human survival. Without pain we could die of an illness, not even realizing that we are ill. Without suffering, we will not grow and evolve. Pain and suffering are needed for our health and growth. Both are uncomfortable. However, we would be far more uncomfortable if we did not have the benefit of experiencing pain or suffering.

It is a source of comfort to us to know that when we are ill we will feel pain as a danger signal and therefore will be able to do something about it. Also, it is a source of comfort to realize that life's suffering can be employed in the service of our growth and development. No life is without suffering, and a life without growth is filled with immense suffering. Therefore, it only makes sense that we learn from our suffering and help ourselves to evolve and grow. This is a creative cycle; the more we learn from our suffering, the less we suffer. Conversely, the more we avoid pain and suffering in life, the more we suffer.

Another example of seemingly contradictory feelings occurs with respect to freedom and discipline. Many people define freedom as the absence of discipline, while true freedom is achieved when there is discipline. Imagine rush hour traffic without the discipline of traffic lights. Compare the conditions of freedom where there is no order with where there is. Order makes freedom possible, and freedom makes order humane. In other words, order prevents chaos and freedom prevents totalitarianism.

These examples about happiness and sadness, comfort and suffering, and freedom and discipline demonstrate the need to apply the principles of unity to our emotions and instead of avoiding certain unpleasant conditions such as sadness, suffering and discipline, try to incorporate them into our life experiences. By doing so, we have lives of less conflict and more concord.

The third aspect of psychological unity occurs with respect to thoughts and ideas. Ideas are the exclusive domain of humans. While I have said that before in this book, I repeat it on purpose. We have a consciousness, an ability to understand and discover, and a capacity to reflect and conceptualize. We acquire knowledge through thinking, inspiration, and inquiry. These capacities define and shape our personalities and the quality of our life. What we think defines who we are and how we live. It is therefore important that we give our thoughts at least equal the attention we give our feelings. In practice, however, most people avoid thinking about their thoughts. We think a lot about what we need, want, and feel. However, we give little thought to our thoughts about who we are and what is the purpose of life beyond survival and feeling good.

Whenever I ask people about what the purpose of this life is, I quite often meet with a bewildered and even hostile response. "What do you mean about the purpose of life?" they ask, then go on to enumerate a number of activities and ideas, most, if not all, of which are about survival, feelings, and relationships. Concerning survival, one simple answer often rolls readily from their lips: to have a good life. But what a good life is, is not very clear. They then talk about happiness, peacefulness, or simply living a life in which they are not badly abused or completely ignored.

Most people's expectations of life are very limited. The horizons of life expand with higher level of consciousness. Most people avoid new consciousness. They are afraid of new ideas because new ideas create a condition of conflict within them. Usually people's views of who they are and what their lives are all about are based on what they have learned from their families and cultures. Their ideas about life have evolved through a mindless process of osmosis. They adopt their ancestors' views, the current public ideas, or their peer group's fashionable belief systems. These ideas are usually accepted without any critical study or reflection.

The most important characteristic of these ideas is that they are the norms of the group to which people belong. By adopting the "norms" of society we then feel "normal." Most people equate "normality" with being "healthy," an equation that is inaccurate and that discourages true change. However, one of the inviolable laws of life is change, so that when ideas do not change to reflect the true conditions of the world, then fundamental disunity develops between the person and the changing world. While the world changes the person does not, and gradually the gap between the two becomes immense.

The most dramatic and far-reaching ideological change taking place in the world today is the realization that humanity is one and that unity is the central ideological challenge of our times. This is so because once we truly understand the concept of humanity's unity and our place in it, then our views about our selves will change dramatically. We will then perceive ourselves not alone and apart, not in constant conflict and competition with others, and not hopeless and impotent in the face of the changes that are swiftly occurring in our world. Rather, we will realize that we are a part of the whole race of humanity, that we belong, that we can accomplish much more through peace and cooperation, and that together we are indeed able both to determine the direction and the nature of the changes taking place in our lives.

Furthermore, our consciousness of unity strengthens our individuality and maintains our diversity. It creates circumstances in which we, as unique individuals with different talents, capacities, and ideas, can build a world large enough for all, belonging to all, and serving all.

There is a tendency for people to think that to make their lives better they should focus on their own selves or, at most, the lives of themselves and their families. Such an approach is counterproductive. When we focus our efforts primarily on ourselves, we limit our world and consequently diminish the opportunities and services that are available to us. Which is better: to belong to a loving family of three or to a loving extended family of thirty-eight? Is it better to belong to a powerful nation among many competing nations or to a united world? In which conditions do we have the greater opportunity for our own personal development? Unity removes obstacles and expands opportunities.

One of the central themes of psychotherapy is self-centredness. We can easily identify the unhealthy and unpleasant consequences of other people's self-centredness as it affects our lives. When people talk about dysfunctional families, troubled marriages, addictive personalities, and loveless homes, they are talking about the selfishness and self-centredness of their parents, their marriage partners, their siblings, their friends, and their own selves. The more self-centred a person is, the more separated that person is from others. Self-centredness and unity are antagonists. A person who endeavours to be a unifier must, by definition, abandon self-centredness.

I have found that the most dramatic change takes place when self-centredness gives way to being directed towards others. This is the quality of *other-directedness*. In other words, change occurs when the person begins to realize that the reality of humanity's unity requires us to improve our individual lives in the context of our collective lives. The idea of *other-directedness* in the context of the unity paradigm is fundamentally different from the practice of giving of oneself without attention to the development of one's own character and life. We, as human beings, must actualize ourselves. We can accomplish this not by excluding ourselves from others, but rather by including others in our efforts. It is a reciprocal, equal, just, and loving process.

So far, we have discussed the notion of unity from biological and psychological perspectives. What remains for us to study is the concept of unity from a spiritual perspective.

SPIRITUAL DIMENSION OF UNITY

The central theme of this book is that we human beings are spiritual in nature. By this is meant that beyond the powers of instincts, emotions, and thoughts, there lies in human beings a capacity that can best be described as the capacity for transcendence and transformation. The uniqueness of human life lies not in our capacity to survive, our ability to feel, or even our ability to learn, even though the human species is far superior to all other beings in these dimensions. Nevertheless, these capacities alone do not completely characterize our humanness. What makes us human is that we are able, if we choose to do so, to transcend the limitations of mere struggles for existence and become both the consciousness and the conscience of our universe. In other words, we can bring about a new, dramatic stage in the evolution of life and civilization. To do so, a new consciousness is needed—divine in its origin, universal in its application, relevant in its concepts, and scientific in its approach.

Among the main dimensions of this new consciousness are the three universal ethical principles of truth, unity, and service. The process of transformation requires the adoption of this set of principles as the framework within which we conduct our lives, reform our marriage and family relationships, reorganize our societies and establish a new world order to replace the present morally and conceptually bankrupt order.

Another aspect of this transformation is the realization on our part that all reforms, be they political, economic, or ideological in nature, regardless of how scientific they are in their content and approach, will fail unless we once again bring God into our lives—but not God as an angry and punitive superman, not as an aimless, careless, unresponsive authority, not as a personal saviour who will admit "chosen" and "good" followers into "heaven," barring everyone else, and not as a powerless, weak, and unfeeling entity unable or unwilling to correct the miseries so prevalent in this world.

Rather, here we are talking about the Creator, All-Knowing, Most Merciful, Most Generous, Who has created us in the image of the Divine, has given us the capacity to know, the ability to love, and the direction to put our love and knowledge at the service of humanity, and Who is assisting us to create an ever-advancing civilization, unified, equal, just and beautiful.

In the nineteenth and twentieth centuries, when humanity, going through the final stages of its collective adolescence, consciously and proudly rejected God, a profound dislocation took place in the human psyche. The consequences of this psychic dislocation have been ominous. When we reject God, we create new gods to fill the spiritual vacuum thus created. Therefore, when humanity rejected its own spiritual reality and severed its relationship with God, at least four developments, all equally destructive to the human psyche, occurred. These developments are: (1) the rise of Marxist communism as a worldview and a form of government, (2) the establishment of materialism as the framework for scientific inquiry and the standard for human accomplishment, (3) the glorification of racism and nationalism as the noble and ultimate accomplishment of human solidarity, and, finally, (4) religious fundamentalism as the exclusive and changeless way to salvation.

The devastation caused by communism is now an established fact of history. In the former USSR and Eastern and Central European countries, one encounters masses of people who are victimized, injured, frightened, and angry. They have no trust in themselves, each other, or their governments. The artificial solidarity that was imposed on the diverse ethnic and religious groups of this vast region of the world dissolved in an instant and the age-old differences, prejudices, and hatreds that had been buried under the oppression of conformity, have surfaced once again. The ravaged landscape, the shattered economies, and the bewildered governments of this part of the world are other examples of the destructiveness of these materialistic ideologies and practices. However, despite the enormous destruction that occurred in these countries, nevertheless the most dramatic outcome of this experiment with humanity is the ultimate victory of the human spirit in the face of all efforts to deny its existence and hinder its development. Everywhere, in the cities and the countryside, in technologically developed or agriculturally centred communities and among those highly educated or masses deprived of it, one sees the remarkable human capacity to bring life and meaning to the lifeless and meaningless conditions in which they live. Therefore, it is not surprising that as soon as the controlling power of the leaders was challenged by the emergence of a new consciousness in the people under their control, the whole system collapsed and after a short period of euphoria, all the conditions of the prerevolutionary era re-emerged. It was as though these peoples and communities had been put in a state of deep freeze, and as soon as the climate began to change, all the issues of the past re-emerged asking for new solutions.

The tragedy of it all is that during this painful period of history, millions of people were sacrificed at the altar of this and similar ideologies, and innumerable lives were wasted under conditions of oppression and control. Notwithstanding these facts about communism as practiced in the former USSR, Eastern European countries and elsewhere, we would be remiss not to refer to the most inhumane and destructive doctrines and practices connected with fascism and Nazism, which have their own uniquely inauspicious place in the annals of human history and have provided us with the most appalling examples of human barbarism and destructiveness.

The effects of capitalistic materialism have likewise been devastating. Materialism, by its very definition, is anti-life. It gives primacy to the material dimension of existence. Consequently, in the materialistic framework, science searches for answers by focusing on life's material properties, society judges the value of the individual according to material accomplishments, and the progress of society is measured in terms of tall buildings, the number of automobiles, refrigerators, television sets owned by families, and the amount of wealth produced by a given population. We pay little attention to the quality of life, the ever-increasing number of homeless people, and the alarming escalation in the rate of violence, addiction, and sexually transmitted diseases that are present not only in the alleyways, stairways, nooks, and crannies of the tall buildings of these same societies, but in the affluent homes and neighbourhoods of their upper and middle classes.

Materialism pays more attention to what people own and produce than to how they live. The standards of society's progress are not measured along such lines as how successful husbands and wives are at developing their equality, how successful parents are in rearing their children to be loving, unifying, and truthful, or how successful we have been in decreasing, and eventually eradicating, the totally barbaric practices of rape and violence against women and children in our families.

There are other yardsticks that a materialistic society tends to ignore. Among them is the prevalence of discrimination, injustice, extremes of wealth and poverty, injustice, expenditures on arms, and sales of arms to individual citizens and other groups and nations. The list goes on.

These are the natural consequences of materialistic societies. It is therefore not surprising that, despite their enormous knowledge and material wealth, those societies that have embraced capitalistic materialism are all afflicted by the disease of materialism itself. North America, Western Europe, Japan, and other nations with similar orientations and perspectives are already either greatly afflicted by these conditions or are rapidly on their way to being so afflicted.

Materialism, by definition, is anathema to spirituality. Materialism and spirituality cannot coexist. However, in a materialistic society, religion can thrive if it allows itself to be used as a commodity. This is exactly what has happened in many of these societies. Religion as a commodity is nothing but a chalice filled with prejudice, divisiveness, and superstition, devoid of spirit.

The third development related to the rejection of God and the consequent dislocation in the human psyche is the continuing rise of both racism and nationalism. The human psyche, by its very nature, needs an object of adoration. If it is not God, then it will be "other gods"—gods of nationalism, racism, hedonism, etc. These "other gods" are the figments of human imagination and are based on the self-centred, self-glorifying, and self-satisfying passions of those who create them. These "other gods" foster people's irrational fears, unreasoned beliefs, and blind prejudices. As humanity becomes aware of its fundamental unity and begins to see its rich diversity as the source of its vitality, life and progress, then it will be able to let go of the gods of racism and unbridled nationalism. Ultimately each and every one of us will realize that "the earth is but one country, and mankind its citizens."[1]

As stated previously, we are now in the final phase of our collective adolescence. Therefore, it is not surprising that we witness a huge worldwide increase in nationalistic and ethnic fervour. These developments are the final efforts of various segments of humanity to establish and affirm their respective identities. From a psychological perspective, this is an essential aspect of the development of human societies (as well as human individuals). Every national and ethnic group, and all the races of the world, need to feel that in the assembly of the world they are equals, that they are all valuable members of the human family, that the unique qualities of each and every one of them are essential for creating a new, ever-advancing, spiritual, and materially progressive civilization.

Once the various nations and races are freed from the clutches of power and control by other groups and are accorded their rightful place in the world of humanity, then we will all be ready to establish a higher level of unity among us. Such a universal unity completely and unhesitatingly preserves, promotes, and appreciates the diversity of all its component parts. It is then that the body of the world of humanity will have finally reached its complete level of assembly and be ready to function within the parameters of a new world order. In this new order every individual, ethnic group, race, and nation will have equal rights, opportunities, and responsibilities.

The fourth and final destructive development that was identified earlier, is the rise of religious fundamentalism. In addition to the pernicious aspects of this development discussed earlier, the following needs to be considered. Religious fundamentalism as practiced today in the West focuses on people's weaknesses, fears, and desperation on the one hand, and on the other, promises cure without pain, salvation without effort, illumination without knowledge, and victory without sacrifice. It is the naive expression of religion in a materialistic society. It makes religion a commodity and worship a form of trade and commerce.

Religious fundamentalism has another form of expression most clearly observed in those regions of the world where religious wars are still fought passionately. These wars are promoted and fueled by doctrines of being the "chosen," the "last," the "only," and the "best." Such doctrines divide people and justify any level of violence and destruction in the name of God. The leaders of such fundamentalist groups, both in the East and in the West, aim at keeping the masses ignorant and frightened.

These approaches to religion are the most glaring rejection of the reality of religion. They have caused not only a profound dislocation in the psyche of all people who practice them but also a deep sense of loss and spiritual deprivation in those who have rejected true religion. This rejection is due to their distaste for religious fundamentalism and the illogical approach to matters of spirituality, morality, and religion.

With this broad review of the implications of the rejection of God and its impact on the world's peoples, societies, and cultures, we now turn our attention to two important issues: the therapeutic process and spiritual transformation. The former is much more popular, but has its limits. The latter is less well known and more difficult to understand.

Life Modification and Limits of the "Therapeutic"

●

In our world today, particularly in the more technologically and economically developed countries and among the more educated and well-to-do populations, "therapy" is viewed as the chief means by which we correct various personal and social problems. Many people have their own therapists, many more seek counselling from a dazzling array of sources ranging from palmists and fortune tellers to gurus, as well as everything from self-appointed therapists to highly trained specialists. Many devotedly follow radio and television programs purporting to enlighten us about ourselves, and still others are dedicated collectors of self-help books.

The very popularity of these services, books, and programs, attests to the important role that "therapy" plays in our world today. Why are so many people seeking therapy? There are many answers to this question. Among them are unhappiness, confusion, fears, anxieties, anger, grief, guilt, poor self-image, lack of self-confidence, lack of motivation, poor relationships, violent relationships, empty relationships, sexual difficulties, boredom, meaninglessness, aimlessness, aging, physical problems, unpleasant or unacceptable and bothersome habits, criminal activities, and addictions to alcohol, drugs, work, sex, relationships, exercise, television, food, lying—indeed almost anything.

The Psychology of Spirituality

Usually the initial, immediate responses to these problems is to search for a cause, offer an explanation, and think of a cure. Of course this is a noble impulse but it is usually neither practical nor effective. The reason is that we usually search for the cause of our problems elsewhere other than within ourselves.

Among the most commonly accepted and established of these external factors are the person's childhood experiences, unhealthy family relationships, unsatisfactory marriage conditions, or stressful work environments. Most psychological theories identify one or more of these external factors as the main, if not the only, cause or causes of emotional and psychological problems. For many years, mothers were the major offenders, then fathers were added to this list. Now fathers, mothers, husbands and wives, children, and society, are all identified as the root causes of most people's problems.

Today, among the most popular psychological theories in North America, are those that relate to dysfunctional families, addictive personalities, abusive relationships, and co-dependencies. Most have gladly and enthusiastically embraced these theories. Some promoters of these concepts claim that more than ninety percent of all families in the United States are dysfunctional. It is quite in vogue today for people to pronounce their families as dysfunctional and themselves as addictive personalities, co-dependent individuals, victims of abuse, and so on and so on.

There are other equally popular schools of thought that consider emotional and psychological problems to be due to chemical and hormonal disorders, genetic factors, or dietary deficiencies. The popularity of these views is apparent from the powerful pharmaceutical and food industries that benefit from the enormous sums people are willing to spend in search of a miracle drug, food supplements, or dietary regimen. Furthermore, these schools of thought have very powerful supporters among scientists and granting agencies.

Today, the psychological disciplines are going through a period of considerable crisis, because recent advances in the understanding of the functions of the brain have made it possible for us to synthesize and isolate chemical agents that are effective, to a greater or less degree, in the treatment of such conditions as depression, anxiety, schizophrenia, and obsessive-compulsive disorders. Many clinicians and researchers now hope for the discovery of the drugs that will ultimately cure all our emotional and mental disorders, providing us the opportunity to live happy and peaceful lives just by taking a few pills each day. Such expectations attest to the shallowness and narrowness of our self-knowledge—who we are, and what it means to be a human being.

Ultimately, as the euphoria about these new developments settles, we will clearly see that all these theories contain certain truths and that each explains one or another aspect of the complex human reality. The psychological theories have correctly identified the primary role of the family and early upbringing in our emotional health. There is no doubt that certain families are much better environments for rearing healthy children than others. Also, there is ample evidence that poverty, prejudice, injustice, violence, and inequality have not only adverse sociological but also profound negative psychological consequences. Turning to other current views on the cause of psychological difficulties there is, likewise, considerable evidence that some emotional and mental disorders are genetic in nature and others have clear organic causes. Recent research is also providing evidence that diet has considerable impact on our emotional states. Furthermore, it has become clearly evident that the institution of the family in our world today is in deep crisis. Marriages are breaking down at alarming rates. Parents are becoming ever more preoccupied with their own personal needs and economic and social pursuits and have increasingly less time, willingness, or ability to parent. The children of the world are growing up in appalling conditions. Millions die of hunger and preventable diseases; millions of others are victims of poverty, violence, and war. And still millions more are reared in conditions of material plenty and spiritual poverty. There are millions of children who are deprived of true education, growing up to be self-centred, instinctually driven, angry, or fearful. These children are not reared or educated to become universally minded, scientifically inquisitive, spiritually enlightened, and morally civilized, in any true sense of those words.

We must very carefully, through the scientific method, identify the essential physical, psychological, and spiritual qualities of a healthy family in order to develop social policies and practices aimed at strengthening the foundation of marriage and family. The neglect of the welfare of the family alone will ensure the return to a new age of barbarism more destructive than any we have so far witnessed in human history.

The tendency to ascribe most current individual and social problems to either psychological or organic causes has no basis in science. This is done primarily because we have not yet developed an integrated model of human reality that includes all these aspects of our being and which explains their relationship to each other. We do not yet have a "unity mindset," the development of which is particularly important in psychotherapy. The therapeutic process, in its true form, is a unifying process which allows for the development of both inner and interpersonal unities.

In the remaining pages of this chapter, I will focus on the qualities of the therapist, the attitudes towards therapy, and the steps one needs to take to achieve inner psychological unity.

QUALITIES OF A "THERAPIST"

To achieve a unity mindset and develop an integrated framework for therapy, the therapist must see, understand, and appreciate the client as a whole and complete human being, as a person with body and mind, emotions and thoughts, and ideas and actions. The therapist must not only see the person as a whole but also love this person in the spiritual and unconditional sense of the word. Love is the elixir of the psychological cure. It creates first a condition of unity between the therapist and the client. It gives them distinctive yet equal places in the relationship. It counters the pernicious forces of power, control, manipulation, and mistrust, and in the process prevents victimization and abuse. Love, pure and unconditional, becomes the motivating force for the growth of the person and helps the individual deal with painful aspects of life with greater assurance and confidence.

The therapeutic process also needs to be encouraging. Encouragement requires a high degree of maturity on the part of the therapist, who must be able and willing to see the positive qualities of the client and not only reinforce them but also celebrate them. It is through this process that a self-doubting, self-rejecting, and self-hating person gradually develops self-confidence, self-acceptance, and self-love.

Once the person has developed a positive sense of self, a totally unexpected new challenge presents itself. Without meeting this latter challenge individuals will not be able to complete their growth and development, will not be free from the psychological disorders with which they are burdened. This challenge is the challenge of selflessness; of becoming other-directed. The therapeutic process, in its most profound form, is a process in which self-centredness is replaced by self-acceptance, which in turn evolves into self-development, and finally is transformed into selflessness.

Each of these stages are healthy under certain, but not all, conditions. Self-centredness is the hallmark of infancy and childhood. Under extreme conditions of illness, deprivation, or danger, adults also become self-centred. However, self-centredness, under ordinary circumstances, is unhealthy during adulthood and must give way to a more mature and healthier condition of self-acceptance. This is the task that under healthy conditions should reach its realization by the end of adolescence. During childhood and adolescence, and under favourable conditions, a high degree of appreciation of one's capacities and abilities must develop so that we can accept ourselves with all our positive qualities, our potentialities which need to be actualized, and our shortcomings which must be overcome. The fact that many people do not achieve self-acceptance is a damning statement on the condition of our world today.

Self-acceptance, by itself, does not provide us with enough strength, insight, and depth to create a happy, meaningful, and constructive life. We need to continue our process of growth and achieve ever higher levels of self-development, which involves at least two tasks. On the one hand, self-development requires that we focus on our capacities of knowledge, love, and will, and make every effort to become more knowledgeable, particularly about ourselves and each other, more loving in our relationships, and more disciplined and creative in our activities. On the other hand, self-development demands that we control and correct our negative and destructive impulses and follow a high level of moral and ethical standards in all aspects of our lives.

Through these combined processes, we begin to develop ourselves in the true sense of the word. Personal growth cannot take place in the context of self-indulgent and undisciplined expression of our wishes and desires. When we truly develop ourselves, we discover that the natural expression of personal growth is through selflessness. By selflessness I mean becoming increasingly less self-focused and more concerned about other people—their needs, their sufferings, their joys, and their accomplishments. It is through this process that a reciprocal relationship of give and take, sharing, cooperation, and unity develops, and the road is paved for spiritual transformation.

Selflessness is a spiritual state. It requires self-love, love of our inner reality and our fundamental nobility. Self-love is the opposite of selfishness. Self-love is possible only when we give and receive love and enter into a unity relationship. This is a creative circle: selflessness requires self-love, which in turn is achieved through loving others, which is only possible through selflessness. The opposite of this creative circle is the vicious circle of self-centreness, which makes both giving and receiving love impossible and results in conditions of estrangement, distrust, and dislike.

When we reflect on the design of creation, it becomes amply obvious that when adolescence is replaced by adulthood, we are biologically, intellectually, and one hopes also emotionally and spiritually prepared to give of ourselves not only at our places of work but also in our marriages, to our partners, and later to our children.

So far I have identified some of the fundamental requirements of a healthy therapeutic relationship. They are the ability of the therapist to see the client as a whole and complete human being, to love unconditionally, and to encourage the process of self-development.

The therapist must also be sensitive to the suffering and pain of others and be able to deal with it in a healthy way. As stated before, pain and suffering are essential aspects of life and growth. The therapist should be able both to see the pain, appreciate its significance, decrease its intensity, assist in identifying its underlying causes, and help to correct the situation.

Finally, the therapist must be aware of his or her own mortality. This is a crucial aspect of the healing art. The healer must deal with the fear of death so that his or her total energy can be committed to life. The fear of death is ever present at the subconscious level and often becomes conscious, particularly when people are suffering and feeling unwell. By being familiar with the forces of life and death, the therapist will be able to increase the optimism, joy, and love for life in the client and to assist in removing the despair, agony, and fear that exist in conditions of stress, be they emotional, physical, or both. By doing so, the therapist increases the healing powers inherent in every individual.

Having described some of the important qualities of the therapist, it will be useful to discuss some of the qualities required of the client.

ATTITUDE TOWARDS THERAPY

Those who decide to enter the therapeutic relationship must, above all, find a therapist they can trust, both with respect to the therapist's knowledge and expertise, and also with regard to the therapist's ethical and moral perspectives and standards. Such a trust is essential for a successful therapeutic alliance, and if it requires several attempts to find the right therapeutic match, it is worth the effort. It is based on this trust that another essential requirement for therapy—cooperation—becomes possible.

The client must be cooperative with the therapist so that the knowledge, expertise, and healing abilities of the therapist can be effectively transmitted to the client. Trust and cooperation remove the obstacles that are usually found in abundance in most human relationships and pave the way for the creation of the essential requisite for a successful therapeutic alliance—unity.

Unity of the individuals involved in therapy makes it possible for the minds to meet, ideas to be shared, emotions to be exposed, hopes to be identified, plans of action to be formulated, and all that is needed to restore health to be made easily accessible. Through this process, the individuals involved begin to feel more in touch with their thoughts and feelings, more aware of their behaviour and less conflicted and distressed. Gradually, a state of inner peace is established and a significant degree of unity of thoughts, feelings, and actions is achieved. Eventually, an integrative process is put into motion that must sooner or later incorporate the spiritual dimension, if those engaged in the therapeutic process are to become their true selves.

A fundamental component of such an evolution is the attitude towards suffering. As stated before, pain and suffering are usually signals that something has gone wrong and must be corrected. As such, pain is a blessing. Furthermore, not infrequently we bring about our own pain and suffering. Consequently, it is important that as soon as we become aware of this fact, we begin to correct the situation. The therapeutic process is an excellent avenue for such self-awareness.

Related to issues of pain and suffering is the inevitability of our own mortality and death. The path of health is through awareness of life and death and their complete interrelatedness. This process of becoming aware of our own mortality is both emotional and spiritual in nature.

As stated before, birth and death are inseparable components of life. As we die from one state, we are born into a new and usually higher state. The therapeutic process, based on the principles of spiritual psychology, demands that we come in touch with our past and leave behind all that was painful and unkind. So it is that we die from our past, are born into our present, and eventually become focused on our future. I will continue with working through our past, present, and future once I have addressed a very key issue, which is that this process calls for understanding and forgiveness.

The question of forgiveness is of special importance, particularly in the present climate of "retaliation and revenge" that is sweeping across the landscape of psychology and psychological praxis. Our capacity to forgive is determined by several factors, among them the level of our maturity and self-confidence, our capacity to appreciate and create unity, and, finally, our ability to transcend our "natural" tendency "to right the wrong by taking revenge."

We will return to these themes in our discussion of the dynamics of spiritual transformation. Before doing so, however, we need to review the process of life modification further, as it is the primary aim of psychotherapy.

All psychological therapies aim at helping people to become more aware of the nature, dynamics, and causes of their emotions, thoughts, and behaviour, and to help them to modify and express them in a "healthier" and more "realistic" manner. Therapists point out that by providing their clients with these insights, which have been hitherto unknown, partially known, or puzzling to them, the clients become motivated to change. Central to this process of change are the client's views and feelings about themselves and others as well as a change in their "unhealthy," "inappropriate," or "unacceptable" behaviour. It is also asserted that psychotherapy helps to bring about a greater measure of maturity and growth in those who engage in it. However, we can only change, grow, and become authentic and realistic according to the way we think about human nature, our expectations of it, and whatever concepts we hold about the purpose of human life and the nature of reality. In other words, we become what we think we are and what we think life is all about. Consequently, most psychotherapies, at best, help us to become as "real," "authentic," and "realistic" as our concepts of reality, authenticity, and objectivity allow. A few examples may help to clarify this point.

At the core of psychoanalytic theory lies the notion that human behaviour is motivated by the forces of our sexual desires, instinctual needs, and aggressive drives. These concepts have been enthusiastically adopted by many individuals and societies in the West, and have provided explanations—indeed justifications—for a preoccupation with sexuality, instant gratification, aggression, and violence in these societies.

Similarly, the behaviouristic model, which perceives humans as machines and animals, seems to have greatly influenced the lives of people who live in the societies that have espoused these views about human reality. There is no doubt that the manipulated, controlled, and mechanized life in both the dictatorial and the industrialized societies is an anathema to our natural and healthy need for autonomy, freedom, and creativity. While we possess considerable power and knowledge, we nevertheless have created a lifestyle more appropriate for machines and animals than for human beings.

These observations do not, in and by themselves, mean that the psychoanalytic or behaviouristic perspectives on human nature are the sole reasons for the woes and evident problems of these societies. What they do suggest is that these concepts have greatly influenced our views about ourselves, helped to explain and legitimize our behaviour, and encouraged the adoption of lifestyles in the framework of these theories.

The impact of these theories are most dramatic in the therapeutic arena. There is ample evidence that over the past half-century therapeutic norms have moved towards encouraging clients to become more concerned about what they want, feel, wish, and desire, and less with the feelings and needs of others. We are constantly, overtly or covertly, encouraged to become more sexually "free"; to display our anger, frustrations, and hostilities with less restraint; to be more "real," "authentic," and basically do our own "thing" at the expense of everyone else. It seems that serious schools of psychotherapy with their well-controlled and well-disciplined orientation are being replaced by new forms of "therapy" that are poorly controlled, shabbily researched, and wanton rather than disciplined.

While some measure of pain and suffering is considered by the major schools of psychotherapy to be necessary and even indispensable to the process of human growth, present popular methods of "therapy" often encourage pain avoidance and, not infrequently, actually provide the clients with suggestions of various forms of instant gratification. The popularity of sexual, sensorial, and chemically induced pleasurable forms of "therapy" are examples of this trend. A more insidious and potentially more damaging form of these "therapeutic sanctions" is the insistent encouragement given to clients by their therapists to do exactly as they please. Here, feelings and instincts are accorded primary importance. The issues of right and wrong, morality, ethics, social needs vis-à-vis individual responsibilities, and short-term gains over long-term consequences are all put in an amoral and relativistic context. These perspectives have their genesis in the prevalent views that human beings are instinctually controlled and that the purpose of life is to obtain gratification and to avoid pain.

Having briefly described these points, the question arises: What is a proper form of psychotherapy? Or perhaps more to the point: What are the contributions of spiritual psychology to the practice of psychotherapy? We have already discussed the central role of knowledge, love, and will in the development of our personality. We have also reviewed the relationship between the disorders of knowledge, love, and will with the most significant human concerns about oneself, others, and time. Now we will address the main elements of psychotherapy within the framework of the psychology of spirituality and, afterwards, focus on the dynamics of spiritual transformation.

Psychotherapeutic practices suggested here are not novel. They are based on established and proven practices developed in this century. However, certain points of emphasis are added and the most effective methods used by different schools of psychotherapy are integrated into this model. Here it should be strongly emphasized that any individual who aspires to be an excellent therapist must study the principles of psychotherapy in a well-established institution of higher learning and obtain the necessary degrees, diplomas and licenses required for engaging in the practice of psychotherapy. The purpose of the psychology of spirituality as put forward in this book is not to negate or deny the many positive contributions that have been made to our understanding of the human psyche and behaviour by the analytical, behavioural, biological, and other schools of psychiatry, as well as the psychosocial and neurological sciences. Rather, my main objective is to demonstrate the absolute necessity of integrating the spiritual and scientific principles in our study of human psychology.

Let us now return to the issue of life modification, which is the main objective of the many schools of psychotherapy. These practices basically involve a review and understanding of our past experiences, present challenges, and future plans.

Understanding the Past

Understanding the past is extremely important because early childhood experiences affect growing children in every respect and determine the extent and quality of their physical health, intellectual development, emotional maturity, social adeptness, and spiritual orientation. In addition, the cardinal human qualities of knowledge, love, and will, and the major human concerns about self, others, and time have their developmental foundation in childhood experiences. Although human beings are endowed with the capacity to determine the nature of their responses to the environment, this ability is present in varying degrees at different stages and conditions of life. During childhood we are to a very large extent at the mercy of our parents and others in our environment.

A healthy environment appropriate for growth and development should at least contain the qualities of love, encouragement, and guidance. Love is a life-generating, growth-inducing, creative force that unites children with their parents and others in their environment, provides children with a sense of basic trust, and enables children to feel secure and peaceful.

The Psychology of Spirituality

Encouragement is the fuel for human growth and creativity. It should emphasize the fundamental nobility and uniqueness of each human being. It should enhance the opportunities for children to develop self-confidence and to become cooperative, sharing, and receptive. These qualities are among the essential ingredients of a mature and healthy human relationship.

Guidance is the third necessary quality of a healthy environment for the growth of children. Children function best when they are provided with adequate guidance in a flexible, loving, and encouraging milieu. Education by example and instruction is the main vehicle for guidance.

This brief outline of the characteristics of a healthy environment for the education and training of children shows that the absence of one or more of these dimensions can cause conflicts and problems. Indeed, at the core of most emotional and psychological problems is the absence of appropriate love, encouragement, and guidance. The outcome of the absence of one or more of these elements is a poor self-image, a distorted view of love, a faulty understanding of reality including the self, and considerable confusion as to the purpose and meaning of life.

The main objective of people's efforts to understand their past should therefore be to comprehend the nature of their misconceptions about themselves (i.e., self-knowledge and self-love) and reality (i.e., the nobility of creation and the purposeful nature of life). In addition, when we reflect on our past we should identify the positive events of our lives. We should remember the loving gesture of a parent, grandparent, teacher, neighbour, or friend. We should recount the encouraging episodes that occurred during our growing years as well as the guidance and advice that we received from various sources.

Therapy need not focus solely on the negative. In fact, the focus on these positive capacities is extremely important because whatever positive qualities we now possess have their roots in our positive experiences of the past. We were somehow introduced to them and were affected by them and then built on them. Therefore whenever we review our past, we should review both the negative but particularly the positive experiences. It is amazing how much we learn by so doing.

There are basically two methods through which we are able to modify our misconceptions. The first is a methodical, realistic, appropriate, and intelligent attempt at self-evaluation and self-understanding with a reflective, humble, and searching attitude. On many occasions we are able to bring about a change in ourselves through these methods. However, it is not always possible to gain insight into our past experience and its effects on us through individual effort alone. Under these conditions professional assistance is required. The outcome of these attempts to understand our past experiences and their effects hopefully will bring about resolution of psychic and emotional conflicts due to unhealthy childhood experiences, identification of positive experiences and capacities we have had, and initial progress towards establishing a clearer and more accurate view of our life at the present.

CHANGING THE PRESENT

The second aspect of life modification concerns our unrealistic appraisal of our present behaviour, how we view ourselves and our world. We have seen how these views are at least partly due to our past experiences. At one level human behaviour is an habitual response to various forms of stimulation coming at us all the time (the present), stimulation which we integrate and understand by way of similar forms of experience in the past. The nature of behaviour depends on our perception of both present and past realities.

We may err in either or both of these perceptions. To change a given type of behaviour, we need motivation, which is partially gained by recognizing that we can alter our unhealthy and unacceptable behaviour and that this is not only possible but also highly desirable. But a far more important source of motivation is our desire to free ourselves from the limitations of an anxiety-ridden, self-centred, egotistic, and materialistic life. It is the motivation to adopt a universal (other-directed) spiritual lifestyle that promotes peace (through being loved and being able to love), calmness (through acquisition of self-knowledge and self-love), and assurance (through trust in the purposefulness and fundamental goodness of creation).

Once again, in studying the present, we must do much more than simply look at what is negative. We are faced with various challenges and difficulties at any time in life. We tend to see these difficulties either as misfortunes, or as the fault of others, or as our own shortcomings. However, most life difficulties are in reality opportunities for learning and growth. These occasions offer us tests, tests from which we may move to greater spirituality as we pass though them. Most of us tend to fear these tests, but life histories are filled with heroic and successful tales of dealing with these tests. So when we are engaged in attempts to modify our approach to life, it is crucial that we identify our own many capacities, which we tend to ignore. The fact is that most of us, in any given day, deal with problems and challenges much more creatively than we realize. The recognition of our inherent abilities is an essential aspect of successful life modification.

The methods used for behaviour change and for the modification of our conceptual framework about ourselves and reality are the same as those described for understanding the past. Here again the basic responsibility is with us ourselves. We need to enhance our self-knowledge and self-love with a high measure of diligence and discipline. Discipline is necessary in any human endeavour and is of paramount importance in the task of life modification. This discipline needs to be all inclusive and to focus on the physical, intellectual, emotional, social, and spiritual aspects of our lives.

Not infrequently, many of us need help in our efforts to modify our behaviour. This assistance might be one or more of the following: psychotherapy, consultation with respected individuals, and encouragement and love from others. And again, we must approach these tasks thoughtfully and with an open mind and open heart. The outcome of these efforts is often a partial or total change in the unhealthy forms of our behaviour.

Having made these two important steps towards life modification, we still need to make another fundamentally more consequential change in our lifestyles. Here I am referring to the third and final step in life modification: planning for the future.

Planning for the Future

Considering the past, the present, and the future involves the duration and the limitations of time—they invoke thoughts of a beginning and an end, union and separation, birth and death. These conditions and occurrences of life are anxiety producing and fear inducing. They create the dread of loss, separation, and extinction, as well as provide the excitement and joy of union, birth, and life. Ultimately, the fear of annihilation and nothingness overwhelms us unless we are able to perceive the spiritual nature of our reality. Materialistically speaking, death is indeed equivalent to annihilation. The concept of annihilation causes human degradation, debasement, and fear. It removes the motivation for growth and feeds into our tendency for instant gratification and a self-centred life devoid of will and motivation.

Human life can be understood as a journey that begins at the moment of conception and continues through the various worlds of existence on an ever-advancing axis of knowledge and love. Life is both eternal and purposeful. Its purpose is to know and to love. These objectives need to be approached in a practical manner so that we will be able to plan the direction and quality of our lives.

Focusing on the past frees us from the constraints of our psychological limitations, while focusing on the future allows us to move toward a spiritual lifestyle. Focusing on the present makes both of these processes possible. Spiritual psychology encompasses these processes and aims at creating unity, both inner and interpersonal. Spiritual psychology, therefore, deals with both issues of psychological life modification and spiritual transformation.

Spiritual Transformation: Concept and Practice

●

Psychological intervention, however important, results at best, in modification of our behaviour. It does not cause spiritual transformation. At the level of biology and psychology, the best we can achieve is to satisfy and discipline our instincts and emotions. This means that, on the one hand, in a state of psychological health we are safe; our instinctual needs are met; our feelings of anger, sadness, anxiety, and fear are decreased and controlled; and our ability to gratify our desires is enhanced; and on the other hand, we achieve these without causing difficulty and harm to others. The best that psychology can achieve is to help us create a humanistic world. But the psychology of spirituality endeavours to transcend the merely biopsychological and to create a spiritual person and a spiritual civilization. A spiritual person transcends the biological and psychological domains. Spiritual psychology does not ignore the biological and psychological aspects of life, nor does it discredit them. Rather, it moves them into the realm of spirituality. This new realm is the domain of knowledge, enlightenment, and truth; of love, cooperation, and unity; and of will, responsibility, and service. Spiritual transformation makes it possible for the person to live within the framework of universal values of truth, unity, and service. Therefore, for each of us to become an integrated person, we need to search for truth, to be truthful and trustworthy and not to lie to ourselves or to others. The human capacity for self-deception is immense, and therefore our efforts to acquire self-knowledge and to seek truth should be equally, if not more, immense.

The same is true of unity. Because unity is the natural outcome of love and because love is essential for the protection of life, we have no choice but to become agents of unity. Every act we perform, every word we utter, and every intention we convey should have, as its main objective, creation of higher levels of unity with all people. Without unity our individual and collective lives are sure to suffer. To be unifiers we need to learn to relate to others with justice, which in turn, calls for the capacity for equality in our relationships.

Finally, the process of spiritual transformation requires us to be of service to one another. We have to be mature enough to be able to put others ahead of ourselves, not because it is a nice or ethical thing to do, but because in the context of a unified world, the welfare of each part depends on the welfare of the whole. In such a condition of human interrelatedness, competition, prejudice, and injustice have no place. Service, in the broadest sense of the word, becomes paramount, both in our individual and our collective lives alike.

Spiritual transformation is a continuous process of death and rebirth to higher levels of awareness and functioning. It calls for detachment from things, abandonment of vain illusions, and contentment in the face of unforeseen tragedies. Death, which is feared by so many, is an ever-present aspect of life. We die many deaths during our lifetime. The world today denies the reality of death. We usually do not allow ourselves to experience the less obvious deaths we encounter in our daily lives. Children growing up and leaving, friends going to other countries, losing a loved one, experiencing divorce, suffering rejection and failure, reading in the newspapers about people who have been killed, learning about thousands annihilated in seemingly "inconsequential" regional wars—these are all examples of deaths that occur in our lives, but to which we do not pay much attention. We suffer the consequences of this denial. We close our hearts and minds. These are the most tragic outcomes of our fear of death and the belief that life ends on this plane. With closed hearts and minds, there is no room for love to grow, for truth to shine, and for acts of service to be performed. In these circumstances lust for power dominates, and injustice and tyranny reign.

Becoming an Integrated Person

Reading these words, you may be daunted by the task. You may protest that spiritual transformation is indeed a tall order and that it is, in fact, impossible to obtain. A tall order it is. Spiritual transformation demands of us much courage, discipline, and detachment. Courage is needed because the journey is lonely and frightening. At every bend there lies a hidden impulse, powerful and demanding; an unconscious wish, forbidden and tempting; and an unresolved conflict, bothersome and persistent. We gain courage through encouragement. In this way, a reciprocal relationship of courage/encouragement must exist within the family, the circle of friends, and co-workers. In the therapeutic milieu, courage is achieved through the encouraging relationship with the therapist. Discipline and its role in all our accomplishments has already been addressed. Suffice it to say that no creative human endeavour is accomplished without the benefit of discipline.

Finally and perhaps most important, there must be detachment. In our lives we tend to put great emphasis on the approval of others. In a society so dependent on imitation, rivalry, and the quest for what is the norm, those who choose to tread the path of spiritual transformation will find themselves alone. They need detachment from the approval of others. This does not mean that they withdraw, or that they do not participate in the active life of society. On the contrary, such detachment provides the necessary freedom to act with authenticity, to love unconditionally, and to be of service without the limitations of expectation for reward.

In short, to achieve spiritual transformation we need to focus on how we can achieve a life characterized by values of truth, unity, and service. To begin with, we have to open our hearts and minds to spiritual issues. We have to raise our children with the spiritual values of truth, unity, and service. All parents teach their children certain values. Central to these should be truth, unity, and service. New generations reared with these values will create a dramatically different world from that which we ourselves have created.

These values, however, like all other human qualities, need to be nurtured throughout our lives. It is here that the spiritual practices of religion assume special significance. Among the most important of these are the universal spiritual practices of prayer and meditation, fasting and self-discipline, and service and sacrifice.

Prayer and Meditation

In the dictionary we read that meditation is an act of deep, continued thought and solemn reflection. A definition that immediately brings to mind our capacity to know, think, reflect, acquire understanding, and seek the truth. As such, meditation is an indispensable aspect of being human. To contemplate and reflect is human, and to do so we need to create an occasion in which we can be silent, able to distance ourselves from the usual everyday concerns, and pose questions to our own self (soul), and to find answers to these questions.

It is primarily through this process that scientific discoveries are made, puzzles are solved, questions are answered, and new insights are gained. In the spiritual context, meditation is an act of deep contemplation of spiritual issues of truth, unity, and service. It is in this context that we ask ourselves how we can become more just and loving, more enlightened and helpful, more universal and worldminded. We need to ask what the purpose of life is and how this purpose can be accomplished. One may, of course, meditate in the opposite direction and try to find answers to such questions as how to cheat others better, how to dominate others, how to kill, how to take revenge, and how to break laws without being caught and punished. Both are the fruits of meditation. A third way that the human power of meditation is used is in respect to gratification of our desires and self-centred pursuits. However, in the context of spiritual transformation, meditation always focuses on that which is creative, constructive, life-enhancing, truthful, just, and beautiful. Spiritual meditation therefore requires discipline and assistance. It does not come about by itself. The greatest assistance for spiritual meditation comes from the act of praying.

While meditation is directly connected with our capacity to know, prayer is indispensable to our capacity to love. Through prayer we commune with the ultimate object of our love. Prayer is love talk. The lover earnestly supplicates the Beloved, humbly entreating the loved one to shower her or him with loving bounties. In the context of spiritual transformation, the loved one is God—the Source of all truth, love, and assistance. Therefore, when we pray we enkindle our soul, open our heart and mind, attract the hearts of other people, and help to create a reciprocal relationship of love, truth, and service.

Becoming an Integrated Person

Many people have difficulty with prayers because when they sincerely and earnestly ask for something from God they often do not receive the desired response. We may pray for healing, and yet the person dies; for money and remain in poverty; for success and still fail. This attitude towards prayer belongs to our individual and collective childhood. The mature human relationship with God calls for the sensitivity to use one's human capacities of knowledge, love, and will. Prayer in its fullest form must take place both in words and in deeds. Healing does not come about through prayers alone. Nor does the defeated, hopeless, and distraught person respond well to medical treatment. A strength of will, a love of life, and a logical approach to healing are the foundations. Meditation and prayer help us obtain a positive attitude at the time of illness and to seek the best medical treatment available. However, in spite of all our prayers and the best medical attention, people die.

It is here that meditation and prayer assume further significance. Reflection on the loss and its reasons not only gives us new enlightenment about our own mortality but also helps us find new treatments, advance our medical knowledge, and learn how better to fight disease. But meditation in the face of loss and death is difficult unless it is assisted by the power of prayer, by connecting oneself with the Source of all knowledge and by entreating God for greater insight. Many times with hindsight, we realize that our prayers were in fact answered.

Aside from these practical issues, prayer is of even more significance in another way. Each human being is ultimately alone. We are connected to people by bonds of marriage, family, friendship, etc. But we are also alone, and we experience this aloneness in the depths of our thoughts and feelings. How often we yearn to share and cannot. We either do not have the words to express our feelings or the ears to hear them or the courage to utter them. But we can share all of this with our Creator. And because everyone else also has similar experiences, if we were all to pray regularly we would, through the spiritual forces of consciousness, unite with one another and feel a profound degree of togetherness. Prayer, then, is a potent force for unity and truth in the world. It connects hearts and minds. When all people pray for peace, justice, freedom, and equality, new waves of awareness are created in the ocean of human consciousness, bringing with them more unity and peace. In this way, prayer becomes an act of service to others and impels us to translate our words into deeds and our thoughts into actions.

I have often been taken aback by the close similarities that exist between therapeutic processes and prayer and meditation. In therapy one engages in deep and continued thought and reflection, which is meditation. Also, during therapy, the client, who is in a state of suffering and pain, entreats the therapist for healing and improvement. This is an act of praying. This is not surprising, because therapists are in a sense the clergy of the materialistic civilization we have created. Their offices function as sanctuary, confessional, and altar, all at the same time. Much power, mystical and mysterious, is both assumed by the therapist and conferred by the client. Consequently, much good can be done and much abuse can take place.[2]

FASTING AND MORAL DISCIPLINE

Earlier in this book it was pointed out that we humans are at the juncture of the material and the spiritual. On the one hand, we are physical beings subject to the laws of biology and physics. On the other hand, we are spiritual beings able to know, love, and will, which are spiritual abilities and the essential properties of our consciousness. It was pointed out that consciousness has a reality of its own. Life is the outcome of the ongoing interface between consciousness and matter. An aspect of life is the tension between the instinctual, which is the property of the body, and the spiritual, which is the property of the soul (consciousness). Human civilization is the outcome of this interface, while human achievements and failures are the respective reflections of the victory of either the spiritual or the instinctual.

For the spiritual to become victorious over the instinctual, for generosity to replace greed, and for love to overcome hate, we need to learn to discipline our instinctual and animal-like appetites, to control our tendency towards violence and hostility, and to replace them with values of truth, unity, and service. Spiritual practices that call for self-discipline, such as fasting, have these outcomes as their prime objectives.

Fasting is a symbol of self-restraint. It brings us more fully in touch with ourselves. It makes us aware that we are stronger than our appetites. It shows us that we can endure hunger, but at the same time it makes us aware how millions of hungry people feel. In a deliberate act of fasting we have the opportunity to break the fast. But the starving masses of humanity fast to death because they have no access to food. They have no choice. Through fasting we become aware once again of the fundamental unity of humanity.

Fasting and other spiritual disciplines, such as avoidance of alcohol and other mind-altering substances, also have profound effects on our lifestyles and the state of our health, both as individuals and as societies. The impact of the absence of spiritual practices of this nature is strongly felt in our world today. Among the major challenges facing humanity in this last decade of the twentieth century are addictions to various drugs and alcohol. Cocaine cartels rule over vast numbers of people and ruin the lives of millions. Drug dealers and drug addicts throughout the world have become agents of crime and death. Alcohol has become the poison that not only kills those who drink but also destroys families, businesses, and even races of people. A spiritual law prohibiting nonmedical use of alcohol and addictive drugs is not an infringement on our freedom, but rather a stronghold within which we can be free. Our concept of freedom is so misguided that we consider order to be the opposite of freedom. But without order there is no freedom. There is only chaos and anarchy.

In addition, spiritual practices such as fasting and praying are acts of love. We are familiar with some varieties of these loving acts. For example, parents remaining hungry while giving their food to children are engaged in an act of love. The same is true for fasting, except that this time the act is performed without the presence of extraordinary circumstances.

SERVICE AND SACRIFICE

The contemporary notion of service is troubling. It conveys the idea of being a servant or slave to someone else in an unequal relationship. Another definition of service is work or duty performed for another such as professional service, repair service, or public service. Service, however, has another meaning: respect, attention, and devotion, as of a lover to a loved one. In the context of the capacities of knowledge, love, and will, and the values of truth, unity, and service, this latter definition is intended. Service, therefore, is the use of the human will for the performance of unifying and truthful actions. This requires a high degree of selflessness, a deep understanding of the fundamental unity of humanity, and complete devotion to truth. More significantly, service is a reflection of our understanding and the acceptance of our own true nature. To the degree that we wish to nurture and develop our humanness, to that degree will we be engaged in acts of service.

Sacrifice has it roots in the Latin word *sacrificium* which is itself composed of two words: *sacer*, meaning sacred, and *facere*, meaning to make. Sacrifice is therefore the act of making sacred.

During our lives we accumulate possessions and positions, and obtain love and powers of various types. We become attached to them and begin to fasten both our minds and hearts on them. As our attachment grows, our minds and hearts become more closed; we become self-centred and frightened. We become self-centred because we possess so much that we fear losing these posessions.

I am reminded of a middle-class family in which the parents and children were happy people. Their home was open to all at all times. Friends felt completely free to stop by, say hello, bring friends with them, drink tea and coffee and go. Sometimes we would bake a cake and take our handiwork to this home, just to sit around eating and enjoying each other's company. There was no pretence and there was a strong sense of unity and togetherness. Then this family won a huge sum of money in a lottery. Overnight everything changed. They moved to a fortresslike home, hired bodyguards, received their calls through an answering service. It was impossible either to see or talk to them. Some years later we learned that the family had dissolved. The husband was in a state of deep confusion and depression. The wife was so angry no one could approach her. The children were the indulged victims of their circumstances: totally self-centred and unprepared to relate to others with comfort or trust. They had dropped out of school. The family was still very rich monetarily, but they were now very poor in everything else that really counted.

As I reflected on this case, one thing was obvious: their new riches were not made sacred. Everything we possess, because we are spiritual in essence, must be made sacred. But how can one do that?

Does giving to a charity make what we have sacred? What about establishing a foundation to do public good in perpetuity in our name or remembrance? Charity, however laudable, seldom makes anything sacred. It is sacrifice that does so, and sacrifice calls for readiness to die and to leave it all behind. We all die and leave everything behind anyway. We basically have no control over the time of our death. What we can control is our life, how we live it, for what purpose, in what manner, and to what end. Looked at in this way, the attitude of sacrifice implies that the quality of our life is such that whenever death comes we are not going to be filled with remorse for neglected acts of kindness and love. This is at the core of spiritual transformation.

Central to the issue of sacrifice is courage to proclaim the truth and the will to acquire qualities of unity and service. We all know how much courage is needed to stand by the truth. That is why we tend to tell small lies. We do so because we know by telling the truth we may have to sacrifice something. "Do you have twenty dollars?" a friend may ask, and we may answer, "no" because we do not wish to part with our money. "Do you believe that blacks are inferior to whites and should be so treated?" a white South African is asked. He may respond "yes" even if he believes otherwise and knows that blacks and whites are equal and should have equal rights. But for him to proclaim the "truth" requires the willingness to sacrifice his standing among his people and therefore he chooses to deny the truth. "Are you involved with another woman?" the wife asks the husband, and he lies and says, "no." But then, the truth is discovered, and the marriage is lost, or the truth is covered up, and the husband's inner peace and integrity are shattered. To sacrifice we need courage to stand by the truth. Or, to put it differently, to have truth we need to sacrifice.

The second meaning of sacrifice has to do with our evolution and development. The process of becoming an integrated person requires the acquisition of spiritual qualities such as truthfulness, unity, and service. But to acquire these qualities we have to be willing to sacrifice our attachment to the instinctual side of our nature. In other words, we have to be willing to make our instincts sacred. But how do we do this? Let us take three basic instincts: sex, hunger, and the need for security.

Throughout history and in all cultures, sex has been made sacred through the institution of marriage. In our times when spiritual values are scarce and considered unimportant, sex has become a public commodity; marriage has lost its sanctity; and human sexual relationships have become vulgar. They are no longer sacred, and consequently love has also lost its sacredness.

Hunger can be made sacred by sharing our food and also by fasting. Through fasting we make both our hunger and our food sacred, and in this process we become aware of hunger as a collective human phenomenon. In our times, food is no longer sacred. That is why so much food is wasted and allowed to rot in one part of the world, while millions of people starve to death in another part. This is done in the name of safeguarding the economy of those who are destroying the food or maintaining political power in those countries in which people are starving.

The need for security is also a basic human instinct. At its elemental level, people attempt to achieve security through self-centred attempts at self-preservation. The most destuctive outcome of this self-centred attitude is creation of a world filled with enough ammunition to destroy the whole planet many times over. Our security comes not from our individual or specific group security, but from world security—our unity. To achieve world unity, we need to sacrifice our self-centred security and to be willing to acquire the spiritual quality of unity which in turn will give us personal security.

On Becoming an Integrated Person: A Postscript

Throughout this book much has been said about spirituality and a spiritual lifestyle. The concept of spirituality presented states that:
- Human beings are created by God as noble beings.
- The basic components of human nature are two: the physical and the spiritual.
- The human soul is what differentiates and distinguishes us from animals. Through the use of our mind, which is the power of our soul, we discover and appreciate the physical laws that provide us with sciences and arts.
- Human knowledge as well as human emotions can be either constructive and unifying, or destructive and disunifying.
- The source of education and guidance of the human soul is the spiritual laws and realities given to humanity through the teachings of the revealers of the major world religions (prophets or manifestations of God) such as Buddha, Moses, Muhammad, Christ, and Bahá'u'lláh, who bring their teachings to humanity in regular intervals according to the level of growth of societies and the needs of humanity at specific times in history.

According to this definition, spiritual individuals are those who make a conscious, deliberate decision to live a life that will allow for an optimal and integrated development of the physical, emotional, intellectual, and spiritual aspects of their human reality, with due consideration to the spiritual teachings appropriate to their own lifetime. Such people bring themselves closer to their own inner reality, to their fellow human beings, and to their Creator. This is achieved through the use of the faculties of knowledge, love, and will, with the help of spiritual and intellectual discipline as well as lofty actions.

It would be of interest to sketch, however briefly, a profile of a spiritual style of living. To do so we need to return to the themes already discussed in this book. In the previous chapters, three major concerns were identified: concerns about self, relationships, and time. How are these concerns dealt with in the context of a spiritual lifestyle?

Those living a spiritual lifestyle are ultimately led to the experience of a profound sense of unity. They begin to realize and experience the fact that human beings, in their true essence, are one and indivisible. They understand that the various dimensions of their being—physical, emotional, intellectual, and spiritual—are but aspects of their fundamental oneness. They know that at the core of their reality lies a noble and spiritual nature, which transcends and incorporates all previous types of existence and which connects humanity with the realm of spiritual realities. This core reality is, at first, in a state of potentiality and actualizes and manifests itself only if we make a concerted effort to ascend to higher levels of growth and maturity through our own knowledge, love, and will, in the light of reason and science along with the spiritual values of truth, unity, and service. In addition, within the framework of a spiritual lifestyle, we become aware of our fundamental unity with our fellow human beings, a unity which once achieved provides us with a universal vision, an unconditional love, and an ongoing desire to serve.

CONCERNS ABOUT SELF IN A SPIRITUAL LIFESTYLE

Materialistic people are lonely people. They are alone in their journey of life, in their struggle for existence, and in their happiness and sadness. They are preoccupied with themselves, their health, their success, their position in society, their acceptance by others, their need to love and be loved at an exaggerated and extreme level. These worries and needs cause materialistically oriented individuals to focus their attention almost exclusively on themselves, and cause them to spend most of their energy and time on their own needs and desires. Self-centredness is the condition and sole outcome of such a process.

Along with their loneliness, materialists feel extremely vulnerable and unimportant. Perceiving oneself to be a mortal animal or a biological machine is obviously not conducive to the development of a sense of self-confidence and self-worth. Consequently, materialists seek power in their quest for security and become competitive in their attempt to feel worthwhile. Power and competition, once combined in the lives of lonely and insecure people, become potent sources of destructiveness and violence.

For spiritual people the process is quite different. Such people realize that they are noble beings who have been created to know and to love. The acquisition of knowledge renders them victorious over ignorance and provides them with true power and strength, power based on reality and a strength that does not fade. Such power is enhanced by the presence of love in the lives of spiritual people.

Contrary to popular beliefs and expectations, material power does not provide a person with a sense of security and confidence. In fact, the more powerful people become, the more insecure they feel because they know that they are very vulnerable and subject to weakness, disease, accident, and death beyond their façade of power. It is in response to these feelings of insecurity that power-seeking individuals begin to compete with others for the purpose of acquiring greater measures of control over themselves and others. Because this process in its very essence is futile, these powerful individuals, in their quest for security, resort to their last weapon—destroying others whom they perceive to be their competitors and enemies. The outcome of all of this is the destruction of themselves and others. Such has been the state of our world to date.

Contrary to power, love provides people with a profound sense of self-worth and self-respect and helps them to establish trustful relationships with others. These are conditions conducive to growth, creativity, unity, and life. Here violence and destructiveness have no opportunity to grow.

The main preoccupations of spiritual individuals become truth and enlightenment on the one hand, and unity and service on the other. Such an interpersonal relationship is characterized by unconditional love, freedom from injustice and prejudice, and the quality of humility. Arrogance and pride have no place in the life of a spiritual person. The concepts of nobility and true equality of all people dictate that we communicate and relate to others with sensitivity, respect, and love.

Humility is another quality greatly needed if one is to live a spiritual life. Humble people are aware that their existence, as well as their potentialities and assets, are gifts bestowed upon them and that their responsibility is to safeguard life and to actualize their potential. They are also aware that this process is only possible if they endeavour to live a life of service and unity.

Another quality of a spiritual lifestyle is detachment. People cannot lead lives of noninvolvement and nonattachment. In fact, we need to belong and to be attached. Because of this the concept of detachment is often poorly understood and at times completely misunderstood. From the perspective of spirituality as defined in this book, detachment refers to that quality which places people in a superior position to their instincts and desires, and instead makes them masters of their own lives and destinies. A detached person acquires and uses material wealth, possessions, and power, not as ends in themselves, but rather as means of acquiring greater heights of knowledge, love, unity, and service. In other words, the quality of detachment renders the person free from attachment to his or her own weakness, mortality, poverty, and material existence and allows that person to be attached to the true source of power, life, and wealth, which is ultimately God.

Concerns about Relationships in a Spiritual Lifestyle

As stated before, loneliness is the outcome of a materialistic approach to life. This loneliness is further enhanced by the materialist's love for power and the tendency to competitive and potentially destructive behaviour. Such conditions are not conducive to the development of positive human relationships. Under these circumstances people grow apart, become suspicious of one another, and deprive themselves of the experience of meaningful communication and intimacy. Alienation and mistrust are the fruits of such relationships, and in spite of their best efforts, the participants in such relationships are not able to develop a cooperative and mature type of communication.

In contrast, interpersonal relationships are, for the spiritual person, the arena within which knowledge and love are put into practice. The acquisition of knowledge demands the search for truth and reality, avoidance of stereotype and prejudice, and the conscious awareness of the total interdependence and unity of humanity. Likewise the power of love functions as a magnet that draws people together, eradicates estrangement, and creates an atmosphere of mutuality, trust, encouragement, and service. In such a relationship the participants feel secure and happy.

All human relationships are greatly helped to remain loving and secure if the participants are joined by a mutual point of attraction. Whenever people are attracted to the same source of meaning, inspiration, and love, they feel closer to one another. The mutual point of attraction helps those involved to overlook the faults and shortcomings of one another, to love unconditionally, to accept without a desire to change others, and not to be unduly disappointed, angry, and rejecting when they do not fulfill our expectations. Because of the importance of finding a mutual point of attraction, we all consciously or unconsciously make such a choice in our interpersonal relationships. Many people tend to choose each other as their mutual points of attraction. Others become attracted to power, fame, wealth, etc. These points of attraction all are temporary and unreliable in character. Consequently, quite often people find themselves disappointed, disillusioned, and discouraged in their love relationships. For the spiritual person, however, the ultimate object of attraction is of a much broader nature.

Spiritual people establish a love relationship with their Creator that is then extended to all people. In such a relationship, loneliness and estrangement are eventually overcome, and harmony and unity are established. Such a relationship must necessarily be characterized by fidelity. Spiritual persons, by definition, are faithful to themselves, to their fellow human beings, and to their Creator. In essence, they make a conscious and deliberate covenant in whatever relationships they engage. This covenant creates the basis for the development of trust, frankness, and honesty in the relationship. In the contemporary world the quality of fidelity is sadly scarce. The root of many problems in interpersonal, marital, familial, and international relationships today is the absence of fidelity. Deceit abounds. Mistrust is so prevalent that true friendship between men and women and people of different persuasions and backgrounds becomes very difficult to establish.

In order to establish a spiritual relationship we need to develop a few qualities. Paramount among these is self-knowledge. The ultimate knowledge is knowledge of self, which is the same as knowledge of God. We can increase this knowledge through the faculty of meditation, through thinking about creation, and through understanding the processes that will enhance growth and maturity as well as through the study of the universal spiritual principles enshrined in religion in its pure and universal essence. While meditation opens the doors of knowledge to us, prayer enhances our capacity for love. Prayer provides an opportunity for people to turn their hearts to the object of their love, to communicate from the position of humility, detachment, and servitude; and to make themselves the recipients of boundless love, mercy, and inspiration. Thus, prayer and meditation, as well as other spiritual disciplines such as fasting, are indispensable parts of a spiritual lifestyle, essential for development of self-knowledge, and highly valuable for creating good relationships.

Concerns About Time in a Spiritual Lifestyle

Of the three major human concerns (self, others, and time), concern about time is the most dramatic. Materialists are in a constant battle with time. They are afraid of time and its passage. Consequently, they preoccupy themselves with the past, dread the future, and are ambivalent about the present. These processes are characteristic of the people of our time—the past is viewed by some with nostalgia, by others with dread, and by others as the time when the direction of their lives was determined, while the future is perceived with suspicion, anxiety, or even horror. To materialistic people, the past is a chance emergence out of nothingness, and the future is a certain return to nothingness. Such ways of thinking cause a profound sense of worry and apprehension. Materialists attempt to alleviate their worry and apprehension with a preoccupation with the present moment. They use alcohol and drugs to dull their senses and decrease their awareness of the past and the future. They become preoccupied with trivia to forget their profound levels of anxiety, material attachment, and insecurity. They focus all their attention on their jobs, health, success, achievement, and similar values. Materialistic individuals, although making tremendous efforts to enjoy the present, in the end find themselves anxious, dissatisfied, unhappy and thus incapable of true enjoyment.

For spiritual persons the situation is different. Time is eternal; the journey of life is an ongoing meaningful journey; and the past, present, and future are various facets of the never-ending process of self-knowledge and self-actualization on the one hand, and the ever-advancing and maturing process of love and unity on the other hand. Spiritual people view their past with gratitude that they were created and see their present as the opportunity to enrich their lives, fulfill their purpose, and actualize their potential. Furthermore, they view their future as yet another stage in the never-ending process of development, maturity, awareness, and enlightenment. They see death as birth into yet another state, more glorious and mysterious than our death from the world of the womb and birth into this life.

For the materialists, death is the very embodiment of nothingness, failure, and deprivation. While the spiritual person prepares for the ongoing journey of life, the materialistic person denies the existence of such a journey.

✧ ✧ ✧

We have now reached the end of this book. I am fully aware that I have only sketched a broad and incomplete outline of such a vast and glorious landscape as that of the psychology of spirituality. No doubt, as humanity enters its age of fulfillment and puts behind the confusions, inconsistencies, and limitations of its collective ages of childhood and adolescence, it will study and understand spirituality in a much more sophisticated and enlightened manner.

The Psychology of Spirituality

We are now approaching an era in which science and religion are reconciled; mind and heart are reunited; men and women are equal; black, white, red, and yellow love one another; justice and unity permeate the politics of the planet; and what once was viewed as utopia may now be the blueprint for the construction of a new global civilization.

Nevertheless, a profound change in our attitude and in our habits must needs occur in order to usher in this new era. Openness is the hallmark of the age of maturity. Mature people and societies possess open minds, open hearts, and open homes. Maturity is an age in which we diligently search for truth, wherever it comes from; unconditionally love one another and celebrate, rather than fear, our diversity; and see the planet earth as our collective home, rather than a battlefield of divergent ideologies, interests, and backgrounds. Already much is happening along these lines. However, for the process to accelerate and succeed, we each need to participate actively in this dramatic process of change, growth, and enlightenment.

It is with these thoughts that this book concludes with the following blueprint for a spiritual lifestyle.

Be generous in prosperity, and thankful in adversity.
Be worthy of the trust of thy neighbour, and look upon him with a bright and friendly face.
Be a treasure to the poor, an admonisher to the rich, an answerer of the cry of the needy, a preserver of the sanctity of thy pledge.
Be fair in thy judgment, and guarded in thy speech.
Be unjust to no man, and show all meekness to all men.
Be as a lamp unto them that walk in darkness,
  a joy to the sorrowful,
  a sea for the thirsty,
  a haven for the distressed,
  an upholder and defender of the victim of oppression.
Let integrity and uprightness distinguish all thine acts.
Be a home for the stranger,
  a balm to the suffering,
  a tower of strength for the fugitive.
Be eyes to the blind, and
  a guiding light unto the feet of the erring.
Be an ornament to the countenance of truth,
  a crown to the brow of fidelity,
  a pillar of the temple of righteousness,
  a breath of life to the body of mankind,
  an ensign of the hosts of justice,
  a luminary above the horizon of virtue,
  a dew to the soil of the human heart,
  an ark on the ocean of knowledge,
  a sun in the heaven of bounty,
  a gem on the diadem of wisdom,
  a shining light in the firmament of thy generation,
  a fruit upon the tree of humility.[3]

Bahá'u'lláh

NOTES

Notes

●

All case histories and clinical vignettes reported in this book are actual cases from the author's practice. However, the names and a few other identifying details have been altered so as to maintain both the integrity and complete confidentiality of each case.

PART ONE: BEGINNINGS

1. Hippocrates, as quoted in Alfred M. Freedman, Harold I. Kaplan, and Benjamin J. Sadock, eds., *Modern Synopsis of Comprehensive Textbook of Psychiatry/II*, 4–5.
2. For more details on Witchcraft Mania and the subsequent state of psychiatry during the Renaissance, see Freedman, Kaplan, and Sadock, eds., *Modern Synopsis of Comprehensive Textbook of Psychiatry/II*, 13-18.
3. See note 2 above.
4. See note 2 above.
5. Bruno Bettelheim, *Freud and Man's Soul*, 4; 5; 11–12.
6. Bettelheim, *Freud and Man's Soul*, 19.

PART TWO: SELF AND SOUL

1. Erich Fromm, *Marx's Concept of Man*, 9.
2. Paul Davies and John Gribbin, *The Matter Myth*, 13.

3. Davies and Gribbin, *The Matter Myth*, 31.
4. Karl Marx, "Preface to a Contribution to a Critique of Political Economy," in *Selected Works*, vol. 1, by Karl Marx and Friedrich Engels, 362-64.
5. Karl Marx and Friedrich Engels, *German Ideology*, 7.
6. For a concise comparative review of views of Plato, Marx, Freud, Sartre, Skinner and Lorenz, as well as Christianity, see Leslie Stevenson, *Seven Theories of Human Nature*.
7. See note 6 above.
8. See note 6 above.
9. See note 6 above.
10. John Wheeler, as quoted in Davies and Gribbin, *The Matter Myth*, 307.
11. Davies and Gribbin, *The Matter Myth*, 307-8.
12. Davies and Gribbin, *The Matter Myth*, 309.
13. Gregory Bateson, cited in Fritjof Capra, *The Turning Point: Science, Society and the Rising of Culture*, 290.
14. 'Abdu'l-Bahá, "Survival and Salvation," in *The Star of the West* 7.19 (March 1917): 190.
15. Paul Davies, *God and the New Physics*, 82.
16. Davies, *God and the New Physics*, 82.
17. Capra, *The Turning Point*, 91-92.
18. Capra, *The Turning Point*, 298.
19. For further description see Ken Wilber, "Psychologia Perennis: The Spectrum of Consciousness," in *Journal of Transpersonal Psychology* 2 (1975).
20. For a full description of these concepts, see Stanislav Grof, *Beyond the Brain: Birth, Death and Transcendence in Pyschotherapy*.
21. 'Abdu'l-Bahá, *Paris Talks, Addresses Given by 'Abdu'l-Bahá in Paris in 1911-12*, 96-98.
22. See 'Abdu'l-Bahá, *Some Answered Questions*, ed. and trans. Laura Clifford Barney, 245-46.
23. The terms "emotions" and "feelings" used here are the same as the term "affect" used in psychoanalysis. There is no clear distinction in the psychiatric literature regarding these terms. For a detailed explanation of the psychoanalytic theory of affects, see David Rapaport, "On the Psychoanalytic Theory of Affects," in *The Collected Papers of David Rapaport*, ed. Merton M. Gill, 476-512.

PART THREE: THE FUNDAMENTALS

1. In formulating the fundamental human capacities to know, love, and will and in identifying them as the properties of the human soul, I have drawn heavily from the Bahá'í writings. The interested reader may wish

to refer to the following sources: Bahá'u'lláh, *Gleanings from the Writings of Bahá'u'lláh*; Bahá'u'lláh, *The Hidden Words of Bahá'u'lláh*; and 'Abdu'l-Bahá, *Paris Talks* and *Some Answered Questions*.

2. The concept that humanity is now in its collective adolescence and is poised for transition to its age of collective adulthood was first introduced by Bahá'u'lláh in the latter decades of the nineteenth century. For a fuller study of these concepts see Bahá'u'lláh, *Gleanings from the Writings of Bahá'u'lláh*; and Shoghi Effendi, *The World Order of Bahá'u'lláh, Selected Letters*.

3. Bahá'u'lláh, *Gleanings from the Writings of Bahá'u'lláh*, 178.

4. Karl Marx, *Selected Writings in Sociology and Social Philosophy*, 177.

PART FOUR: WHEN THINGS GO WRONG

1. The concept that our understanding of spiritual realities is relative and not absolute is of major significance. At the root of all religious hostilities and differences lies the notion of "possession of absolute truth" and therefore "the only right religion." For more details about the concept of the relativity of religious truth, see Bahá'u'lláh, *The Kitáb-i-Íqán, The Book of Certitude*, and, the Bahá'í concept of progressive revelation as explained in William S. Hatcher and J. Douglas Martin, *The Bahá'í Faith: The Emerging Global Religion*.

2. For a more detailed analysis of the authoritarian personality, see H. B. Danesh, *Unity: The Creative Foundation of Peace*, 49-51.

PART FIVE: FROM ADOLESCENCE TO MATURITY

1. For a more detailed look at the unity paradigm, see Danesh, *Unity: The Creative Foundation of Peace*.

2. Bahá'u'lláh, *Gleanings from the Writings of Bahá'u'lláh*, 250.

3. See 'Abdu'l-Bahá, *Some Answered Questions*, 233-35.

4. For more information about anatomy and the functions of the brain, see Richard M. Restak, *The Brain: The Last Frontier*.

5. Paul Maclean, cited in Restak, *The Brain: The Last Frontier*, 52.

6. Restak, *The Brain: The Last Frontier*, 53.

7. Paul Maclean, cited in Restak, *The Brain: The Last Frontier*, 53.

8. Edward O. Wilson as reported in Restak, *The Brain: The Last Frontier*, 74.

9. Edward O. Wilson, *Sociobiology: The New Synthesis*, cited in Restak, *The Brain: The Last Frontier*, 75.

10. Edward O. Wilson as reported in Restak, *The Brain: The Last Frontier*, 78-79.

11. Restak, *The Brain: The Last Frontier*, 82.
12. Restak, *The Brain: The Last Frontier*, 82.
13. A. R. Wallace and Charles Darwin, cited in Restak, *The Brain: The Last Frontier*, 76-77.
14. Edward O. Wilson as reported in Restak, *The Brain: The Last Frontier*, 77.
15. Edward O. Wilson as reported in Restak, *The Brain: The Last Frontier*, 77.
16. Jonas Salk, cited in the *Omni Interviews*, 99.
17. Russell Fernald, a neurobiologist at Stanford University, in his studies of the African cychild fish has discovered that certain behavioural changes resulted in the *cellular change* in their brain. Dr. Lawrence Hartman, in his presidential address at the 145th annual meeting of the American Psychiatric Association in 1992, referred to these findings and then observed: "With better (and less intrusive and harmful) tools (as, for example, some of our new neuroimaging techniques), we already are to some extent, and soon will be to a greater extent, able to demonstrate many similar bits of biosocial and biopsychosocial continuity in humans." For further details see *The American Journal of Psychiatry*,149, 9 (September 1992): 1135-41.
18. For more detailed description of left/right brain functions, see Robert Ornstein, *The Psychology of Consciousness*.
19. Ornstein, *The Psychology of Consciousness*, 83.
20. Grof, *Beyond the Brain*, 21.
21. Grof, *Beyond the Brain*, 21-22.
22. Grof, *Beyond the Brain*, 22.
23. Wilder Penfield, *The Mystery of the Mind*.
24. Jonas Salk, cited in *Omni Interviews*, 100.
25. Cyril Ponnamperuma, cited in *Omni Interviews*, 6.
26. Cyril Ponnamperuma, cited in *Omni Interviews*, 7.
27. See the interview with Roger Sperry in *Omni Interviews*, 187-207.
28. See the interview with Roger Sperry in *Omni Interviews*, 199-200.
29. See the interview with Karl Pribram in *Omni Interviews*, 136-51.
30. Roger Sperry, cited in *Omni Interviews*, 191.
31. Roger Sperry, cited in *Omni Interviews*, 194.
32. Karl Pribram, cited in *Omni Interviews*, 148.
33. Albert Hofmann, cited in *Omni Interviews*, 159.
34. Roger Sperry, cited in *Omni Interviews*, 197.
35. For a comprehensive perspective on the spiritual concepts of evolution and consciousness, see 'Abdu'l-Bahá, *Some Answered Questions*, particularly Part 4, "On the Origin, Powers and Conditions of Man", 205-96.
36. Cyril Ponnamperuma, cited in *Omni Interviews*, 4.
37. Karl Pribram, cited in *Omni Interviews*, 139.
38. Karl Pribram, cited in *Omni Interviews*, 137-38.

39. Roger Sperry, cited in *Omni Interviews*, 198.
40. Roger Sperry, cited in *Omni Interviews*, 195–96.
41. Roger Sperry, cited in *Omni Interviews*, 196.

PART SIX: BECOMING AN INTEGRATED PERSON

1. Bahá'u'lláh, *Gleanings from the Writings of Bahá'u'lláh*, 250.
2. For further elaboration on the roles and effects of prayer and meditation in our spiritual development, see the address by 'Abdu'l-Bahá cited in *Paris Talks*, 173–76.
3. Bahá'u'lláh, *Gleanings from the Writings of Bahá'u'lláh*, 285.

BIBLIOGRAPHY

Bibliography

'Abdu'l-Bahá. *Paris Talks, Addresses Given By 'Abdu'l-Bahá in Paris in 1911-1912.* 11th ed. London: Bahá'í Publishing Trust, 1969.
———. *Some Answered Questions.* Collected and translated from the Persian by Laura Clifford Barney. 3d ed. Wilmette: Bahá'í Publishing Trust, 1968.
———. "Survival and Salvation." *The Star of the West,* 7.19 (March, 1917). Oxford: George Ronald, 1978. Reprinted.
Abraham, Karl. "Notes on Psychoanalytical Investigation and Treatment of Manic-depressive Insanity and Allied Conditions." *Selected Papers on Psychoanalysis.* New York: Basic Books, 1953.
Arieti, Silvano, ed. *American Handbook of Psychiatry.* Vol. 1. New York: Basic Books, 1963.
Bahá'u'lláh. *Gleanings from the Writings of Bahá'u'lláh.* Translated by Shoghi Effendi. 2d ed. Wilmette: Bahá'í Publishing Trust, 1976.
———. *The Hidden Words of Bahá'u'lláh.* Translated by Shoghi Effendi. Wilmette: Bahá'í Publishing Trust, 1939.
———. *The Kitáb-i-Íqán, The Book of Certitude, Revealed by Bahá'u'lláh.* Translated by Shoghi Effendi. 2d ed. Wilmette: Bahá'í Publishing Trust, 1950.
Bettelheim, Bruno. *Freud and Man's Soul.* New York: Vintage Books, 1984.
Bonime, Walter. "The Psychodynamics of Neurotic Depression." In *The American Handbook of Psychiatry* Vol. 3. New York: Basic Books, 1966.
Capra, Fritjof. *The Turning Point: Science, Society and the Rising of Culture.* Toronto: Bantam Books, 1983.

Danesh, H. B. *Unity: The Creative Foundation of Peace.* Toronto: Association for Bahá'í Studies and Fitzhenry Whiteside, 1986.

———. "The Violence-Free Society: A Gift for Our Children." *Bahá'í Studies.* Vol. 6. Ottawa: The Canadian Association for Studies on the Bahá'í Faith, 2d ed., 1979.

Davies, Paul. *God and the New Physics.* London: J. M. Dent and Sons, 1983.

Davies, Paul, and John Gribbin, *The Matter Myth.* New York: Simon and Schuster, 1992.

Darwin, Charles Robert. *The Origin of Species.* London: John Murray, 1859.

Freedman, Alfred, Harold I. Kaplan, and Benjamin J. Sadock, eds. *Modern Synopsis of Comprehensive Textbook of Psychiatry/II* Second Edition. Baltimore: The Williams and Wilkins Company, 1976.

Freud, Sigmund. "Mourning and Melancholia." In *Collected Papers.*Vol. 4. London: Hogarth Press and Institute of Psychoanalysis, 1925.

———. *New Introductory Lectures on Psychoanalysis.* Translated and edited by James Strachey. New York and London: W.W. Norton & Company, 1965.

Fromm, Erich. *Marx's Concept of Man.* New York: Frederick Ungar Publishing Co., 1981.

Gabbard, Glen. "Psychodynamic Psychiatry in the 'Decade of the Brain'." *The American Journal of Psychiatry,* 143, 8 (August 1992): 996-97.

Grof, Stanislav. *Beyond the Brain: Birth, Death and Transcendence in Psychotherapy* New York: State University of New York Press, 1985.

Hartmann, Lawrence M.D. "Reflections on Human Values and Biopsychosocial Integration." *The American Journal of Psychiatry* 149.9 (September 1992): 1135-41.

Hatcher, William S., and J. Douglas Martin. *The Bahá'í Faith: The Emerging Global Religion.* San Francisco: Harper & Row, 1984.

Klein, Melanie. *Contributions to Psychoanalysis, 1921-1945.* London: Hogarth Press and Institute of Psychoanalysis, 1948.

Lorenz, Konrad. *On Aggression.* Reprint. London: Methuen & Co. Ltd., 1970

Marx, Karl. "Preface to a Contribution to a Critique of Political Economy." In *Selected Works.* Vol. 1, by Karl Marx and Friedrich Engels. Moscow: Foreign Languages Publishing House, 1955.

———. *Selected Writings in Sociology and Social Philosophy.* Translated by T.B. Bottomore and edited by T.B. Bottomore and M. Rubel. London: Penguin Books, 1963.

Marx, Karl, and Friedrich Engels. *German Ideology,* edited with an introduction by R. Pascal. New York: International Publishers, 1939.

Mendelson, Myer. "Neurotic Depressive Reaction." In *Comprehensive Textbook of Psychiatry.* Edited by Alfred M. Freedman and Harold I. Kaplan. Baltimore: The Williams and Wilkins Company, 1967.

The Omni Interviews. Weintraub, Pamela, ed. New York: Ticknor & Fields, 1984.

Ornstein, Robert. *The Psychology of Consciousness.* New York: Penguin Books, 1986.

Penfield, Wilder. *The Mystery of the Mind.* Princeton: Princeton University Press, 1976.

Rapaport, David. *The Collected Papers of David Rapaport.* Edited by Merton M. Gill. New York and London: Basic Books, 1967.

Restak, Richard M. *The Brain: The Last Frontier.* New York: Warner Books, 1979.

Shoghi Effendi. *The World Order of Bahá'u'lláh, Selected Letters.* 2d ed. Wilmette: Bahá'í Publishing Trust, 1974.

Skinner, B.F. *Beyond Freedom and Dignity.* New York: Alfred A. Knopf, 1971.

Stevenson, Leslie. *Seven Theories of Human Nature.* New York and Oxford: Oxford University Press, 1974.

Wilber, Ken. "Psychologia Perennis: The Spectrum of Consciousness." *Journal of Transpersonal Psychology,* no. 2 (1975).

Wilson, Edward O. *Sociobiology: The New Synthesis.* Cambridge: Harvard University Press, 1975.

INDEX

Index

'Abdu'l-Bahá, 38-39, 43-44
acceptance of others, 93
action, 101-2, 168
addiction, 17, 212
Agrippa, Cornelius, 14-15
alcohol
    destructive, 233
    and free will, 139-40
alertness, 168
American Bill of Rights, 140
animals: see also reptiles
    follow instincts, 45-46, 149
    no power of knowledge, 49-50, 149
    no power of love, 49-50
    no power of will, 47, 50
    no spirituality, 6, 149, 237
attraction, 68-70, 72, 151
authoritarian personality, 134-37, 156

Bahá'u'lláh, 44n, 67n, 178, 237
beauty, 69-70
behaviour
    aggressive aspects, 16
    and creativity, 133-34
    sexual aspects, 16
behaviourism
    and current life styles, 219
    definition, 26
    and feelings, 171
body
    and death, 35, 55, 57
    and mind, 35-36, 41-42, 48
    and self, 45
    and soul, 11, 14, 38, 43-45, 50, 199
brain
    cortex, 42, 168-69, 175-80
    evolution of, 42-43, 175-78
    functions, 168-70
    hypothalamus, 170
    and intelligence, 191
    and knowledge, 179
    limbic system, 42, 170-75
    and love, 179-80
    mammalian, 168, 170
    and mind, 186-88, 192
    neocortex, 42-43
    neomammalian, 168
    paleomammalian, 168
    and soul, 181-84
brain stem: see cortex
Buddha, 44n, 67n, 178, 237

Canadian Charter of Human Rights, 140
case studies
 death and dying, Dawn, 53-62
 disorder of knowledge, Mary, 119-22
 disorder of love
  David, 126-29
  Jane, 129-32
 disorder of will
  Joseph, 134-38
  Sandy, 157-58
 in search of meaning, Carol, 7-12
 integration of relationships
  Bruno, 95-96
  Peter and Patricia, 96-97
 integration of self
  Rosanna, 88-89
  William, 87-88
 integration of time
  Juliana, 106-7
  Justin, 103
  Susan and John, 104-6
  Timothy, 102-3
 knowledge and trust, couple, 151
 love and unity
  Carl, 153-54
  couple, 154
 self-knowledge and truth, Jan, 150
 will and service, Chief Executive Officer, 158-59
charity, 165
children
 and death, 53, 56, 60-62, 103-4
 need encouragement, 222
 need guidance, 222
 need love, 221
choice, 32, 182-83
Christ, 44n, 67n, 178, 237
code of ethics, universal, 161-66
co-dependency, 212
communism, 25-26, 206-7
competitive relationships, 77, 94, 124-25
complementary relationships, 77
Confucius, 178
consciousness: see also mind; soul
 capacity to choose, 47
 characteristics, 189

core of realities, 24
definition, 39, 191-92
and evolution of brain, 172-74, 177-78
levels or domains, 43
"life force", 186-88
link with soul, 36-37
needed for feeling, 48
and self-knowledge, 198
containing relationships, 76-77
cooperative relationships, 78, 94-95, 124-25
cortex of brain, 42, 168-69, 178-80
creation
 and evolution, 190
 main activity of love, 69
 of universe, 189
creativity
 less important in materialism, 30
 of soul, 38
 and will, 133-34
cultural differences, 4, 95-96

Darwin, Charles Robert, 176, 184
Darwinism, 25, 27
death: see also dying
 as the end, 8
 and body-mind duality, 35
 coping with, 53-54, 123
 effect on children, 103-4
 fear of, 53-54, 99-100, 102-3
 and God, 54
 in materialistic view, 30
 and knowledge, 54-58
 and love, 54-55, 58-59
 and physicians, 3, 8
 planning for, 224-25
 and prayer, 231
 and spiritual transformation, 228
 tests self, 54-55
 therapeutic attitude to, 216-18
 and will, 54-55, 59-60
decision-making, 101-2
desire, 101-2
devil, 14
diet, 212-13
disease, 54-55
divorce: see marriage

Index

drugs
agents of crime and death, 233
and psychological problems, 212-13
dualism, 18-19, 36, 41, 45
dying: see also death
effect on children, 53, 56, 60-62
effect on family, 9-12
effect on friends, 12
effect on parents, 53, 58-59, 102-3
effect on patient, 7-12
support groups, 53

education: see ignorance
emotions: see feelings
empathy, 93
encouragement
in childhood, 222
in therapeutic relationship, 214
equality, 94-95
ethics: see also morality; values
important to spirituality, 160
and service, 164-66
and truth, 161-62
and unity, 163-64
ethnology, 27
evil
ancient beliefs, 13
and mental illness, 13-15
and physical conditions, 13-15
evolution
biological, 42, 169, 175-78, 184-85, 188, 191
material world, 43
metabiological, 185, 188-91
prebiological, 185
psychological, 42
spiritual, 42-44, 170, 174, 176-80, 181-84, 188-91
values, 43
existentialism, 26
experience
and feelings, 34-35
and human nature, 33-34
and spirituality, 35

facial expressions, 171-72
families
"dysfunctional", 212-13

healthy, 213-14
fascism, 207
fasting, 232-33
feelings
and brain, 168
bridge body and mind, 48, 50
characteristics, 48
and experience, 34-35, 47-48
instinctual, 183
and limbic system, 170-74
physical, 48-49
psychological, 49
purpose of, 43-44
spiritual, 49-50
and unity, 200-202
forgiveness, 218
freedom: see also will
from selfishness, 140-42
personal, 139-40
and poverty, 140
social, 140
Freud, Sigmund, 14-15, 26, 75
friends as patients, 3-4
future, planning for, 224-25

genetic code, 190
genetic disorders, 212-13
Gökel, Rudolf, 15
God
the Creator, 187, 189-90
and death, 54
in behaviourist view, 26
in existentialist view, 26
in religious view, 31
in spiritual view, 28
knowledge of, 66-67
manifestations, 67n
and prayer, 230-32
rejection of, 205-6, 208-9
relationship with humans, 43, 65-66, 237, 241
religious fundamentalism, 209
source of unity, 205
and will, 73
gratification, 130-32, 151, 167
Grof, Stanislav, 43
guidance in childhood, 222

265

heart, 39
Heraclitus, 14
Hippocrates, 14
history of psychology, 13-16
hormonal disorders, 212-13
human capacities
  disorders of, 115-40
  healthy development of, 147-48
  integration of, 80-81, 142, 160
  knowledge, 63-67
  love, 63, 67-70
  versus instincts, 168
  will, 63, 70-73
human concerns
  integration of, 80-81, 87-89, 95-97, 102-8, 237-38
  relationships, 76-78, 91-95, 240-42
  self, 75-76, 83-89, 238-40
  time, 79-80, 99-102, 242-43
human nature
  and experience, 33-34
  machinistic, 24-25
  material view, 24-27, 29-30, 237
  spiritual view, 27-29, 31-32, 237
humans
  can transcend instincts, 46-47, 168, 232-33
  relationship with God, 65-66, 237, 241
hypothalamus, 170, 172-74

ignorance, 4
immortality, 99-100
individualism: see uniqueness of people
information processing, 168
Innocent VIII, 14
instincts
  animalistic, 45-46, 149
  and brain cortex, 183
  humans can control, 46-47, 168, 232-33
  making sacred, 235-36
  materialistic view, 24
  physical feelings, 48-49
  and unity, 199-200
integration: see also unity
  body and mind, 41-42, 48
  and brain structure, 168
  goal of, 168
  knowledge and relationships, 80-81, 91-93
  knowledge and self, 80-81, 83-84
  knowledge and time, 80-81, 99-100
  love and relationships, 80-81, 93-94
  love and self, 80-81, 84-85
  love and time, 80-81, 100-101
  self, 50, 63, 72-73
  through spirituality, 17-19, 227-28
  will and relationships, 80-81, 94-95
  will and self, 80-81, 86-87
  will and time, 80-81, 101-2

knowledge
  and brain, 179
  and death, 54-58
  disorders of, 115-22, 135-36, 159
  human power, 19, 49-50, 149, 237
  intuitive/creative, 64
  integration with relationships, 91-93, 241
  integration with self, 83-84, 239
  integration with time, 99-100, 243
  and meditation, 230
  of God, 66-67
  of reality, 115-18
  of self, 66-67, 72, 115-17
  of the world, 115-17
  rational/logical, 64-66
  and soul, 37-38
  spiritual/divine, 64-66
  and truth, 148-51

"life force", 185-86
life modification
  changing the present, 222-24
  goal of therapy, 218
  planning the future, 224-25
  understanding the past, 221-22
limbic system: see also brain, mammalian
  and consciousness, 173-74
  and feelings, 42, 170-74
  functions, 170
Lorenz, Konrad, 27
love

Index

attraction, 69-70, 72, 151
and brain, 179-80
competitive, 124-25
cooperative, 124-25
and death, 54-55, 58-59, 123
definition, 67, 68
disorders of, 123-33, 136-37, 159
growth of, 124-25
human power, 19, 50
in childhood, 221
integration with relationships, 93-94, 241
integration with self, 84-85, 239
integration with time, 100-101, 243
in therapy, 214
nature of, 123-25
and prayer, 230-31
self-centred, 124-25, 204, 215
spiritual reality, 117-18
unconditional, 124-25
and unity, 151-55, 163
and war, 68
love object, 124, 126-29
love relationships
disorders, 123
growth of, 151-53
in materialistic view, 29

marriage
competitive, 96-97
lack of growth in, 104-6
and love, 118
strengthening, 213-14
Marxism: see communism
Marx, Karl, 25-26, 67
materialism
antilife, 207-8
as way of life, 29-30, 238-43
basic concepts, 24
behavioural, 26-27
Darwinian, 25, 27
denies soul, 25
ethnological, 27
existential, 26
framework of science, 206-7
and knowledge, 66
Marxist, 25-26
prevents freedom, 141
psychoanalytic, 26
and religion, 208
view of consciousness, 41
material life style
concerns about relationships, 240-41
concerns about self, 238-39
concerns about time, 242-43
maturity
of humanity, 66
of therapist, 214
meaning of life: see purpose of life
medicine
focuses on knowledge, 112-13
inhumane, 7, 9
meditation, 230-32
mental illness and evil, 13-15
mind: see also consciousness; soul
as biological entity, 25
and body, 35-36, 41-42, 48
and brain, 186-88, 192
definition, 39
and self, 45
and soul, 36-38
morality: see also ethics, 28
mortality: see death
Moses, 44n, 178, 237
motivation to change, 223
movasat, 94-95
Muhammad, 44n, 178, 237

nationalism, 206, 208
natural resources, 29
Nazism, 207
neocortex, 42-43
neomammalian brain, 168

oneness: see unity
others-directedness, 204

pain, 201, 217-18
paleomammalian brain, 168
past, understanding, 221-23
patients
cultural differences, 4
death, 3
loved ones, 3-4
physical conditions

biochemical causes, 16
and evil, 13-15
physical causes, 18
psychical causes, 18
physicians
and death, 8
feelings, 4
and spiritual dimension, 9
Pinel, Philippe, 15
Plato, 14, 178
poverty
affects life chances, 4
and freedom, 140
power, authoritarian personality, 134-37
prayer, 230-32
present
changing, 223-24
time concern, 99-100
primary union, 101
psyche, definition, 39
psychoanalytic theories
and current life styles, 219
parts of the whole, 213
popular, 212
psychology
analytic approach, 15-16
biological approach, 16-17
prescientific approach, 13-15
spiritual approach, 17-19, 23
psychotherapy
changing the present, 223-24
client's attitudes, 217
current methods, 26, 219-20
goals, 218-20
knowledge, 116
like prayer, 232
planning the future, 224-25
popularity of, 211
stages of, 214-15
therapist's attitudes, 214-17
understanding the past, 221-23
purpose of life
faced with death, 55, 60
and healing, 111-13
in materialistic view, 29
in spiritual view, 31-32
lack of, 5-6
personal discovery, 11

spiritual dimension, 6
and unity, 202

racism, 206, 208
reality
as soul, 36-38
knowledge of, 115-18
of love, 117-18
spiritual, 117-19
rejection
by loved one, 123
of God, 205-6, 208-9
relationships
abusive, 212
competitive, 77, 94, 124-25
complementary, 77
containing, 76-77
cooperative, 78, 94-95, 124-25
in spiritual life style, 240-42
integration with knowledge, 91-93
integration with love, 93-94
integration with will, 94-95
of love, 76-78, 151-52
primary human concern, 76
and service, 165
and truth, 162
and unity, 163
with God, 43, 65-66, 237, 241
with nature, 29, 38, 163-64
religion
ancient beliefs, 13-14
ascendancy, 14
decline, 16
founders, 44n
fundamentalism, 206, 209
and human knowledge, 192-93
in materialistic society, 208
and physical knowledge, 65-66
and spirituality, 27-28, 31, 229-36
struggle with science, 171-73
and truth, 118-19
religions, and spiritual reality, 118, 121-22, 237
reptiles, human evolution, 169
reptilian brain: see cortex

sacrifice
definitions, 234-35

and spiritual transformation, 234-36
sameness of people, 91-92
Sartre, Jean-Paul, 26-27
science
    and human knowledge, 193
    struggle with religion, 171-73
    and truth, 118-19
secondary union, 101
self
    and body, 42, 45, 50
    definition, 45
    in spiritual life style, 238-40
    integration of knowledge, love and will, 63, 72-73
    integration with knowledge, 63-67, 83-84
    integration with love, 63, 67-70, 84-85
    integration with will, 63, 71-73, 86-87
    and mind, 45
    physical, 44-45
    primary human concern, 75-76
    spiritual, 44-45
    and world views, 47
self-acceptance, 84-85, 215
self-centredness, 124-25, 204, 215
self-confidence, 86-87
self-control, 86
self-discovery, 83
self-experience, 83
self-growth, 84-85, 215-16
selfishness, 140-41
self-knowledge
    case study, 119-22
    and feelings, 172-73
    in spiritual life style, 242
    of the past, 221-23
    and reality, 115-17
    required for unity, 199-200
    ultimate goal, 66-67, 83-84
selflessness, 216, 234
self-love, 216
self-preoccupation, 84-85, 125
self-responsibility, 86-87
separation, 101, 123
service
    definition, 165
    and ethics, 164-66

and spiritual transformation, 205, 228, 233-34
and will, 156-60
sex, making sacred, 235-36
Skinner, B.F., 26-27
Socrates, 178
soul: see also consciousness; mind
    as reality, 36-38
    and body, 11, 14, 38, 43-45, 50, 199
    and brain, 170, 181-84
    and death, 55, 57
    definition, 39
    denied by scientists, 18
    in material view, 25
    and knowledge, 37-38
    and mind, 36-38
    psychoanalytic theory, 15-16
    and truth, 149
spirit, definition, 39
spiritual evolution
    definition, 189
    and evolution of brain, 174, 176-80, 181-84
    nature of, 189-91
    third stage of evolution, 42-44, 170
spirituality
    as way of life, 31-32, 238
    basic concepts, 28, 41
    and ethics, 160
    and experience, 35
    and healing, 112-13
    history, 13-16
    human characteristic, 6, 149, 237
    inner peace, 72
    and knowledge, 66
    modern scepticism, 27-28
    promotes freedom, 141-42
    psychology of, 17-19, 23
    and reality, 11-19, 80-81
    and religion, 27-28
spiritual life style
    blueprint, 245
    concerns about relationships, 240-42
    concerns about self, 238-40
    concerns about time, 242-43
spiritual transformation
    achieving, 227-29

moral discipline, 232-33
prayer and meditation, 230-32
service and sacrifice, 233-36
suicide
    as quest for reunion, 103-4
    purpose in life, 5-6
    and self-knowledge, 119

therapist client relationship, 17, 214-17, 221
thought
    by neocortex, 42-43
    and unity, 202-3
time
    in spiritual life style, 242-43
    integration with knowledge, 99-100
    integration with love, 100-101
    integration with will, 101-2
    primary human concern, 79-80
truth
    and ethics, 161-62
    and knowledge, 148-51
    and sacrifice, 235
    and spiritual transformation, 205, 227-29
    with oneself, 162
    with others, 162

uniqueness of people, 91-92, 153
United Nations Charter of Rights, 140
unity: see also integration
    biological, 198-99
    and ethics, 163-64
    and feelings, 200-202
    and instincts, 199-200
    in therapeutic relationship, 217
    and love, 70, 151-55, 163
    of people, 91-94
    psychosocial, 199-204
    spiritual, 204-9, 228-29
    and thought, 202-3
    universal, 198, 208-9
universe, creation, 189

values: see also ethics
    evolution, 43
    good and evil, 36
    love and hate, 36
    of society, 6, 187
Vives, Juan Luis, 14

war, and love, 68
Weyer, Johann, 15
Wilber, Ken, 43
will: see also freedom
    abuse of, 72
    and alcohol, 139-40
    and death, 54-55, 59-60
    definition, 70, 72
    disorders of, 133-38, 142, 159-60
    and God, 73
    human power, 19, 47, 50
    integration with relationships, 94-95
    integration with self, 86-87
    integration with time, 101-2
    role in life, 71-72
    and service, 156-59
witchcraft, 14-15
women
    rights, 15
    witchcraft, 14
world views and self, 47

Zoroaster, 178